ORDINARY
SUFFERING OF
extraordinary
SAINTS

D0109080

vincent j. o'malley, c.m.

Our Sunday Visitor Publishing Division
Our Sunday Visitor, Inc.
Huntington, Indiana 46750

893

This book is dedicated to my dear nieces and nephews,
whom I once held in my arms, and now I hold in my heart:

Stephen, Scott, and Christopher Brunner;
Anne Marie, Stephen, Lisa, and Michele Fiducioso;
Maureen, Brian, Fiona, and Sheila McGinley;
Patrick, Hilary, Casey Anne, and Kevin Minix;
Monica, Andrea, Kathleen, and Emily O'Malley;

that you might respond as did the saints
to life's unexpected but inevitable sufferings:
full of faith, hope, love, and eventual joy.

Topical Table of Contents

Part 2: Family and Friends

Part 3: Life in the Church

Part 4: Life in the World

Introduction

This is not your typical saint book. It is a book that explores a side of the saints that is often not emphasized in many hagiographies.

While Christians recognize Jesus as the Suffering Servant, and Mary as the Mother of Sorrows, few Christians are knowledgeable about the ways in which the saints also suffered.[1] The saints were not immune to the afflictions common to all people. This book presents the ordinary sufferings of extraordinary people, that is, the saints and others renowned for their holiness.

The Catholic Church highly esteems the saints. They believed in God, imitated Jesus, and received the Holy Spirit, who animated their daily lives. The saints are respected because they successfully modeled their lives on Jesus' life.

The Church distinguishes three levels of praise: *latria, dulia,* and *hyperdulia. Latria,* which means worship in Latin, is given only to the persons of the Holy Trinity: God the Father, Jesus, and the Holy Spirit. The saints are never *worshiped* in Catholic liturgical life.

The honor paid to the saints and the angels is called *dulia.* It is praise, but not worship. The veneration of the saints and angels is due to their cooperation with God's grace. The special praise given to the Blessed Virgin Mary is called *hyperdulia.* This highest honor given to any human is owed to Mary because of her unique role in the Incarnation.

The saints exemplify Christian living.[2] "There is a constant in the identification of Christian saints, namely, the witness to the intimate and infinite love of Jesus Christ. . . . The saints in any age are transparent in their pointing to the new creation in Christ."[3]

The saints pray for people who beseech them for assistance. In the same way that Christians will ask other Christians to pray for them, the Church teaches that these holy people who are now living in glory are able to intercede for us, if we seek their aid.

Finally the saints inspire believers to live holy lives. Since the saints were ordinary people who attained extraordinary holiness, their example gives believers hope that they too might attain holiness if they open up themselves to God's grace as the saints did. In summary, the saints provide Christians with example, intercession, and inspiration.

Unfortunately, too often the saints' witness to the path of holiness has been lost because of the desire to make them so heroic that their human weakness almost vanishes from the stories of their lives. The sad result of such hagiography is that the example and inspiration, the model and hope, that the saints could offer ordinary believers in their own pursuit of holiness might often be lost.

The reader will discover in this book that the saints carried in their lives the same crosses ordinary persons bear. But in imitation of Jesus, the saints were not crushed by the weight of the cross; rather, they bore its weight and drew closer to Jesus as a result.

Suffering is universal and inevitable; no one escapes it. It is mysterious; no one can fully understand it. Deeper meaning unfolds for those who dare to explore its depths.

The faith-filled Christian response to suffering is to use the experience and the process to identify with Jesus. Jesus suffered, died, and rose for the salvation of all people. He instructs whoever wishes to be his disciple to "deny himself and take up his cross and follow me."[4]

Jesus teaches his disciples that they must die in order to live with him: ". . . unless a grain of wheat falls into the earth and dies, it remains alone; but if it dies, it bears much fruit."[5] Believers learn that acceptance of suffering for the sake of Jesus and his kingdom is part of the cost of discipleship: ". . . he who loses his life for my sake will find it."[6]

Is it accurate to view suffering as a punishment from God? In the New Testament, when Jesus heals the man born blind, the disciples inquire, "Rabbi, who sinned, this man or his parents, that he was born blind?" (John 9:2). Jesus replies, "It was not that this man sinned, or his parents, but that the works of God might be made manifest in him" (John 9:3). Jesus came to heal and forgive sins, not to punish on account of sins.

This book has a pastoral purpose: to offer example and encouragement to all suffering people. The words of the saints themselves are included to enable the reader to sense the depth of feeling that the saints experienced in their sufferings. It is hoped that the reader will identify with the saints' sufferings and, like the saints, imitate Jesus in his path of holiness.

The one hundred six saintly persons included in this book consist of sixty-eight men and thirty-eight women, who represent every century and every continent except Australia, which to this date claims no saint, although a native nun recently was beatified.[7] An effort has been made to include saints who are contemporary, lay, and representative of the New World. Of the one hundred six saints included, therefore, thirty-five lived in the nineteenth and twentieth centuries, eighteen were married, fourteen were single, and eighteen ministered in the Americas.

Almost all the persons whose stories are told in this book are designated as Venerable, Blessed, or Saint. Their title indicates their stage of progress of ecclesiastical recognition for the cause of canonization. Seven other persons, however, are included whose title is "servant of God." Their causes for canonization have been accepted for investigation, but they have not yet advanced beyond the initial stage.[8] Six of these seven have died after 1963, which allows little time for the process of canonization that usually requires decades, if not centuries, of investigation before approbation.[9] The intention in including these contemporaries is to provide current examples of suffering by persons who enjoy the *fama sanctitatis*, that is, "the reputation of sanctity." This reputation is one of the first considerations in the process of investigation toward canonization. The intention is not to anticipate the Church's decision on such matters. Whether or not these persons might be recognized as saints someday is the will of God and the work of ecclesiastical authorities.

Endnotes

1. Jesus is called the Suffering Servant in imitation of the four poems of Isaiah: 42:1-4, 49:1-6, 50:4-9, and 52:13 through 53:12, which record the dialogue between Yahweh and his servant regarding the God-given call to mission, the servant's felt inability to complete the mission, the internal and external difficulties experienced in mission, and the servant's death and recompense, which action by Christ is redemptive for all people.

    Mary has been called the Mother of Sorrows by theologians and spiritual writers ever since the fourth century. These authors provided various interpretations and enumerations, from five to fifteen, of her sufferings. The number of sorrows always paralleled the number of joys. In the fifteenth century a priest, John of Coudenberg from the Low Countries, founded confraternities of devotion to the sorrows of Mary. He fixed the number at seven, and a century later the Servites popularized these confraternities and their devotion. These seven sorrows consist of the prophecy of Simeon (Luke 2:34-35), the flight into Egypt (Matthew 2:13-14), the loss of the child Jesus in the Temple (Luke 2:41-52), the carrying of the cross (Luke 23:26-31), the crucifixion (Luke 23:32-49), the taking down from the cross (Luke 23:50-53), and the burial of Jesus (Luke 23:54-56).

2. Because spiritualities differ according to cultures and centuries, appropriate adaptations need to be made according to time and place.

3. Shawn Madigan, "Saints, Communion of Saints," in *The New Dictionary of Catholic Spirituality*, ed. by Michael Downey (Collegeville, Minn.: The Liturgical Press, 1993), p. 850.

4. Matthew 16:24.

5. John 12:24.

6. Matthew 10:39.

7. Mary MacKillop (1842-1909), native-born Dominican Sister, was beatified in 1995.

8. Catherine de Hueck Doherty (1896-1985), Dorothy Day (1897-1980), Pope John XXIII (1881-1963), Joseph Cardinal Bernardin (1928-1996), Louis Martin (1823-1894), Mother Teresa of Calcutta (1910-1997), and Archbishop Oscar Romero (1917-1980).

9. Only Louis Martin died before 1963, having died in 1894. The causes of canonization for him and his wife have been submitted to the Congregation for Sainthood Causes. Together they were declared servants of God in 1994.

PART
1

Sickness and Death

Dorothy Day

Dorothy Day (1897-1980) has been described as "a feisty, street-smart, yet compassionate American Mother Teresa — but a Mother Teresa with a past."[1] The same observer adds:

> I think Dorothy Day is quintessentially American. . . . And in her life she struggled with questions that, some 50 years later, would be the nerve issues of contemporary American Society: feminism and women's rights, sexuality and commitment, abortion, single-motherhood, the balancing of career and family, non-violent conflict resolution, the option for the poor, the jobless, the homeless, the hunger for transcendent meaning.[2]

Young Dorothy was a rebel. She resisted all authorities: parents, family, church, and government. She refused to conform to traditional social expectations regarding dress, diet, and behavior. She marched in public protests against the Vietnam War and on behalf of women's rights, the Birth Control League, the labor movement, communism, and American Blacks' civil rights. She was jailed on three occasions.

Dorothy fell into numerous heartbreaking romantic relationships and trysts. Almost all of these relationships evaporated. At twenty, she fell for a thirty-year-old hard-drinking egocentric womanizer named Lionel Moise. He told her outright, "But you know you love babies. And if you had one, I'd leave you. . . . I'll take what I can get out of you."[3] Dorothy was determined to seduce him. No matter how many times he walked out on her or berated her, she continuously sought him out in the streets and cafés of Greenwich Village. She wanted to lose her virginity, and it was Moise with whom she wanted to experiment. " 'I've got to have you,' she told him. 'I love you. I do love you. It's a fatal passion. . . . I don't give a damn about marriage.' "[4] Their on-again off-again affair evolved into her moving in with him at his 35th Street apartment in midtown Manhattan.

The experience with Moise was more than what she bargained for. Their first days of living together were blissful. She loved performing the household chores of picking up and ironing his clothes. She was "his woman."[5] She enjoyed sex with him, the wilder the better. Two or three months passed and she became pregnant. She refused to have the child. She refused to move home because her mother had warned her, "Don't get caught! Whatever you do, don't get caught."[6] In one of her three auto-biographical novels, Dorothy describes herself as June, and Moise as Dick in the story of her having an abortion.[7]

> June lay on a single cot bed in the home of Dr. Jane Pringle, a six-room flat in a huge apartment house on the upper East Side. Pretty soon it would all be over with. It ought not to take but a few hours more the doctor said. Just to lie there and endure. Three hours seemed an eternity but the minutes sped by very fast. One pain every three minutes. How fast they came! It seemed that the moments of respite could be counted in seconds. The pain came in a huge wave and she lay there writhing and tortured under it. Just when she thought she could endure it no longer, the wave passed and she could gather up her strength to endure the next one.[8]

"A life that had begun an unwilled journey. . . . It was the realization of this that became a part of Dorothy's person and, finally, changed her life."[9] Moise promised that he would pick her up at the abortionist's apartment. He never showed. She sat on the outdoor steps waiting for two hours. "When the clock struck ten, she gave up hope, and putting on the scarf and hat, she left the house and waited on the corner for a taxi. She would rather go home alone than have Dr. Pringle find out that Dick had not called for her. If anyone pitied her, she would find it very easy to begin pitying herself."[10]

Ashamed, hurt, and finally more realistic, she took herself home. Moise had left a note saying he was leaving her. The note concluded, "Don't build up any hopes. It is best, in fact, that you forget me. [Signed] Your ever devoted swain."[11]

Years passed and Dorothy found the meaning for which she had been searching. She dedicated her life to Jesus Christ, the Catholic Church, the pursuit of social justice, and the service of the poor. With her typical determination, she pursued and found Jesus. She is considered now by many to be a candidate for sainthood.

ALCOHOLISM

Bl. Matt Talbot

This lad from Dublin contracted what is called euphemistically "Irish flu." Matt Talbot (1856-1925) began drinking before his teen years and continued his habit until he was twenty-eight. He broke the habit only after the habit had broken him and deprived him of self-control, friendships, and finances.

Matt grew up as the second of twelve children in a working-class family. As soon as this eleven-year-old completed his only year of formal education, he went to work. He proved to be a responsible and likable worker. He labored ten hours a day, six days a week. His first job was as a messenger boy at a wine merchant's store. Whenever the men were loading and unloading crates of wine, some crates became damaged and their contents then became available for free tasting. Within a few months, young Matt was imitating the actions of the grown men. He quickly showed the effects of his drinking in his face and gait. He never missed work, however, and he prided himself on that trait.

> Matt opened bottles more and more frequently. After a while, he started his workday with a wine breakfast at 7 a.m. He kept the wine intake at as steady a pace as possible throughout each day, in between deliveries, during warehouse tasks. It was easy he realized, and it took more and more to satisfy him. As he celebrated his thirteenth birthday, he pondered all that had happened to him in a year. The first thing he thought about in the morning was wine. As his eyes opened and looked up at the barren ceiling of the Talbots' crowded flat, Matt pictured a plush, chilled bottle, begging to be drunk.[12]

His parents noticed the effects of alcohol on their son. The father grew frustrated at Matt's behavior and beat him. The father took Matt away from the wine distributor and found his son a job at the same place where the father worked at the Port and Docks Board of Dublin. Here there was no wine. Instead, there was whiskey. The foreman motivated the men by providing free whiskey. Despite the presence of his father, Matt continued his drinking.

At seventeen, the son, wanting to be freed from his father's supervision, found work at a brickyard. The workday began at six o'clock in the morning, and immediately after work, Matt dashed to the pub, where he stayed until one or two o'clock each morning. He adhered to this schedule for the next twelve years. He joined in the drinkers' storytelling, singing, joking, and cursing. Eventually, he simply handed over his weekly pay to the bartender, who would allot him drinks throughout the week, as long as the pay lasted. Sometimes Matt would have to scrape together money when his pay no longer covered his bar bill. On one occasion, he sold his shoes for a drink and arrived home barefoot on a cold winter's night. Another time, Matt distracted a working fiddler while Matt's drinking companion stole the musical instrument, ran to and sold it at a pawn shop, returned, and treated his friend to drinks.

At twenty-eight, Matt missed work for the first time. In fact, he missed an entire week. Knowing Saturday was payday and feeling better, he meandered to the intersection between his workplace and the pub. He planned to intercept his friends and join them in their customary activity. When his group of friends arrived, they ignored him. No one offered to treat him. He refused to beg from them. He went home in disgust. That was early in 1884.

That same day, he went to confession for the first time in three years. He took the pledge not to drink, at first for three months, then for one year, then for the rest of his life. He performed daily acts of penance and fasting. He rose each morning at two o'clock to pray. At the local church, he would often kneel outside, waiting for the priest or sexton to open the doors. Inside, he took the same posture. For the next forty years, he never again touched alcohol.

Bl. André of Montreal

Brother André Bessette (1845-1937), the devotee of St. Joseph and publicly renowned miracle-worker of Montreal, was a kind but occasionally irascible man. While hundreds of thousands annually sought cures and hundreds received cures from him, nevertheless, his short-tempered manner sometimes chased away the miracle-seekers. He was asked if he realized how gruff and angry he appeared at times. He responded, "Not at all. I realized it only afterwards."[13]

He roughly rebuked people for two behaviors especially: immodest dress and improper intentions in seeking a miracle. To a woman whose young daughter was wearing a great deal of makeup, he said, "Is she your daughter? If I were you, I would not boast of it."[14] To a woman wearing a low-cut dress who was complaining of chest pains, he commented, "It is surely not because your collar is too tight."[15] To a young woman whose skirt was particularly short, he asked: "Were you afraid of entangling yourself in your skirt?"[16] One woman whom he insulted ran away in tears, but realized she had nonetheless been cured, returned chastened and forever grateful.

Sometimes André perceived that people approached him with the wrong intentions. After a tourist asked him if he worked cures by hypnotism, André ordered the ushers to forcibly escort the nonbeliever outside. André scolded a woman who appeared to be laughing at him, saying that her prayers would never be answered until she learned to pray properly. One time, the chaplain of the king of England asked to visit with André and proceeded to tell André how impressed was the king with André's good work. "Brother André listened to all that reverently for two or three minutes, and then he said, 'You will excuse me; many sick people are here today.' "[17] To his confreres in religious life who sometimes criticized him for traveling long distances and even overnight under the guise of visiting the sick, he retorted, "You know it is not forbidden to travel in order to do good to our fellow men."[18]

Granted, André lacked sophistication and subtlety. He had grown up on a farm, the sixth of ten children, and later worked at physically demanding unskilled jobs before entering religious life at thirty. Orphaned at twelve, he had received almost no formal education and throughout his life could hardly read or write. His manner was simple and direct. He related in that way with God and everyone whom he met. This simplicity was both a blessing and a curse. While never intending to offend people, he oftentimes did so. André himself would weep after learning he had made others cry.

ASTHMA

St. Bernadette Soubirous

At Lourdes, France, Bernadette Soubirous (1844-1879) grew up in abject poverty. "The family were living in the dark airless basement of a dilapidated building."[19] Bernadette fell sick during the cholera epidemic of 1854 and never recovered.

Between February 11 and March 4, 1858, Bernadette experienced daily apparitions of the Blessed Virgin Mary in a cave along the Gave River. On February 25, Mary made a spring of water flow in the area of the now famous grotto. On March 25, the Blessed Mother identified herself as the Immaculate Conception and requested that a chapel be built at the site.

Throughout her entire convent life, Bernadette experienced sickness. After just a few weeks of entering into the convent at twenty-two, she became so sick that she received the last rites. She recovered and lived until thirty-five, but suffered from asthma and tuberculosis much of the time. During the last four months of her life, she was confined to bed. Her body ached with every movement. Bed sores plagued her. Ankylosis of the knee caused her whole leg to swell grotesquely. She passed many sleepless nights. A frequent priest-visitor describes her ills.

> Chronic asthma, chest pains, accompanied by spitting up of blood, went on for two years. An aneurysm, gastralgia, and a tumor of the knee developed. Finally, during the last few years she suffered from bone decay, so that her poor body was the vessel of all kinds of pain and suffering. Meanwhile abscesses formed in her ears . . . inflicting partial deafness on her. This was very difficult for her and ceased only a short time before her death. After she made her perpetual vows (September 22, 1878), her sufferings redoubled in intensity and ceased only at her death. Her ambition, which she concealed as much as she could, was to be a victim for the Heart of Jesus.[20]

Although she received excellent care from the doctors and sister-nurses, nothing lessened her pain. During her last week on earth, she begged her doctor, "Look among your drugs . . . for something to revive me. I feel so weak I can hardly breathe. Bring me some strong vinegar to sniff."[21] A few days later she said, "This morning, after Holy Communion, I asked our Lord for five minutes' relief so that I could talk to him leisurely. But he did not choose to give me them."[22] She commented to one of her religious sisters, "I have been ground in the mill like a grain of wheat. I would never have thought that one must suffer so much to die."[23] The next day, she added, "How right the author of the *Imitation of Christ* was in telling people that they must not wait for the last moment to serve God. One is capable of so little!"[24]

She continued to receive visitors. Many of them kept requesting her prayers for themselves, but all she wanted to do was to die.[25] She commented about her visitors: "I like to see the backs of people's heels rather than the tips of their noses. When one is suffering, one needs to be alone."[26] She said to one visitor, "Mademoiselle, I am in a great deal of pain. I cannot embrace you, but I will pray for you."[27] In her last hours, those attending her prayed with her, as Bernadette had requested.[28] She simply held the crucifix in her hands. Making the sign of the cross, she took a few sips of water, bowed her head, and gave up her soul to God.

Joseph Cardinal Bernardin

"I am Joseph your brother," spoke Joseph Bernardin (1928-1996) as he greeted the people of Chicago in 1982 at his installation as archbishop of the country's largest archdiocese. The intimacy and simplicity of his greeting was repeated in his 1997 posthumous publication, *The Gift of Peace*, in which he describes a number of past struggles.

Bernardin writes comfortably about his personal sufferings. He admits to having a spiritual crisis as a young priest when he believed that he "could not continue on."[29] He reveals his pain about his family's poverty, his father's death, his growing up in a single-parent home, his mother's sickness, his distaste for administration and preference for pastoral ministry. He attributes his ability to respect others to his public high school experience in which "I learned early in life how to live with people whose beliefs differ from my own."[30] The issues he encountered daily throughout his ministry provided him with a profound opportunity to connect with God and God's people.

In November 1993, Bernardin was "startled and devastated" to hear that a former seminary student claimed that Bernardin had sexually molested him.[31] The accusation was the topic of national news for a hundred days. At the end of February 1994, the young man, dying of AIDS, recanted his story. In December 1994, the cardinal and young man, each accompanied by a friend, met, chatted, and expressed mutual pardon and repentance; the young man participated in a Mass celebrated by Cardinal Bernardin.

The cardinal exults after the previous year, "I began 1995 as a liberated man."[32] In June, however, he was diagnosed and operated on for pancreatic cancer. The chance of malignancy was "99 percent plus."[33] The cancer remained in remission for fifteen months and then Bernardin died in November 1996. The cardinal writes openly in his Pastoral Letter on Healthcare in October 1995 about his feelings, his faith, and the community he felt with fellow cancer patients.

> When I entered the Loyola University Medical Center last June, my life had been turned completely upside down by the totally unexpected news that what I had been experiencing as a healthy body was, in fact, housing a dangerous, aggressive cancer. The time since the diagnosis, surgery, and postoperative radiation and chemotherapy

has led me into a new dimension of my lifelong journey of faith.

I have experienced in a very personal way the chaos that serious illness brings into one's life. I have had to let go of many things that had brought me a sense of security and satisfaction in order to find the healing that only faith in the Lord can bring.

Initially, I felt as though floodwaters were threatening to overwhelm me. For the first time in my life I truly had to look death in the face. In one brief moment, all my personal dreams and pastoral plans for the future had to be put on hold. Everything in my personal and pastoral life had to be reevaluated from a new perspective. My initial experience was of disorientation, isolation, a feeling of not being "at home" anymore.

Instead of being immobilized by the news of the cancer, however, I began to prepare myself for surgery and postoperative care. I discussed my condition with family and friends. I prayed as I have never prayed before that I would have the courage and grace to face whatever lay ahead. I determined that I would offer whatever suffering I might endure for the Church, particularly the Archdiocese of Chicago. Blessedly, a peace of mind and heart and soul quietly flooded through my entire being, a kind of peace I had never known before. And I came to believe in a new way that the Lord would walk with me through this journey of illness that would take me from a former way of life into a new manner of living.

Nevertheless, during my convalescence I found the nights to be especially long, a time for various fears to surface. I sometimes found myself weeping, something I seldom did before. And I came to realize how much of what consumes our daily life is trivial and insignificant. In these dark moments, besides my faith and trust in the Lord, I was constantly bolstered by the awareness that thousands of people were praying for me throughout the Archdiocese and, indeed, the world. I have been graced by an outpouring of affection and support that has allowed me to experience ecclesial life as a "community of hope" in a very intimate way.[34]

DEATH IN CHILDBIRTH

Bl. Hedwig of Poland

Hedwig (1371-1399) is identified in all the major dictionaries of saints as blessed, even though her cause for beatification was never completed.

She was the youngest daughter of King Louis of Hungary, whose uncle was the king of Poland. When her uncle and father died, she succeeded them and reigned simultaneously on both thrones. For political purposes, she was asked at thirteen to marry Jagiello, the duke of Lithuania. The arranged marriage had one condition: that the husband and the citizenry of his territory would convert to Christianity. Jagiello agreed. Their bond "began a four-hundred-year alliance between Poland and Lithuania."[35]

At his baptism, Jagiello took the name of Ladislaus. He then oversaw the baptism of his people.

> We read strange stories of the "conversion" of the Lithuanian people — how the temples of the false gods were destroyed wholesale, and how men, women and children drawn up in platoons, were sprinkled [for their baptism] by the bishops and priests, every division receiving the same name.[36]

While Hedwig's husband, Ladislaus, was feared because of the way he mistreated his people, she was loved for her kind manner and practical charity toward the sick and poor.

When Hedwig became pregnant, Ladislaus was ecstatic. He purchased extravagant gifts for the anticipated child. Hedwig, meanwhile, showed little interest in these material goods. She spent her time in prayer, asceticisms, and practical preparations. She thanked God for this pregnancy, since she had been unable to conceive during the previous decade. She gave birth to a daughter. Everyone rejoiced. Shouts of joy, however, turned into tears of mourning when, a few days later, the new mother died.

Bl. Herman the Cripple

Herman (1013-1054) was born severely deformed and crippled. His parents placed him at age seven in the Abbey of Reichenau on an island in Lake Constance, Switzerland, where he remained for the rest of his life.

At twenty, Herman took vows as a monk, dedicating himself to prayer and study. He wrote a mathematical-astronomical text and invented instruments to use in his research. He wrote poetry and music. The hymns *Salve Regina* ("Hail Holy Queen") and *Alma Redemptoris Mater* are attributed to him. He wrote one of the earliest medieval chronicles of world history and "became known to scholars all over Europe for his keen mind."[37] His contemporaries regarded him as "the wonder of the times."[38]

St. John of God

After hearing a sermon preached by John of Ávila, John of God (1495-1550) went berserk and was detained for nine months in an insane asylum. Prior to his insanity, John had been a soldier, shepherd, and store owner. He had left his native Portuguese village to fight for the Spanish count of Oporusa against the French and Turks. During his enlistment, John had given up the practice of religion and morality. He spent his time drinking, gambling, and fighting. When his military days were over, he found employment as a shepherd. With time to reflect on his sinful past, he experienced a conversion.

He traveled to Algiers in North Africa, intending to ransom Christian slaves and die a martyr at the hands of the Muslims. After a priest counseled him that it was not necessary to fulfill a private vow to die a martyr, John returned to Spain, where he opened a small religious goods store. After three years' success, he opened another religious goods store in the cathedral city of Granada. At forty-three, John appeared settled in his personal and professional life.

Then the famous preacher John of Ávila visited Granada. John joined many others in listening to the saintly priest. John's heart was deeply touched. A wave of remorse surged within him. He stood up in the cathedral, beat his breast, and shouted out that he desperately needed God's mercy. He ran from the church into the city streets. He pulled out the hair from his beard. He stripped off most of his clothes. He tore apart with his teeth the secular books he had been selling. He threw himself down onto the muddy road. He begged God for forgiveness and publicly confessed his sins. He urged onlookers to throw rocks and mud at him, since he felt he deserved mistreatment. The children complied. Onlookers shouted, "See the madman!"[39] Friends intervened and carried him to the preacher whose sermon had occasioned the bizarre behavior. The preacher calmed the penitent. As soon as they separated, however, John renewed his antics. A firsthand account in the earliest biography of John of God describes the situation.

> The common people believed him to be insane. But John, inflamed by God's grace, wanted only to die to himself for love of God.

So that all might think falsely of him and despise him, he got up from the garbage heap and ran through the principal streets, jumping and doing all kinds of foolish things. The children and the mob followed him throwing stones, mud and other filth at him. He bore it all patiently and with joy, as if he were at a banquet, happy to attain the fulfillment of his desire, to suffer for Him whom he loved so much, without harming others. He carried a wooden cross in his hand and gave it to everyone to kiss. Some told him to kiss the ground for the love of Jesus Christ, and he immediately obeyed, even though the ground was muddy, or if a little child asked him to do it. He repeated it every day with much devotion, so that he often fell exhausted and weak because of the ridicule, the shoving and the blows heaped upon him; and for the want of food, so that he could barely stand upright. In spite of all this, he was not yet satisfied, offering his body to the stones and blows the children rained upon him, supporting it all cheerfully and without complaint or refusal.

Two citizens who had pity on John took him by the hand and, forcing a path through the crowd, brought him to the Royal Hospital, where the insane of the city were received and treated. They requested the superintendent to take him in and put him in a room away from everyone, in order that he might get some rest and perhaps be cured of his madness.[40]

John of Ávila oftentimes visited John in the asylum. The preacher advised the penitent to focus no longer on performing penances for past sins but to focus on doing good deeds in the present for others. The penitent patient listened. He applied in the asylum the good advice he received and recovered marvelously. Upon his release, John rented an apartment in which he sheltered and cared for the abandoned sick. In the marketplace, he earned a little money that he shared with the poor. His ministry attracted donors and followers and it laid the foundation of the religious order of the Brothers of St. John of God.

EXCESSIVE FASTING

St. Clare of Assisi

For almost half of her life, that is, the last twenty-eight years, Clare of Assisi (1194-1253) suffered uninterrupted ill health. Within two months after Clare's death, the pope appointed a commission to examine the cause for her canonization. This board interviewed under oath fifteen religious sisters who had lived with Clare and five laypersons of Assisi who had known her before she entered the convent.

The nuns spoke at length about Clare's ill health, which they generally attributed to her severe austerities of diet and self-discipline. They noted that Clare ate nothing on three days of the week and fasted on bread and water the other three days, but never on Sundays. On the Lord's Day, she permitted herself to drink a little wine when there was some. During Lent and the two months between the Feast of All Saints and Christmas, she practiced special abstinences. Clare spent long hours in prayer, to which they attributed her many miracles.[41] One nun observed, "She seemed to have the life of an angel in that her holiness was obvious to all those who knew and heard her."[42] The combination of much prayer and penance seemed to have resulted in a visible radiance. The testimony of one sister is representative of what the others reported.

> This witness also said the blessed mother [Clare] kept vigil so much of the night in prayer, and kept so many abstinences that the sisters lamented and were alarmed. [The witness] said that because of this she herself had sometimes wept. Asked how she knew this, she replied: because she saw when Lady Clare lay on the ground and had a rock from the river for her head, and heard her when she was in prayer.
>
> She said she was so strict in her food [intake] that the sisters marveled at how her body survived. She also said blessed Clare fasted much of the time. Three days of the week, Monday, Wednesday, and Friday, she did not eat anything. She said on the other days she kept such abstinence that she developed a certain illness so Saint Francis together with the bishop of Assisi commanded her to eat on those three days at least a half a roll of bread, about one and a half ounces.
>
> She also said the blessed mother was assiduous and careful in her prayers, lying a long time upon the ground, remaining humbly prostrate. When she came from prayer, she admonished and comforted her sisters always speaking the words of God who was always in her mouth, so much so that she did not want to speak or hear of vanities. When she returned from her prayer, the sisters rejoiced as though she had come from heaven.[43]

The lay witnesses included a relative, a next-door neighbor, two friends, and an employee of the family. They testified that Clare had lived a holy life before she entered the convent. One witness sums up the words of the others: "Asked what good deeds she did, he replied that she fasted, prayed, and willingly gave as many alms as she could. When she was sitting with those in the house, she always spoke of the things of God."[44]

The testimony of witnesses and other data were compiled into an official biography entitled *The Legend of Saint Clare.* This legend was based on well-documented sources of personal witnesses and critically verified miracles. Under the legend's chapter titled "Her Sickness And Prolonged Illness," one reads: "For forty years she had run the course of the highest poverty, when, preceded by a number of illnesses, she was obviously approaching the prize of her exalted calling."[45] The following poetry by a contemporary describes Clare.

> Since the strength of her flesh had succumbed
> to the austerity of the penance
> [she had practiced] in the early years,
> a harsh sickness took hold of her last years,
> so that she who had been enriched
> with the merits of [good] deeds [when] well
> might be enriched with the merits of suffering when sick.
> For virtue is brought to perfection in sickness.[46]

As soon as she died, a brief announcement was distributed "to all the sisters of the order of San Damiano throughout the world," noting Clare had long suffered without complaint.[47]

> Wounded by the sting of a lingering sickness and delayed by
> the tenderness of subsequent old age, she did not break into grumbling out of weakness nor did she open the door of her mouth to complain. Moreover, the more strongly she was stung by the barbs of sickness, so much more did she devoutly offer a song of praise to the Lord.
> How great was the bond of seriousness with which she was bound![48]

GAMBLING

St. Camillus de Lellis

Camillus de Lellis (1550-1616) gave himself wantonly to fighting, drinking, and gambling. On numerous occasions, he gambled away everything he owned, including the proverbial shirt off his back. His childhood interest in playing cards developed into a habit, which burst into an addiction.

At seventeen, he joined his father and two cousins as mercenaries fighting with the Venetians against the Turks and was wounded in action. The injury in Camillus's left leg cleared up, but the infection traveled to his right foot and ankle. The nature of the wound has never been identified, but it was incurable and it periodically flared up. This affliction never left him. Coming home from war, he encountered two Franciscans. "Impetuously he resolved and even vowed to become a Franciscan."[49]

In March 1571, Camillus entered the famous Roman hospital for incurable patients. At the end of the month the burly ex-soldier was hired as a staff employee. By the end of the year, however, he was fired. Hospital records indicate that Camillus "was an appalling hot-head, constantly quarrelling with one or another of the servants. Being obsessed with card-playing, he would often desert the service of the sick and go off across the Tiber to play with the Tiber boatmen."[50] Unemployed, he reenlisted in the Venetian army. At Corfu, he fell ill with dysentery and received the last rites. He recovered and returned to war.

After Venice signed a peace treaty with the Turks in March 1573, Camillus returned to Rome. He took up his usual pastime and lost all his money. He found a temporary job as a security guard before sailing to Palermo, where he gambled away again his earnings. Sailing for Naples, he encountered a terrible storm, during which he renewed his vow to become a Franciscan. Before following through on his vow, he decided to gamble one last time. One quick game became many games! At Naples, once again, he lost everything.

> Back at Naples, he quickly forgot the perils he had come through and his vow. He gambled unrestrainedly day and night, almost without rest. He wagered and lost all his service bonus, his sword, his hook-gun, his powder flask, his cape — everything, except the trappings of his sword and the essential garments he wore. The inherent needs of life and the inclemency of the weather seemed of no concern to him. But for Camillus, gambling was a perturbed and painful struggle with hopelessness and death. In spite of the crippling losses he incurred, he hung on to the terrible illusion that, sooner or later, fortune would smile on him, and this was fatal. Although reduced to misery, he refused to believe that his good fortune lay in any other direction.[51]

Camillus headed north, ending up at Manfredonia. A Capuchin asked Camillus if he wanted to work in a construction project. Camillus pondered the offer, walked away from it, then ran back to it when he discovered farther on that work and money were difficult to find. He worked hard for two straight weeks. When he asked for a day off, he was refused. He became so enraged that he bit his own hand. He took the time off anyway. Upon his return, the Capuchins rehired him and even gave him a raise.

The guardian in a neighboring friary spoke to Camillus about God's love and Camillus's mania for gambling. The friar told his penitent to "spit in the devil's face" when confronted by thoughts of sin.[52] While riding on a mule the next day, Camillus jumped off the beast, threw himself to the ground, and in a flood of tears, begged God to help him turn his life around. He knew his gambling was out of control. He wrote to a friend, "I have just returned from the war with a lot of money and I lost it all playing cards. I beg you not to mention my plight to anyone when you return to Bucchianico; I am so ashamed of myself."[53]

Between 1575 and 1584, he entered the Capuchins twice and twice was asked to leave because the sore on his leg kept reopening. He tried to enter the Friar Observantines, but they rejected him for health reasons. In order to soothe his scrupulous conscience about his private vow, the priests provided him with a letter explaining that their statutes prohibited them from accepting someone not in good health. During this same period he returned to work at the hospital where he had been a patient. He rose through the ranks, eventually becoming the supervisor of all personnel and finances. On the advice of his confessor, Philip Neri, Camillus founded a community of men committed to faith-inspired service of the sick. This group worked, prayed, and lived together. This community became known as the Order of Brothers Hospitalers.

GRIEF FROM DEATH OF A BEST FRIEND

Bl. Raymond of Capua

Raymond of Capua (1330-1399) and Catherine of Siena (1347-1380) became best friends during their six-year relationship. Because she was emerging as a controversial public person who had already attracted a "family" of disciples among clergy and laity, the Dominicans appointed Raymond to guide her.

> She was a saint who mixed fearlessly in the world and spoke with the candor and authority of one completely committed to Christ. At the same time she was a woman, young and with no social position. She was accused of hypocrisy and presumption. At this critical

point it was her Dominican affiliation that saved her. Summoned to Florence to give an account of herself to the general chapter of the order held there in May and June of 1374, she satisfied the rigorous judges, and her work was given official Dominican protection. The chapter appointed Bl. Raymond of Capua as director of Catherine and her followers.[54]

These two saints combined efforts on many occasions. They assisted the victims of a local plague, collaborated in a crusade against the Turks, and persuaded the pope to end the seventy-year Avignon Papacy and return to Rome. In all their activities, Catherine was the charismatic leader and Raymond was her staunch supporter.

Their friendship was tested when Raymond misjudged Catherine. She had asked him to sail to France to seek the king's support for the Roman-elected pope against the Florentine-elected pope. Raymond began but aborted the mission because he learned that enemies were lying in wait to kill him in France. He then wrote to Catherine, expressing the hope that she would not love him less because of his cowardice. She responded with a stinging reply, not because he failed to complete the mission but because he failed to understand her limitless love for him. She writes:

> You began to doubt whether my love and concern for you had decreased. But you did not realize, that you yourself showed this to be the case, that my love had increased while yours had diminished. I love you with the love with which I love myself. . . . So my love for you is greater than before, not less.[55]

Having remained in Genoa after his aborted mission, Raymond paused for a moment in front of a statue of the Blessed Virgin Mary and had a mystical experience. He writes:

> Suddenly there was a voice, though there was no sound in the air; the words sounded not in my bodily ears but in my mind, and I heard them more clearly than if they had come from the mouth of someone standing only a yard away. This is the only way I can think of describing the voice, if voice it can be called, since there was no sound attached to it. However that may be, these words resounded distinctly in my mind: "Fear not: I am here for your sake; I am in heaven for your sake. I will protect you and defend you. Go on your way in confidence, and do not lose heart: I am here for your sake."[56]

Initially, Raymond thought that the voice belonged to the Blessed Mother. Later, he discovered that the voice was Catherine's. When writing the biography of Catherine, he learned that her parting advice to her disciples was to turn to Raymond for his advice, since she said, "I shall always be with him." Raymond writes:

> At this point, as I have been told by those present at the time, she suddenly lost all her strength; but despite this she continued to give holy advice to the children, both present and absent, whom she had generated in Christ. At this last moment she remembered me too, and said, "In all your doubts and needs turn to Friar Raimondo, and tell him not to be discouraged or lose heart, whatever happens, for I shall always be with him to save him from any danger; and when he does anything he shouldn't, I shall tell him, and see that he mends his ways and improves." They told me that she said this many times, for as long as she could speak.[57]

Raymond and Catherine were best friends in life and at death. Even in her physical absence, Catherine gifted Raymond with her spiritual presence. How fortunate he was to have been appointed to help her, since she never stopped helping him.

GRIEF FROM DEATH OF A CHILD

St. Elizabeth Ann Seton

Within a space of four years Elizabeth Ann Seton (1774-1821) lost her eldest and youngest children: Anne Marie, nicknamed Nina, at sixteen, and Rebecca at twelve. Elizabeth was well accustomed to death: in the previous decade, she had lost her father, husband, and three sisters-in-law, whom she calls her "soul's sisters."[58] But the death of her children unnerved Elizabeth.*

> She would say later, "After Nina was taken I was so often expecting to lose my senses, and my head was so disordered that un-

---

*The reader may notice errors or inconsistencies in grammar, syntax, and punctuation in excerpts attributed to St. Elizabeth Ann Seton. Evidently the editors of these excerpts decided to transcribe them verbatim. This applies also to two other stories about her under the titles "Abandonment by many friends" and "Single parent." Moreover, a number of excerpts pertaining to other stories in this work have similar irregularities.

less for the daily duties always before me I did not know much of what I did or what I left undone." For six months she remained virtually inconsolable. Although surrounded by her community and students, and still possessed of two other daughters and two sons, she longed for death, writing to a friend, "The separation from my angel has left so new and deep an impression on my mind, that if I was not obliged to live in these dear ones I should unconsciously die in her."[59]

Elizabeth had centered a special affection on her firstborn child. The mother anticipated a lifelong friendship with her daughter. On New Year's Eve in 1798, reflecting about the future together, Elizabeth writes a letter to her not-yet-three-year-old Nina:

> The last, the first and every day of the year my thoughts and time are yours my Anna, but I enjoy a peculiar pleasure in devoting an hour generally appropriated to amusements, to you my precious child, in whom my greatest delight and amusements are centered. May the giver of all good grant his protection to you, and assist me in my endeavors to promote your future and good advantage. The blessing and attentions of the tenderest parents and most affectionate friends are constantly yours, and by your conduct you will confer the gratification of our fondest wishes, or inflict the most bitter disappointment. In you I view the friend, the companion, and consolation of my future years — delightful reflection.[60]

Nina was the only child who accompanied her parents to Italy when her father was sick. She shared her mother's affection for the Catholic faith and encouraged their formal conversion. Nina, more than the other children, resembled her mother in appearance and personality. After her husband died, Elizabeth confided in Nina more than the other children. And so, when death took Nina, part of Elizabeth died too. Elizabeth describes her wide-ranging feelings at her daughter's graveside:

> On the grave of Anina — begging crying to Mary to behold her Son and plead for us, and to Jesus to behold his Mother — to pity a mother — a poor poor mother — so uncertain of reunion — then the Soul quieted even by the desolation of the falling leaves around began to cry out from eternity to eternity thou art God — all shall perish and pass away — but thou remainest forever — then the thought of our dearest stretched on the cross and his last words coming power-

fully, stood up with hands and eyes lifted to the pure heavens, crying out, forgive they know not what they do.[61]

In the same year that Nina died, Rebecca fell while playing. From that day forward, she needed to use a crutch. Her mother observes: "By much suffering, [Rebecca] is preparing and hastening, I believe, to her happy eternity."[62] Four years later, Rebecca lay on her deathbed. She ached with every movement. Her mother observes:

> Poor darling, once when writhing herself out of our hands till her poor lame knee fell to the floor, sweating and panting half scream-ing she stared her big eyes and said to us as if in consultation "I am almost tempted to beg our Lord to ease me, do you think it will dis-please him" — and with such faith when permitted she begged him let her have only a moment to get in a posture, and actually was eased enough to get in bed — almost gone though — we have all sobbed round her like babies at that silence which succeeded.[63]

St. Gregory Nazianzen

We distinguish the father and son who bear the same name by calling them the elder (c. 276-374) and the younger (c. 329-389). Gregory the el-der converted from a pagan syncretistic religion to Christianity at his wife's urging. After a career as a government official, the elder was ordained a bishop at fifty-two and served in that capacity for the next forty-five years. The father influenced his son in becoming a priest. The younger, brilliant in mind and spirit, is known in history as "the theologian."

Throughout the eulogy at the funeral, the son praised the father with numerous appellations from the Scriptures, for example, man of God, faithful servant, and wise shepherd. He calls his father a seaman's skilled pilot and a beacon for people's lives. The son describes his father's origins as undistinguished stock. The younger esteems his father's integrity, since "he held the highest offices in the state, yet did not enrich himself by a single penny."[64] He contrasted his father to more popular preachers, say-ing that "while he bore off second prize in oratory, he took the first in piety."[65] His father's brief lapse into heresy is explained in that "in his guile-lessness he had not been on guard against guile."[66] He repeated his father's principle regarding bestowing alms: "For it is far better to be generous to the unworthy for the sake of the worthy than to deprive the worthy out of fear of the unworthy."[67]

The son continues, "But his noblest and most characteristic quality, recognized even by the multitude, was his simplicity and his guileless and forgiving disposition."[68] The father acted so kindly "that while he was not the only one to deliver censure, he was the only one to be both loved and admired by those he reproved."[69] The younger notes how fitting a "memorial of his magnanimity" is the place of worship built by his father's congregation and using much of the father's own money.[70]

The final paragraphs of Gregory's funeral oration are addressed, in part, to his deceased father, and to his grieving mother who would die within a few months.

To his father, Gregory the younger inquires rhetorically if he is satisfied with the 13,500-word eulogy.

> What do you say, my father? Is this enough, and do you accept this eulogy accompanying you to the tomb as recompense for those labors you undertook for my education? And according to your old custom, do you grant peace to my discourse, and set a limit upon it, shunning excess, that it may be of right measure? Or do you require some addition? You bid me cease, I know, for I have spoken long enough.[71]

To his mother, he addresses the following:

> Does the thought of separation grieve you? Then let hope cheer you. Is widowhood a grievous burden? Yet it is not grievous to him. And where is love's goodness if it gives the easier role to itself and the more arduous one to its neighbor? Why should it even be grievous at all to one who is soon to be dissolved? The appointed day is near at hand; the pain will not last long. Let us not be ignoble thinking to give weight to the merest trifles. Great is the loss we have suffered, for great was the blessing we enjoyed.[72]

GRIEF FROM DEATH OF A HUSBAND

St. Jane Frances de Chantal

Jane's (1572-1641) husband, Christopher, died at thirty-seven in a hunting accident when he and a companion were riding on horseback "with their shotguns cocked and loaded."[73] She was twenty-nine, at home, eight-and-a-half months pregnant with their seventh child. Upon hearing of the tragedy, Jane (or Jeanne) ran to her husband's side.

> As soon as he saw her, he said, "Darling, heaven's judgment is just; we must resign ourselves to it. I'm going to die." "No, no," she answered, "we'll get you well." "It's no use," said Christopher. Jeanne started to say something about the carelessness of the friend who had accidentally shot him. "Please," said the wounded man, "let us respect heaven's Providence; let us consider this as having come from heaven." And to the distraught M. d'Anlezy: "Dear cousin, dear friend, it just happened; it wasn't your fault. I beg you, don't commit the sin of hating yourself when you haven't done anything wrong. Think about God and remember you're a Christian."
>
> M. de Chantal was carried back to the castle. He lived another nine days, in excruciating pain. He urged Jeanne to imitate him in forgiving d'Anlezy and in accepting all this with resignation. But she could not. "Lord," she prayed, out of her mind with grief, "take everything I have, my family, my goods, my children, but spare this dear husband whom you have given me." Christopher then had his pardon inscribed in the parish register "so no one will prosecute M. d'Anlezy."[74]

Depressed for the next four months, Jane could neither forget her husband's death nor forgive his killer. She withdrew from social activities and parental responsibilities. For five years, Jane avoided her husband's companion. Then one day he asked her to be the godmother of his new child. Overwhelmed by mixed emotions, "she burst into tears! She accepted the offer to become a godmother, a relative, of a child of the man who killed her beloved husband."[75]

After her husband's death, Jane asked Francis de Sales to be her spiritual director. He guided her along the way of *douceur* (French for "gentleness, sweetness, softness"). He encouraged her to start a community of uncloistered nuns who would serve people in the streets and their homes. In 1610, Jane and Francis co-founded the Visitation Order. The order grew so remarkably that by the time of her death, Jane had founded sixty-six convents.

In 1632, Jane's daughter lost her husband through sickness. She became depressed. The mother visited her daughter and the two spoke at great length. At the daughter's request, Jane wrote down her words of advice, which reflected Jane's experience three decades earlier.

You wanted to have my advice in writing, so here it is. My greatest wish is that you live like a true Christian widow, unpretentious in your dress and actions, and especially reserved in your relationships, having nothing to do with vain, worldly young men. Otherwise, dear, even though I am very sure that your conduct is above reproach — I feel more sure about it than of my own — others could question and criticize it if you entertained such persons in your house and took pleasure in their company. Please trust me in this, for your honor and mine, as well as for my peace of mind. I know very well, darling, of course, that we can't live in the world without enjoying some of its pleasures, but take my word for it, dearest, you won't find any really lasting joys except in God, in living virtuously, raising your children well, looking after their affairs and managing your household. If you seek happiness elsewhere, you will experience much anguish, as I well know.[76]

St. Francis Borgia

Francis (1510-1572) and Eleanor married when both were nineteen. Theirs seemed like an ideal marriage. Each year, for eight consecutive years, they were blessed with a new infant son. Francis, being a Borgia, possessed extraordinary bloodlines: great-grandson of a pope and a king, and cousin to the reigning emperor, King Ferdinand. Eleanor served as lady-in-waiting to Queen Isabella. The young couple enjoyed enormous political titles and privileges.

Eleanor's health had never been strong after a miscarriage in 1540. In the spring of 1543, Francis and Eleanor were informed that the employment they had been promised by the Spanish prince and his fiancée would not materialize, which broke Eleanor's heart. Her health continued to spiral downward. Francis writes about Eleanor in November 1544:

> A few days ago she was so bad that we were afraid that we should lose her. Our Lord has restored her a little. She is now able to dress herself and lie out of doors. . . . I am taking her to the mountains, away from Gandía, which is too near the sea. I hope God will cure her and that the prince will tell us to come. While waiting, we are getting ready so as to start as soon as God has given the duchess the strength we want for her.[77]

The duchess's health improved temporarily. The ever-hopeful Francis writes in May 1545, "Thank God she is better than last year. . . . May our Lord reward you for your prayers for her and me. We recommend ourselves to you the more as our leaving for the court draws near. They are pressing it on their side, and as the patient has improved in health, we cannot resist."[78]

Almost a year later, however, in March 1546, Francis is resigned to the inevitable, "for she travels swiftly to death."[79] On March 27, at age thirty-seven, Eleanor died.

> Her weakness had increased so rapidly that after each relapse recovery was slower and less complete. Francis was faced by the prospect of losing her who for so long had shared his every thought and wish, of being left with the care of eight children, Carlos, the eldest, only fifteen, Alfonso, the youngest just eight. He multiplied his already generous alms to the poor of Gandía, ordered prayers and Masses through the duchy for his wife's cure. When not at her bedside he was on his knees in his little private oratory before the Crucifix.[80]

In June, he writes: "Our Lord has willed to call back to himself the duchess whose death leaves this house so dejected and tearful as anyone can think. By the mercy of Our Lord God, however, her life was spent so much in His service, and the end of her life was so Christian, that we are left with good reason to believe that her soul is in heaven by the merits of Jesus' most precious blood."[81]

Eleanor was deceased only a few weeks when Francis petitioned for membership in the Society of Jesus. The superior general, Ignatius Loyola, advised Francis to settle his responsibilities to his children and his finances. Within two years of Eleanor's death, Francis arranged for the care of his sons and the estate. Privately he took temporary vows and, two years later, he took permanent vows.

Francis achieved great success as a Jesuit. Ordained a priest at forty, he was named the superior general of all Jesuits fifteen years later. During six years as general, this second founder of the Society of Jesus increased the community's membership and its number of institutions and sites, including among the Native Americans in what is now New York state and the provinces of Quebec and Ontario.

St. Thérèse of Lisieux

Thérèse's (1873-1897) mother died when Thérèse was four. The death left an indelible emotional mark on the child. Writing her autobiography as a twenty-four-year-old religious sister, Thérèse divided her life into three stages: young girl (until her mother's death), adolescence, and religious life. As a little girl, Thérèse felt loved by her mother, father, and four elder sisters. She enjoyed their attention, affection, company, conversation, and playfulness. She describes herself as a joyful, confident, strong-willed child. And she recounts stories exemplifying all these traits.

But her mother's death dealt her a severe blow. She writes: "Every detail of our mother's illness is still with me, especially the last weeks she spent on earth."[82] She remembers the bedroom scene in which her mother lay dying and received the last sacraments, while Thérèse knelt and her father stood crying. She describes the coffin as "huge and grim."[83] She adds that the two youngest sisters threw themselves into the arms of the two eldest sisters, viewing them now as their mothers. Her mother's death ended Thérèse's first stage as a carefree and confident little girl. Her autobiography is addressed in part to her blood sister, who was also her religious superior. This sister had requested Thérèse to provide for posterity the story of her life.

> The moment Mummy died, my happy disposition changed completely. I had been lively and cheerful, but I became timid and quiet and a bundle of nerves. A glance was often enough to make me burst into tears. I was only happy if no one took any notice of me, and I couldn't endure being with strangers. I was never cheerful except in the family circle, and there the greatest love and kindness surrounded me. Daddy's affection seemed enriched by a real motherly love, and I felt that both you and Marie were the most tender and self-sacrificing of mothers. God's little flower would never have survived if He had not poured his warmth and light on her. She was still too frail to stand up to rain and storm. She needed warmth, the gently dropping dew and the soft airs of spring. She was never without them, for Jesus gave them to her, even amidst the bleak winter of her suffering.[84]

St. Augustine of Hippo

Augustine (354-430) shed copious tears at his mother's death. He and she were more than child and parent; they were best friends.

Augustine left home at the age of sixteen to study at the university at Carthage. Two years later, he took a mistress, with whom he lived for approximately twelve years. They had a son, Adeodatus. At twenty-nine, Augustine left Carthage for Rome, and his mother, Monica, followed him there. Three years later, he moved to Milan. So did Monica. She indefatigably prayed and pleaded for his conversion. Her entreaties succeeded when he was thirty-three. He sent his mistress home to North Africa, and he converted to Christianity. With her prayers answered, Augustine's mother felt free to die.

Augustine writes often and movingly in his *Confessions* about the profound conversations that he and his mother shared. One story he relates took place during the last week of Monica's life, while he and she were standing at a window overlooking a garden, in the city of Ostia on the Tiber River. Augustine writes:

> The two of us, all alone, were enjoying a very pleasant conversation, "forgetting the past and pushing on to what is ahead." We were asking one another in the presence of the Truth . . . for you are Truth . . . what it would be like to share the eternal life enjoyed by the saints, "which eye has not seen, nor ear heard, which has not even entered into the heart of man." We desired with all our hearts to drink from the streams of your heavenly fountain, the fountain of life.
>
> That was the substance of our talk, though not the exact words. But you know, O Lord, that in the course of our conversation that day, the world and its pleasure lost all their attraction for us. My mother said: "Son, as far as I am concerned, nothing in this life now gives me any pleasure. I do not know why I am still here, since I have no further hopes in this world. I did have one reason for wanting to live a little: to see you become a Catholic Christian before I died. God has lavished his gifts on me in that respect, for I know that you have even renounced earthly happiness to be his servant. So what am I doing here?"
>
> I do not remember how I answered her. Shortly, within five days or thereabouts, she fell sick with a fever. Then one day during the

course of her illness she became unconscious and for a while she was unaware of her surroundings. My brother and I rushed to her side but she regained consciousness quickly. She looked at us as we stood there and asked in a puzzled voice: "Where was I?"

We were overwhelmed with grief, but she held her gaze steadily upon us and spoke further: "Here you shall bury your mother." I remained silent as I held back my tears. However, my brother haltingly expressed his hope that she might not die in a strange country but in her own land, since her end would be happier there. When she heard this, her face was filled with anxiety, and she reproached him with a glance because he had entertained such earthly thoughts. Then she looked at me and spoke: "Look what he is saying." Thereupon she said to both of us: "Bury my body wherever you will; let not care of it cause you any concern. One thing only I ask you, that you remember me at the altar of the Lord wherever you may be." [85]

In 1430, nearly eleven hundred years after her death, a number of Monica's relics were transferred from Ostia, not to North Africa, but to the Church of St. Augustine in Rome at the behest of Pope Martin V.

GUNSHOT

St. Charles Borromeo

Charles Borromeo (1538-1584) was a prodigious student and Church leader. He completed his doctoral degrees in civil and canon law by age twenty-one. The next year, the pope, who was Charles's maternal uncle, named Charles a lay cardinal of the Church, administrator of the prestigious see of Milan, and secretary of state for the papacy. Charles advised the pope to reconvene the interrupted Council of Trent, during which "Charles played a leading role."[86] Charles then was ordained at twenty-five a priest and bishop, retaining responsibility for the see of Milan. He later founded a community of diocesan priests, who are now called the Oblates of St. Charles. He assisted priests working in England during the height of the English persecution of the Catholic Church. He organized, in the absence of civil response, the Church's response to the needs of the poor at Milan, feeding thousands during a three-month famine, and caring for the sick during a two-year plague.

In an age tarnished by loose discipline among clerics and civil officials, Charles publicly criticized leaders who were derelict in duty and, needless to say, made enemies. In 1569, a priest, Gerolamo Donato, known as Farina, attempted to assassinate Charles. The assassin was paid for his deed by three former provosts of his Humiliati order.

> The preparations were long and intricate, especially to find the sum of money that Farina demanded. They first thought of theft, pretending that thieves had broken in from the outside, then of strangling the provost who had charge of the strong box and make it look as if he had committed suicide. Finally they stole the sacred vessels. But Farina, having received the money, fled to Corfu without even attempting to perpetrate his crime on the Cardinal. Two years later he returned with the same dark design and this time, unfortunately, he found an opportunity to put it into effect. Again and again he lay in wait at the entrance of the church of St. Barnabas, which St. Charles was accustomed to frequent. But it seemed easier to take the Archbishop by surprise in his private chapel in the evening, where access was free to all because St. Charles wished that any of the people who cared to do so might be free to come and pray with him. Thus it happened that on the evening of October 26, 1569, Farina dared to go into this private chapel, where the Archbishop was singing the psalms with his household. Coming as close to the Cardinal as he could, he aimed his arquebus and fired the shot.
>
> There was general confusion. Only the saint remained tranquil and serene. Happiness quickly followed the confusion for, to the surprise of all, the shot which had been fired at the Archbishop's back had glanced off harmlessly. All proclaimed it a miracle. The saint, in his humility, wrote to Ormaneto that God had miraculously saved his life not because of his own merit but "undoubtedly because of the place where we were or because of my episcopal dignity or perhaps to give me more time to do my penance, for I need it."[87]

Ecclesiastical and political dignitaries, as well as common folk, sent messages of sympathy and prayer to the cardinal. Charles thanked God publicly, then visited a monastery to thank God privately.

> The deed remained shrouded in mystery for several months. St. Charles was very glad of this because he was accustomed to say: "The misstep of a single one of my priests would cause me far more sorrow than if all the powers in the world would conspire against my life." Finally, thanks to the perspicacity of the Bishop of Lodi, the first traces of the conspiracy were found. Farina was discovered and ar-

rested in Piedmont where he had gone into hiding among the soldiers of the duke of Savoy. The trial took place in Rome, St. Charles having declared that he did not intend to prosecute his assassins. The principal culprits were condemned to death. On August 11, 1570, Farina and his accomplices, that is, the three former provosts, were sentenced in Milan according to the law and customs of the time.[88]

Bl. Damien the Leper

When Father Damien de Veuster (1840-1889) volunteered for the leper colony at Kalaupapa on the island of Molokai, he left behind his comfortable parish in Honolulu on Oahu, Hawaii's main island, where he had served since ordination in 1864. At Kalaupapa, "officially, Damien was the pastor of the Catholics in the colony, but actually he served as the lepers' physician, counselor, house-builder, sheriff, gravedigger and undertaker."[89]

Prudent persons advised Damien to adhere to proper medical precautions so as not to contract the dreaded Hansen's disease, the "official" name of leprosy. Observers described him, however, as reckless in exposing himself to contact with the lepers' skin, blood, body fluids, clothing, and even the air they breathed. But Damien wondered how he could do otherwise without separating and isolating himself from the very people to whom he was sent to serve. He was their constant companion and friend. Of course, when building homes together, he occasionally cut himself with a saw or a hammer. When working side by side, he occasionally lay down his pipe, which his leprous coworkers picked up and puffed. When administering the sacraments, how could he avoid touching the lepers' hands, faces, forehead, lips, and tongues? Because Damien visited the lepers in their hovellike homes, how could he not breathe their air? In the rectory, his leprous cook dipped her infected fingers into the food that she prepared for him. Despite all the precautions he might take, how could Damien be the lepers' priest and not expose himself to the possibility of contracting leprosy?

In 1873, Damien began his ministry at Molokai. Within one year, "he felt a kind of tingling or burning sensation on his feet and legs."[90] Within the next few years, the same symptoms occurred, but more frequently and more intensely. One arm and his back developed dry spots, symptomatic of Hansen's disease.[91]

By 1879, all symptoms disappeared. Damien, his religious superiors, and the entire leper colony rejoiced. Two years later, however, the rejoicing ended. Sharp pains returned to Damien's leg. His sciatic nerve caused excruciating pain. In 1884, after bathing his feet in boiling water, he discovered that large blisters had surfaced and that he had not even felt the burning through his insensate legs. One year later, "a small leprous tubercule manifested itself on the lobe of the right ear."[92] Diagnosis confirmed the condition, which Damien accepted, as leprous.

> The (leprous) marks were discovered on my left cheek and ear. My eyebrows are beginning to fall out. Soon, I will be disfigured entirely. Having no doubts about the true nature of my disease, I am calm, resigned and very happy in the midst of my people. God certainly knows what is best for my sanctification and I gladly repeat: 'Thy will be done!' "[93]

Damien alerted his priest-brother, but fearing the impact of the news on his elderly mother, Damien told her some but not the whole truth. Months later, however, she died soon after some friend ran to read her the newspaper account that "the flesh of the leper priest at Molokai was falling off in hunks."[94] Damien writes in 1885: "I'm having a hard time saying Mass; I have to sit down to preach; and since I can no longer walk, I ride around in a wagon. So, in the midst of our patients, I myself am playing the part of a sick man."[95]

Religious authorities asked Damien if he wished to leave the island in order to receive better medical treatment. The saint declined, saying, "I would not be cured if the price of my cure was that I must leave the island and give up my work."[96] The priest who had set out to become all things to all people, succeeded marvelously. He became a saint for all the world to know, esteem, and emulate.

MENTAL ILLNESS

St. Benedict Joseph Labre

Four times Benedict Joseph (1748-1783) tried to become a priest and four times he was sent home. At age twelve, Benedict was advised by his priest-tutor to discontinue plans for the priesthood, since the youth, oddly, would study only the Scriptures and the lives of the saints, while ignoring all other academic subjects. Beginning at age eighteen, Benedict attempted, over a period of four years, to enter three different communities. Both the

Cistercians and Carthusians gave him a period of probation, then declared him unfit. The Trappists refused him outright. Benedict writes to his parents partway through this series of rejections:

> This is to tell you that the Carthusians have judged me not a proper person for their state of life, and I quitted their house on the second day of October. I now intend to go to La Trappe, the place which I have so long and earnestly desired. I beg your pardon for all my acts of disobedience, and for all the uneasiness which I have at any time caused you. By the grace of God I shall henceforth put you to no further expense, nor shall I give you any more trouble. I assure you that you are now rid of me. I have indeed cost you much; but be assured that by the grace of God, I will make the best use of and reap benefits from all that you have done for me. Give me your blessing, and I will never again be a cause of trouble to you. I very much hope to be received at La Trappe; but if I should fail there, I am told that at the Abbey of Sept Fonts they are less severe, and will receive candidates like me. But I think I shall be received at La Trappe.[97]

Disappointed but feeling compelled to dedicate his life to God, Benedict spent four years traveling from shrine to shrine in western Europe throughout France, Switzerland, Italy, Germany, and Spain. He returned four and five times to the same shrines. He walked everywhere, wearing broken-down shoes and a threadbare cloak. He carried only a sack and a few books. He ate little, and "if charitable people failed to offer him food, he would pick up orange peels, cabbage stalks, or mouldy fruit from refuse heaps, or would do without."[98] Whatever food or money was given to him by passersby, he gave away most and kept a little for himself. He spoke with almost no one. He slept wherever the end of the day brought him, in an open field or a shack. Oftentimes he was beaten physically by people who mocked or feared him. He writes occasionally to his parents to update them on his intentions:

> You have heard that I have left the Abbey of Sept Fonts, and no doubt you are uneasy and desirous to know what route I have taken, and what kind of life I intend to adopt. I must therefore acquaint you that I left Sept Fonts in July; I had a fever soon after I left, which lasted four days, and I am now on my way to Rome. I have not traveled very fast since I left, on account of the excessively hot weather which there always is in the month of August in Piedmont, where I am now, and where, on account of a little complaint, I have been detained for three

weeks in a hospital where I was kindly treated. In other respects I have been very well. There are in Italy many monasteries where the religious live very regular and austere lives; I design to enter into one of them, and I hope that God will prosper my design. Do not make yourselves uneasy on my account. I will not fail to write you from time to time. And I shall be glad to hear of you and my brothers and sisters; but this is not possible at present, because I am not yet settled in any fixed place; I will not fail to pray for you everyday. I beg you that you will pardon me for all the uneasiness that I have given you; and that you will give me your blessing, that God may favor my design. I am very happy in having undertaken my present journey. I beg you will give my compliments to my grandmother, my grandfather, my aunts, my brother James and all my brothers and sisters, and my uncle Francis.[99]

In 1774, he put down roots in Rome. He spent his nights as a homeless man among the ruins of the Colosseum. He spent his days praying at churches, especially those celebrating the Forty Hours Devotion. He seemed to be absorbed genuinely in prayer. His demeanor was pious and devout. At a local hostel he always yielded the higher place in line to others, slept on a plank, and ate only after everyone else had eaten. His regular confessor wrote an article in which he describes "the beggar of Rome":

> In the month of June 1782, just after I had celebrated Mass in the church of Saint Ignatius belonging to the Roman College, I noticed a man close beside me whose appearance at first sight was decidedly unpleasant and forbidding. His legs were only partially covered, his clothes were tied around his waist with an old cord. His hair was uncombed; he was ill-clad and wrapped about in an old and ragged coat. In his outward appearance he seemed to be the most miserable beggar I had ever seen.[100]

Homeless beggar that he was, nonetheless, people recognized and appreciated his virtue. At his death, adults nodded in agreement as the children raced through the city streets shouting: "The saint is dead."[101]

St. Anthony Mary Claret

Anthony Mary Claret (1807-1870), founder of the Missionary Sons of the Immaculate Heart of Mary, known popularly as the Claretians, paid a high price for his reform movement. He endured fourteen assassination attempts for preaching often against maintaining mistresses and mistreating slaves. After serving seven years as archbishop of Santiago, Cuba, he reluctantly accepted appointment as chaplain to the queen of Spain. Early on, when she asked him what favor she might grant him, he replied, "You may let me resign."[102]

In Santiago, Anthony was attacked by a hired killer whose release from jail Anthony had secured one year earlier at the tearful request of the parents. In his autobiography, Anthony relates that on February 1, 1856, he had just finished preaching about Mary's giving her son to suffer and die for all people. He was walking home with four priests and the sacristan, who led the way with a lantern because of the darkness of the night at 8:30. Crowds filled the main street and greeted him kindly. A gentleman knelt down in front of the archbishop, as if to kiss his ring.

> Suddenly and without warning, he raised his hand in which he grasped a razor, and with all his might executed a downward stroke which was supposed to have lacerated my neck. Luckily I had been walking with bent head and with my right hand holding a handkerchief over my mouth so as not to catch cold after preaching. Instead of striking my neck, as he had intended, the would-be assassin made a gash on my left cheek from the ear to the chin. Fortunately, the brunt of the blow fell on my arm which had been upraised to cover my mouth, as I have said.
>
> The knife thrust ripped open the flesh of my face until it had struck the very bones of my upper and lower jaws, causing blood to spurt from the outside of the face as well as to the inside of the mouth. I tried at once to check the flow of blood by clasping my cheek with my right hand, while with my left hand I pressed and stemmed the blood coming from the wound in the right arm. As the incident had happened near a pharmacy, I beckoned my companions to take me there, saying: "Let us enter here, and we shall have all we need for dressing the wounds." Requests for assistance were speedily sent to the physicians who had attended the services. . . .

On my part, I felt perfectly quiet and tranquil. The doctors said that all the blood I lost was not less than four and one-half pints. The loss of so much blood made me weak, and I felt like fainting. However, I felt better after they gave me a little vinegar to revive me.

When I had regained a little more strength, they carried me to my residence in a stretcher. I cannot explain the pleasure, joy, and happiness my soul experienced in seeing that come to pass which I had so long desired, namely, to shed my blood for Jesus and Mary, and to be able to seal the truths I had been preaching with the very blood of my veins.[103]

Immediately following the attack, Anthony interceded again on his assailant's behalf. The enraged populace was circulating rumors that a mob might force its way into the jail and do successfully to the assassin what he had failed to do to the archbishop. When Anthony learned of this threat, he urged the jailer to release the assassin and allow him to sail home across the Atlantic Ocean to the Canary Islands. Because the young man had no money, Anthony paid the passage.

OLD AGE

St. Vincent de Paul

Vincent de Paul (1580-1660) had experienced much sickness before he reached old age. A companion provides an account of Vincent's medical history, which the saint confided to a young sick confrere.

> "Do not be afraid, my Brother," he would say; "when young I had the same illness, and I recovered. I was afflicted with asthma, but now it is gone. I had a rupture, and God cured me. I suffered from neuralgia; it has disappeared. Lung trouble and stomach weakness were among my afflictions, but I have outlived them. Be patient, there is reason to hope that your sickness will pass away, and that God plans to make use of your services."[104]

Fifteen years before he died, Vincent lay on what he and others expected to be his deathbed. Already sixty-five, he had been suffering for years with intermittent fevers, which lasted from three days to three weeks and from leg ulcers, which pained him continuously. Now he had fallen into delirium. Friends and confreres gathered at his bedside, but Vincent recovered. He renewed his schedule of rising at four o'clock each morning and sleeping only a few hours each night. "Drowsiness and weakness overcame him during his visits and occupations. But instead of yielding to the pressure of sleep, he would rise from his chair and remain standing, or assume an uncomfortable position in order to keep awake."[105]

Old age, though, was taking its toll. His legs were wearing out. Since age fifty-two, he could no longer walk long distances and traveled instead by horseback. At sixty-nine, he could not ride a horse any more and instead was forced to use a horse-drawn carriage — which embarrassed him, since usually only the wealthy enjoyed this mode of transportation. He referred disparagingly to this vehicle as his "ignominy."[106] When he was seventy-six, leg ulcers prohibited him from bending his knees for genuflecting or even walking without the use of a cane. At seventy-nine, he depended on crutches. Four years before he died, he lost his appetite and failed to take the nourishment necessary to sustain him. The next year his eyesight worsened rapidly. Two years before he died, this near-octogenarian was thrown from his carriage, smashing his head into the stone pavement, and lacerating his head severely.

During the last two years of his life, he never left home. In the community house, he struggled to attend daily Mass and spiritual exercises. For Mass, he allowed himself the indulgence, usually restricted to bishops, of vesting at the altar, about which he joked, "See how I have become a dignitary?"[107] During his last year, he could walk only as far as the chapel for the infirm confreres. No longer able to celebrate Mass, he could only assist at Mass. "In order to go from his room to the chapel, he had to drag himself along on crutches, and the effort reopened his wounds and aggravated his pain."[108] Community members offered either to carry him to the chapel or to construct an altar in the room adjoining his bedroom so that he could assist at Mass while remaining in his room. At first, he refused to listen to these suggestions; he wanted no special treatment. A few weeks later, however, he changed his mind. In his last weeks on earth, a urinary blockage caused him excruciating pain that caused him to cry out, "Oh, my Saviour! my good Saviour."[109] He spent his last days and nights racked with pain.

Vincent finally divulged some of what he had been suffering. He wrote to a friend, "I have been concealing my condition from you as much as possible lest a knowledge of my illness might sadden you."[110] He admitted to a confrere, who noted Vincent's worsening condition, "It is true that I feel their [sufferings] increase from the soles of my feet to the top of my head. But what an accounting I shall have to render at the tribunal of God, where I must soon appear, if I do not make good use of them."[111]

His eighty-year-old body had worn out. He had spent over half of his life caring for the suffering sick and poor. Now he himself was experiencing sickness and its attendant suffering. The day before he died, he assisted at Mass from his bed and prayed with visitors. Around sunrise the next day, while sitting in a chair close to the fireplace, he died peacefully, without a struggle.

POISONED, SURVIVED

St. Benedict of Monte Cassino

Benedict (c. 480-c. 547) is the recognized founder of Western monasticism. His communities of men and women monks incarnated his vision of moderate monasticism, so that monks both worked and prayed as well as lived in a supportive community of federated monasteries under one spiritual leader while eschewing excessive asceticism. The Benedictine Rule became paradigmatic for monks for the next thousand years. "In the course of the Middle Ages all of occidental monasticism had been gradually subjected to the Rule of St. Benedict."[112]

The historical moment in which Benedict grew up was challenging. "Overrun by pagan and Arian tribes, the civilized world seemed during the closing years of the fifth century to be rapidly lapsing into barbarism: the Church was rent by schisms, town and country were desolated by war and pillage, shameful sins were rampant among Christians as well as heathens, and it was noted that there was not a sovereign or a ruler who was not an atheist, a pagan, or a heretic."[113]

In his early teen years, Benedict left his home in Nursia, in central Italy, to pursue at Rome his literary studies, which he completed around age twenty. He then fled the dissoluteness of the city in search of a haven for virtue. He traveled thirty miles to Enfidde, where he lived in a community of ecclesiastical students before living as a hermit for three years at Subiaco.[114]

Monks from Vicovaro, near Subiaco, visited Benedict to ask him to serve as their new abbot, since the previous abbot had just died. Benedict initially refused. He explained that he anticipated conflict between their lifestyle and his. When they begged him, he relented. Before long, the inevitable conflict took place. Benedict was too demanding for this community. One disgruntled monk tried to poison him to death, which Benedict discovered. The saint returned to Subiaco, where monastic life flourished until a priest named Florentinus fabricated a scandal about

Benedict. Benedict then left Subiaco and walked to Monte Cassino, where he established the monastery known now as the font of civilization and Christianization of western Europe.

Information about the attempted poisoning of Benedict comes from *The Dialogues of Gregory the Great*. Gregory wrote this story less than fifty years after the death of Benedict, based on the personal testimony of Benedict's own monks and other disciples.

> At the monastery he watched carefully over the religious spirit of his monks and would not tolerate any of their previous disobedience. No one was allowed to turn from the straight path of monastic discipline either to the right or to the left. Their waywardness, however, clashed with the standards he upheld, and in their resentment they started to reproach themselves for choosing him as abbot. It only made them the more sullen to find him curbing every fault and evil habit. They could not see why they should have to force their settled minds into new ways of thinking.
>
> At length, proving once again that the very life of the just is a burden to the wicked, they tried to find a means of doing away with him and decided to poison his wine. A glass pitcher containing this poisoned drink was presented to the man of God during his meal for the customary blessing. As he made the sign of the Cross over it with his hand, the pitcher was shattered even though it was well beyond his reach at the time. It broke at his blessing as if he had struck it with a stone.
>
> Then he realized it had contained a deadly drink which could not bear the sign of life. Still calm and undisturbed, he rose at once and after gathering the community together he addressed them. "May almighty God have mercy on you," he said. "Why did you conspire to do this? Did I not tell you at the outset that my ways of life would never harmonize with yours? Go and find yourselves an abbot to your liking. It is impossible for me to stay here any longer." Then he went back to the wilderness he loved, to live alone with himself in the presence of his heavenly Father.[115]

POISONED

Bl. Juvenal Ancina

Juvenal (1545-1604) left the Piedmont region to come to Rome with the newly appointed ambassador to the Holy See, whose personal physician he was. At Rome, he gave up a lucrative career as a medical professor and doctor in order to join the Oratorians. Juvenal rose quickly through the community's administrative ranks. Four years after being ordained, he was sent to Naples, where he enjoyed great success in preaching, convert-making, and organizing assistance to the sick and poor. After ten years in Naples, he was assigned to continue his ministry at Rome. After six years in that position, Juvenal was named bishop of Saluzzo.

In the town of Saluzzo a certain friar was carrying on an affair with a nun. News of this reached Juvenal. He called in the two and reasoned gently with them, warning that if their conduct continued, he would use strong measures to stop it. Shortly thereafter, Juvenal was officiating at services and dining with the Conventual Franciscans. The criminal friar took the opportunity to poison the bishop's wine. Before vespers, he fell ill. Four days later, he was restricted to bed and ten days after consuming the poison, Juvenal died.[116]

STABBED

St. Josaphat

Josaphat (c. 1580-1623) was the monastic name chosen by John Kunsevich. He dedicated his life to uniting the Roman Church and the Eastern Orthodox Church, a movement that had been started in 1595 by the metropolitan of Kiev and bishops in the Bylorussian and Ukrainian regions. For this purpose, Josaphat left his native Vladimir, Poland, and studied the languages and rites of the Eastern Church at Vilna, Russia. Beginning at twenty-four, he became in quick succession monk, priest, abbot, bishop, and, at thirty-nine, archbishop of Polotsk, Lithuania.

> Josaphat was confronted with an eparchy [diocese] which was as large in extent as it was degraded in life. The more religious people were inclined to schism through fear of arbitrary Roman interference with their worship and customs; churches were in ruins and benefices were in the hands of laymen; many of the secular clergy had been married two and three times and the monks were decadent.[117]

Josaphat's prayer and pastoral conduct inspired many conversions. He provided disciplinary rules for the clergy and published a catechism for the laity. He prohibited political interference in ecclesiastical matters.

These reforms created enemies. Some bishops, therefore, convened in Josaphat's absence an assembly that elected Meletius Smotrytsky, in place of Josaphat, as the archbishop of Polotsk. A monk named Silvester politicked in surrounding towns to win support for Smotrytsky. Although the king and nobility supported Josaphat, the dissident clergy and masses of people rioted in favor of Smotrytsky. The clergy spread the rumor that Josaphat wanted to subject the Eastern peoples to the Western Church. Not only the Byzantine clergy actively opposed Josaphat but also the Roman bishops chose not to defend him because "he maintained the right of the Byzantine clergy and customs to equal treatment with those of Rome."[118]

Josaphat planned a canonical visit to Vitebsk, even though "the people of Vitebsk so hated their archbishop that they resolved to kill him."[119] A priest by the name of Kamin publicly collected the signatures of people willing to kill Josaphat. Josaphat knew what awaited him. He spoke repeatedly about his impending death: "I am going to Vitebsk to meet a martyr's death; if only I could be made worthy to give up my life and blood for God."[120]

At Vitebsk, the conspirators and rumormongers had generated a storm of hostility. "Like a good shepherd, he [Josaphat] visited homes, settled quarrels, admonished sinners, confessed the repentant, preached the word of God in the churches, and conducted church services."[121] He even invited one of the chief conspirators, Naum Wowk, to dine with him in the archbishop's residence as an expression of forgiveness and peace. Wowk refused.

After two weeks, the conspirators grew anxious. They had hoped that their confrontations with Josaphat's followers would have provoked a fight. Josaphat spoke to the mob about the situation:

> You people of Vitebsk want to put me to death. You make ambushes for me everywhere, in the streets, on the bridges, on the highways, in the market-place. I am here among you as your shepherd and you ought to know that I should be happy to give my life for you. I am ready to die for the holy union, for the supremacy of St. Peter and of his successor the Supreme Pontiff.[122]

The frustrated conspirators met at city hall and arranged that on November 12 they would kill the archbishop. On the evening of November 11 they sent the priest Elias Davydovych to the archbishop's residence to shout insults. On the advice of a Roman priest, Josaphat gave permission, in accord with canon law, to arrest Elias if he persisted. A councilman warned Josaphat "that the leaders of the conspiracy had formed a plot to have him killed, but that the leaders themselves planned to leave the city while the plot was carried out so that no suspicion would fall on them."[123]

About six o'clock the next morning Elias renewed his shouting and rock-throwing. An aide arrested him and immediately the conspirators sprang into action. "Soon the bells of all the churches in Vitebsk, as well as those of the city hall, began ringing."[124] Several thousand people gathered. Shots rang out. Axes were slung against the fences and doors of the residence. "The people began to shout, 'Strike him.' 'Kill him.' "[125] Josaphat ordered that Elias be released, which quieted the mob for a moment, until they received directions to push forward with their attack. The mob burst into the palace and beat up the servants. Josaphat, who had been praying, faced the mob.

> Then, as was his custom, he spoke to the rebels very gently: "Children, why do you beat my servants? If you have anything against me, here I am!" But no one raised a hand against him. Suddenly, however, two men rushed in from another room, and seeing Josaphat standing there before them, with his hands folded on his breast, one of them struck him with a club, while the other split his head open with axe. As he fell, others began to assail him with every sort of weapon. In the midst of these blows, Josaphat cried out, "O my God!" — perhaps he was about to say — "do not lay this sin to my enemies." The murderers then dragged him from the hall into the courtyard where they shot him in the head and continued to beat him long after he was dead.

The mob vandalized the home and drank the wine cellar dry. Somebody stood Josaphat's body upright, and mockingly invited the archbishop to preach, then angrily thrust the body to the ground. Others carried the corpse into the street, where onlookers mutilated the body.

> Finally, they took the body to a very high hill from which they threw it down to the banks of the river, shouting as they did so, "Hold on tight, bishop, hold tight!" Then, going down to the riverside, they put the remains of the body into a small boat and rowed it to a place they knew to be very deep. There, filling the hair shirt with rocks, they tied it to the remains of the body, and having weighted it in this way, they sank it in the river, confident that no one would ever find it again.[126]

Archrival Smotrytsky, who had orchestrated the assassination, repented of his deed and became reconciled with Rome. Josaphat was the first among the Eastern Uniate saints to be canonized.

Bl. Padre Pio

Several hundred persons have received the stigmata since the time of the first stigmatist, St. Francis of Assisi. The stigmata "are signs on a person's body of the passion of Christ, usually wounds on hands, feet, and side, appearing without external causes."[127] The stigmatists' wounds may be either visible or invisible, permanent or impermanent, oozing blood occasionally or constantly.

Padre Pio (1887-1968) was the first priest to have received the stigmata; Francis of Assisi was never ordained. Pio's wounds were invisible and impermanent in their original weekly redness and constant pain from 1910 until September 20, 1918, when the five wounds burst forth in a flood of blood that continued daily until he died fifty years later. One of the four medical doctors who examined Pio describes the wounds:

> In the palm of his left hand, more or less corresponding to the middle of the third metacarpal, I saw the existence of an anatomical lesion, round in shape, with clearly defined outer edges. In size it is little more than 2 cm. (about 3/4 of an inch) in diameter. . . . The lesion is covered with a reddish brown scab which appears on any normal wound. . . . But in the case of Padre Pio's wounds, the edges of the scab detach themselves and begin to flake towards the center of the wound. Eventually the whole scab falls off. The wound is continuously bloody and keeps forming this kind of a scab. . . . The area of the lesion in the palm which I have just described has a clearly marked border, so that the surrounding skin, when I examined it with a powerful magnifying glass, showed no signs of edema, no sign of redness, no sign of infection, and not the tiniest indication of having been struck. . . . The metacarpal bone shows no anatomical discontinuity, and although slightly enlarged in the middle section it appears to be regular in the rest of its length. On the reverse side of the same left hand, more clearly in line with the metacarpal bone of the third finger, and therefore, not corresponding exactly with the palm side, there is also a lesion similar to the other one in shape and appearance, which

seems to be more restricted and apparently with a more superficial scab. Lesions which exist on both sides of the right hand can be similarly described. During my examination, tiny and continuous drops of blood oozed out of the lesions.[128]

The doctor added that the wounds on the feet and chest were similar in nature to those on the hands: in the surrounding tissue no traces of redness, edema, or infection occurred. The wounds on the feet were slightly smaller than two centimeters. The wound on the left side of the chest was an upside-down cross, about seven centimeters by four centimeters, which bled in greater quantity than the other wounds.[129]

Pio suffered intense pain. A visiting devotee once knelt down, then grabbed and kissed Pio's very swollen feet, causing Pio to cry out in excruciating pain. Another visitor asked the priest if the marks of Jesus hurt him, to which Pio replied, "Do you think he gave me this for decoration?"[130] Walking was difficult; his gait resembled a shuffle.

Pio's wounds bled profusely, about a cup of blood each day.[131] Until the last three years of his life, he himself bandaged these wounds two or three times daily. His bandaged hands, he covered with fingerless mittens. His chest, he wrapped from his waist to his armpits. Over his feet, he wore dark woolen socks. These socks, mittens, and bandages were always blood-soaked when he changed them. He never experienced anemia until the last months of his life. His meals amounted to only five hundred to six hundred calories daily, which is much less than the usual adult minimum of fifteen hundred calories.[132] His wounds could be seen by onlookers only during Mass, when he raised his hands beyond his long-sleeved garment.

Pio suffered professionally also. When news of his stigmata percolated among the townsfolk, visitors flocked to San Giovanni Rotundo. At first, hundreds; then, thousands; and in the last year of his life, one-and-a-half million people visited the remote mountain town. Religious authorities were skeptical about the reported stigmata and were wary of the crowds. Five times between 1919 and 1923, Capuchin and Vatican authorities attempted to transfer Pio to another Capuchin house. Each time, however, the news leaked out to the townsfolk who boldly and sometimes violently protested and prohibited the removal of their revered padre. Frustrated in transferring Pio, the Vatican put its plans on hold.

The Vatican renewed its efforts in 1931. The townsfolk detected these visits by officious priests, suspected their purpose, and stormed the monastery. Delayed but not defeated, the Vatican ordered Pio "to desist from all activity except the celebration of Mass."[133] Initially, only a very few persons were permitted to attend his Mass; and eventually, only the servers.

For two years, 1931-1933, Pio was restricted to solitary confinement. Again the people rioted and threatened physical harm to those who hid Pio. Finally the pope himself intervened, reversed the ban, and wrote to the local archbishop: "I have not been badly disposed toward Padre Pio, but I have been badly informed about Padre Pio."[134] Within the next year, Pio was gradually permitted to celebrate Mass publicly, then to hear confessions of men, and eventually to hear the confessions of women.

Pio experienced not only the stigmata but also many other phenomena. It is verified that he experienced bilocation (being in two places at the same time), discernment of spirits (ability to read people's souls even before they spoke), speaking in tongues (speaking languages that he had never studied), and charismatic aromas (scents of perfume emanated from him).

STROKE

Louis Martin

St. Thérèse of Lisieux's saintly father was Louis Martin (1823-1894), who suffered a series of strokes throughout the last six years of his life.[135] He had enjoyed robust health and he never even visited a doctor until age fifty-three, when a poisonous fly bit him behind his left ear. Within weeks, the "epithelioma" bite ballooned from a speck to the size of the palm of a hand.[136] The bite's effects pained him for the rest of his life, and family members wondered if his later cerebral troubles were related to the bite. Ten years later, with his wife having died and his having retired as a watchmaker, Louis suffered his first stroke. Louis's daughter Céline describes the incident:

> On May 1, 1887, on awakening, he had an attack of paralysis, which affected his whole left side. With his usual energy, he wished nevertheless to go with us as he did every day to the seven o'clock Mass, in order to receive Holy Communion on the opening of the month of May. He spoke rather inarticulately, and painfully dragged his leg.[137]

He recovered his good spirit, but not his good health. Within the year, he suffered two more strokes. Movement in his legs slowed, and his memory lapsed. The next year, further debilitation in walking, talking, and remembering took place. Nonetheless, he continued his travels to

Paris, Le Havre, and Alençon to conduct personal business, but his failure to return on time and even on the appointed day caused great anxiety to his family members and friends. He often carried large sums of money, and the family worried that he might be beaten or even killed by robbers.

His health soared and plummeted like a roller-coaster ride of recovery, relapses, and ever-worsening strokes. The situation depressed him and his family. His daughter Céline writes to her three sisters in the convent that "tears came easily and frequently to his eyes" whereas "before his illness I never saw him shedding tears, except when our mother was receiving Extreme Unction" (in 1877).[138] Céline continues, "Papa seems to have become so old and so worn. If you saw him every morning kneeling at the altar-rail for Holy Communion! He leans and helps himself along as best he can. It would make you cry!"[139]

Feeling helpless, Céline and her sister Léonie and Uncle Isidore Guérin transferred "the venerable patriarch"[140] to the hospital at Caen so that he could receive proper medical treatment by specialists. "He went there without knowing where he was being taken, but he realized it as soon as he entered. His first reaction changed into sentiments of humility and surrender to Divine Providence."[141] The two daughters took lodging with the Daughters of Charity of St. Vincent de Paul at Caen, and visited their father for hours at a time, every day, for three months. These two daughters kept their sisters in the convent informed by means of frequent correspondence. Louis passed his time praying for the conversion of sinners and exchanging pleasantries with passersby. The nurse-sister in charge writes: "He is really admirable. Not only does he never complain, but everything we give him is 'excellent.' "[142] She observes about the relationship between the father and his family: "It is touching to see the affection of this patriarch for his family."[143] His health, however, kept worsening. Céline writes:

> At present his legs are becoming numb and it is only with difficulty that he took a walk around the garden with us. At first, while leaning on my arm, he let go of Léonie's. But gradually he was losing control, and he could not have gone on long without falling. He realized that, for he leaned against the wall, saying that he was not tired but that everything was swimming around him. Léonie then gave him her arm.[144]

Poor health prevented Louis from attending various family functions, including Thérèse's veiling ceremony, a cousin's wedding, and a vacation trip. In May 1892, the hospital released Louis after determining that they could provide no further physical assistance and that his being at home might have emotional benefit. In summer 1893, Uncle Isidore Guérin took Louis and the family on vacation, despite the inconveniences of transporting the wheelchair, the hospital bed, and lifting Louis's limp body to and from the horse-drawn carriage and the train.

In May 1894, Louis suffered another stroke and received the last rites. Family members rushed to his bedside. He recovered, but one week later, he suffered a heart attack. Again, family rushed home. Céline writes, "While running the whole way home, I did not know whether I would find him better or dead."[145] Another month passed, and another heart attack occurred, less violent but more prolonged. Within twenty-four hours, with his breathing labored and his body turning icy cold, Céline prayed for a miracle. Louis opened his eyes for the last time, looked at her with affection, closed his eyes, and died.[146]

Catherine de Hueck Doherty

On at least three occasions, the world-famous foundress of the Friendship House Movement and the Madonna House Apostolate considered suicide. In public life, Catherine de Hueck Doherty (1896-1985) was a renowned Christian heroine, a servant of the poor, a contemplative in action, the lay spiritual adviser to countless priests and nuns, and author of thirty books. In private, however, she found life so burdensome that she turned toward suicide.

The first occasion took place after the Finnish Communists attacked, imprisoned, and almost starved to death Catherine and her husband because they were Russian nobility.

> Catherine's body swelled, her teeth loosened, and her hair fell out in clumps. Shivering from the cold, she lay close to the stove. Thoughts of closing the flue and ending the pain by asphyxiation tormented her. "All you need is a slight movement of your arm, and you have death, which now becomes a real friend and merciful," she kept thinking.[147]

When the war's tide turned, German soldiers rescued the baron and baroness. The couple fled from Russia in 1920 and emigrated to New York City in 1924. There, Catherine suffered both poverty in her job as a laundress and sexual harassment in her employment as a waitress. Depression led to despair. She wandered onto the Brooklyn Bridge, about which she writes: "I experienced a powerful temptation to end my life."[148] She explained:

> I found a space between the wires where I could slip through. I looked down and prepared to jump. Do you know what I saw? I saw Christ mirrored in the water! In a panic, I stopped, turned and ran. I ran down the bridge so fast that a policeman yelled, "Hey, lady, slow down! You're shoving people around!" I was running away from the vision, which probably was no vision at all. But at that moment it was very real to me, and it saved my life.[149]

A third episode resulted from the abuse she suffered from her husband of fifteen years. "He was a well-known womanizer and everybody liked him. He loved a good time. He loved to party."[150] But his wife lamented: "Lord, you see how Boris, little by little, is killing my life."[151] He had a string of mistresses. He spent about one hundred dollars a month on his favorite mistress and about twenty-five dollars per month on his wife and young son.[152] The whole city knew of Boris's affairs and gossip abounded. She felt "completely humiliated."[153] She sensed an inner voice calling her to suicide. Her priest-confessor urged her not to think about the word or ways in which she might end her life. He would bark, "SUICIDE. No! No! Faith is stronger than all that. You shall win the victory. It is not suffering that you must fear, but discouragement and sin."[154] After she separated from her husband, he begged her to give him another chance. She relented, but later regretted it. During one weekend at their summer cottage, Boris renewed his physical and verbal abuse and "goaded me beyond all endurance."[155] She ran from the house, jumped into a rowboat, and rowed furiously to the middle of the lake.

> Yes, as I gazed into the water I realized that I had been tired for a long, long time. I had been tired since I left home at age 15 or 16. Then I closed my eyes and thought about what the waters offered me: home . . . birches . . . sparkling sunshine . . . Russia . . . mother and father. I began to hear my mother playing Debussy on the piano by the soft light of the three-branched candelabra. All the while the water lapped gently around the boat, and the oars made funny little noises as they floated with the current; and the fog was coming closer.
>
> Then a most strange thing happened. It's very hard to explain. It wasn't the sun, because the sun was going down. It was more like a

shimmering curtain. It moved in folds, as curtains do. Suddenly, it stood between me and the fog.

I woke from my dreaming and realized that I was standing on the last bench of the boat. I hadn't noticed that I was standing there, and that somehow I had gone from one end of the boat to the other. But I "woke up" from my dream. Above all, I woke up from despair, and from the gray-black fog which vanished at the coming of the shimmering curtain. With great energy I rowed back to the house.[156]

Catherine literally placed herself near the edge and end of her life on several occasions.

St. Thérèse of Lisieux

The life of Thérèse of Lisieux (1873-1897) seems, at first glance, idyllic. Both of Thérèse's parents possessed a local reputation for sanctity, and, in fact, their causes for canonization have begun. All five surviving daughters entered the Carmelite convent. At fifteen, Thérèse spoke face-to-face with the pope to request permission to enter early into the Carmelite convent. Precocious at twenty, she was appointed acting mistress of novices. Her spiritual life and writings are so simple yet profound that she was named posthumously a Doctor of the Church. And along with the ubiquitous Francis Xavier, the cloistered Thérèse has been named patron of the foreign missions because of her prayers for missionaries and her desire to labor in the missions, namely, Hanoi, Vietnam.[157]

She suffered terribly, however, claiming, "Never would I have believed it was possible to suffer so much."[158] In her autobiography, Thérèse divides her life into three stages. The first stage (birth to four and a half years of age) was the happiest, during which "truly, the whole world smiled on me."[159] The second stage (four and a half to fourteen) was "the most unhappy one."[160] During that time, her mother died and Thérèse's two eldest sisters, upon whom she depended as new mothers, both entered the convent. At ten, she suffered a nervous breakdown, during which "she had terrifying hallucinations, thrashed about in her bed, even banged her head against its wooden posts."[161] At twelve, she experienced scrupulosity, from which she never fully recovered. Two years later, she overheard her father describe her as immature, to which criticism she responded positively and immediately, and to which she refers as her "Christmas miracle." Her third stage (fifteen to the time of her death) covers her life in Carmel, her father's stroke and aphasia, his subsequent placement in a mental hospital for four years, and her physical and spiritual suffering, which is described below.

Tuberculosis struck Thérèse on Good Friday, 1896, and took her life on September 30, 1897. "During the first hours of Good Friday," Thérèse woke up spitting blood.[162] The next morning, the same symptoms reoccurred. "The disease was claiming victims throughout France by the hundreds of thousands, and almost every week someone — usually a young person — died from it in Lisieux."[163] She described her initial reaction to this sickness as: "The hope of going to heaven transported me with joy."[164] By Easter Sunday, however, her response had changed to:

> He (Jesus) allowed pitch-black darkness to sweep over my soul and let the thought of heaven, so sweet to me from my infancy, destroy all my peace and torture me. This trial was not something lasting a few days or weeks. I suffered it for months and I am still waiting for it to end. I wish I could express what I feel, but it is impossible. One must have traveled through the same sunless tunnel to understand how dark it is.[165]

Her physical and spiritual well-being pained her right up to the day she died. "My sufferings increased whenever I grew wearied by the surrounding darkness and tried to find peace and strength by thinking of eternal life."[166] But thoughts of heaven and eternal life only raised doubts for her. She began to sympathize with the atheists of her era, calling them brothers, and saying she would be "glad to sit at their tables and eat their food."[167] She referred to this period as her "night of nothingness."[168]

In January, she moved to the infirmary. By mid-August, she could no longer receive Holy Communion. So excruciating was her pain and so depressed was her spirit that in the last moments of her sickness "she was tempted to suicide."[169] On the day of her death, her sister relates the following situation and conversation: "In the morning, I was with her during the Mass. She didn't speak a word to me. She was exhausted, gasping for breath; her sufferings, I thought, were indescribable."[170] She frequently proclaimed her love for God: "O my God! I love God! . . . Yes, He is very good, I find Him very good."[171] Her sister attempted to console Thérèse, saying, "God is going to aid you, poor little one, and it will soon be all over;" to which Thérèse replied, "Yes, but when?"[172] Six o'clock that evening, while looking at the crucifix, Thérèse spoke her final words: "Oh! I love Him! My God . . . I love You!"[173]

Endnotes

1. Jack Wintz, "Dorothy Day: Father Kieser's New Film," in *St. Anthony Messenger*, January 1996, p. 30.
2. Ibid., p. 32.
3. Dorothy Day, *The Eleventh Virgin* (New York: Albert And Charles Boni, 1923), pp. 258-259.
4. Ibid., p. 258.
5. Ibid., p. 134.
6. Ibid., p. 298.
7. Dorothy Day, *From Union Square to Rome*, 1939; *The Long Loneliness*, 1952; and *The Eleventh Virgin*, 1923; p. 123.
8. Ibid., p. 304.
9. Ibid., p. 141.
10. Ibid., p. 308.
11. Ibid., p. 311.
12. Susan Helen Wallace, *Matt Talbot: His Struggle and His Victory Over Alcoholism* (Boston: St. Paul Books and Media, 1992), p. 7.
13. Henri-Paul Bergeron, *Brother André, the Wonder Man of Mount Royal*, tr. by Réal Boudreau (Montreal: St. Joseph's Oratory, 1988), p. 113.
14. Ibid., p. 114.
15. Ibid.
16. Ibid.
17. Bernard LaFreniere, *Brother André, According to Witnesses* (Montreal: St. Joseph's Oratory, 1990), p. 30.
18. Bergeron, ibid., p. 117.
19. *Butler's Lives of the Saints*, ed. by Herbert Thurston and Donald Attwater, four volumes (Westminster, Md.: Christian Classics, 1990), vol. II, p. 109.
20. René Laurentin, *Bernadette of Lourdes*, tr. by John Drury (Minneapolis: Winston Press, 1979), p. 55.
21. Ibid., p. 228.
22. Ibid., p. 229.
23. Ibid., p. 231.
24. Ibid., p. 232.
25. Ibid., p. 223.
26. Ibid., p. 224.
27. Ibid., p. 225.
28. Ibid., p. 235.
29. Alicia von Stamwitz, in *The Liguorian*, May 1986, p. 2.
30. *Current Biography*, ed. by Charles Mortiz and others (New York: The H. W. Wilson Co., 1982), p. 31.

31. Joseph Bernardin, *The Gift of Peace: Personal Reflections* (Chicago: Loyola Press, 1997), p. 19.

32. Ibid., p. 51.

33. Ibid., p. 59.

34. Ibid., pp. 108-110.

35. John J. Delaney, *Dictionary of Saints* (Garden City, N.Y.: Doubleday and Co., Inc., 1980), p. 277.

36. Butler, vol. I, p. 445.

37. Delaney, p. 282.

38. Butler, vol. III, p. 638.

39. Francis De Castro, *The Life of St. John of God*, tr. by Benignus Callan (published privately by the Irish Province of the Hospitaller Order of St. John of God, 1983), p. 13.

40. Ibid., pp. 15-16.

41. Clare of Assisi, *Clare of Assisi: Early Documents*, tr. and ed. by Regis J. Armstrong (New York: Paulist Press, 1998), pp. 149-150.

42. Ibid., p. 151.

43. Ibid., p. 131.

44. Ibid., p. 173.

45. Ibid., pp. 224-225.

46. Ibid., p. 225.

47. Ibid., p. 122.

48. Ibid., p. 123.

49. Cyril Charlie Martindale, *Life of Saint Camillus* (New York: Sheed and Ward, 1946), p. 7.

50. Ibid., pp. 14-15.

51. Mario Vanti, *St. Camillus de Lellis and His Ministers of the Sick*, tr. by Charles Dyer (Manila: St. Camillus College Seminary, n.d.), p. 25.

52. Ibid., p. 31.

53. Ibid., p. 24.

54. Kenelm Francis Foster, "Catherine of Siena, St.," in *New Catholic Encyclopedia*, vol. 3, p. 259.

55. Vincent J. O'Malley, C.M., *Saintly Companions* (New York: Alba House, 1995), p. 10.

56. Raymond of Capua, *The Life of St. Catherine of Siena*, tr. by George Lamb (New York: P. J. Kenedy and Sons, 1960), p. 337.

57. Ibid., p. 336.

58. Ellin Kelly and Annabelle Melville, eds., *Elizabeth Seton: Selected Writings* (New York: Paulist Press, 1987), p. 36.

59. Ibid.

60. Ibid., p. 75.

61. Ibid., p. 304.

62. Ibid., p. 281.

63. Ibid., p. 318.

64. Gregory Nazianzen, "Four Funeral Orations," tr. by Leo P. McCauley, *Funeral Orations by Saint Gregory Nazianzen and Saint Ambrose* (New York: Fathers of the Church, Inc., 1953), p. 123.

65. Ibid., p. 132.

66. Ibid., p. 133.

67. Ibid., p. 134.

68. Ibid., p. 137.

69. Ibid., p. 139.

70. Ibid., p. 153.

71. Ibid., p. 155.

72. Ibid., pp. 155-156.

73. André Ravier, *Saint Jeanne de Chantal: Noble Lady, Holy Lady*, tr. by Mary Emily Hamilton (San Francisco: Ignatius Press, 1983), p. 51.

74. Ibid., p. 52.

75. Ibid.

76. Francis de Sales and Jane de Chantal, *Letters of Spiritual Direction*, tr. by Peronne Marie Thibert, intro. by Wendy M. Wright and Joseph F. Powers, *The Classics of Western Spirituality* (New York: Paulist Press, 1988), pp. 217-218.

77. Margaret Yeo, *The Greatest of the Borgias* (London: Sheed and Ward, 1936), p. 117.

78. Ibid.

79. Ibid., p. 118.

80. Ibid.

81. *Sanctus Franciscus Borgia, Quartus Gandiae Dux Et Societatis Jesu*, vol. II (1530-1550), Matriti, Typis Augustini Avrial, 1903, p. 522, letter no. 234, tr. by Ms. Ana Spitzmesser, Assistant Professor of Foreign Languages at Niagara University.

82. Thérèse of Lisieux, *The Autobiography of St. Thérèse of Lisieux: The Story of a Soul*, tr. by John Beevers (Garden City, N.Y.: Image Books, 1957), p. 28.

83. Ibid., p. 29.

84. Ibid., pp. 29-30.

85. Augustine of Hippo, *The Confessions of Saint Augustine*, Book 9.10-11, as found in *The Liturgy of the Hours*, vol. IV (New York: Catholic Book Publishing Co., 1975), pp. 1352-1354.

86. Delaney, p. 114.

87. Cesare Orsenigo, *Life of St. Charles Borromeo*, tr. by Rudolph Kraus (St. Louis: B. Herder Book Co., 1943), pp. 126-127.
88. Ibid.
89. R. E. Carson, "Damien, Father (Joseph De Veuster)," in *New Catholic Encyclopedia*, vol. 4, p. 627.
90. Vital Jourdain, *The Heart of Father Damien: 1840-89,* tr. by Francis Larkin and Charles Davenport (Milwaukee: The Bruce Publishing Co., 1955), p. 249.
91. Ibid., p. 250.
92. Ibid., p. 251.
93. Ibid., p. 253.
94. Ibid., p. 258.
95. Ibid., p. 257.
96. Ibid., p. 253.
97. Alban Goodier, *Saints for Sinners* (San Francisco: Ignatius Press, 1993), p. 160.
98. Butler, vol. II, p. 107.
99. Goodier, p. 163.
100. Ibid., pp. 166-167.
101. Ibid.
102. Leonard Foley, *Saint of the Day. A Life and Lesson for Each of the 173 Saints of the New Missal*, vol. 2 (Cincinnati: St. Anthony Messenger Press, 1974), p. 133.
103. Anthony Mary Claret, *The Autobiography of Anthony Mary Claret*, tr. by Louis Joseph Moore (Compton, Calif.: Claretian Major Seminary, 1945), pp. 154-155.
104. Abbé Maynard, *Virtues and Spiritual Doctrine of St. Vincent de Paul*, rev. by Carlton Prindeville (St. Louis: Vincentian Foreign Mission Press, 1961), p. 292.
105. Ibid., p. 287.
106. Ibid., p. 288.
107. Ibid.
108. Ibid.
109. Ibid., p. 289.
110. Ibid.
111. Ibid.
112. Françoise Mallet, "Benedict, St.," in *New Catholic Encyclopedia*, vol. 2, p. 272.
113. Butler, vol. I, p. 651.
114. Subiaco was named formerly Sublacum, which was located near the artificial lake built by Nero.

115. Gregory the Great, *Life and Miracles of St. Benedict*, tr. of Book 2 of *Dialogi et vita* by Odo J. Zimmermann and Benedict R. Avery (Westport, Conn.: Greenwood Press, Publishers; 1980), pp. 9-11.

116. Butler, vol. III, p. 455.

117. Ibid., vol. IV, p. 338.

118. Ibid., p. 339.

119. Demetrius Wysochansky, *St. Josaphat Kuntsevych, Apostle of Church Unity* (Detroit: Basilian Fathers Publications, 1987), p. 224.

120. Ibid., p. 225.

121. Ibid., p. 227.

122. Butler, vol. IV, p. 399.

123. Wysochansky, p. 229.

124. Ibid., p. 230.

125. Ibid.

126. Ibid., pp. 233-234.

127. William J. Short, "Stigmata," in *The New Dictionary of Catholic Spirituality*, ed. by Michael Downey (Collegeville, Minn.: The Liturgical Press, 1993), p. 947.

128. John A. Schug, *Padre Pio: He Bore the Stigmata* (Huntington, Ind.: Our Sunday Visitor, Inc., 1975), pp. 79-80.

129. Ibid., p. 82.

130. Charles Mortimer Carty, *Who Is Padre Pio?*, tr. by Laura Chanler White (Rockford, Ill.: Tan Books and Publishers, Inc., 1974), p. 9.

131. Ibid., p. 87.

132. Ibid.

133. Ibid., p. 103.

134. Ibid., pp. 105-106.

135. Louis Martin and his wife, Zélie Guérin Martin, were regarded as saints by their contemporaries. Their causes for canonization were submitted to the Vatican: Zélie's in 1959 and Louis's in 1960.

136. Sister Genevieve of the Holy Face, *The Father of the Little Flower* (Dublin: M. H. Gill and Son, Ltd., 1959), p. 87.

137. Ibid., p. 88.

138. Ibid., pp. 89-90.

139. Ibid., p. 93.

140. Stephane-Joseph Piat, *The Story of a Family. The Home of the Little Flower*, tr. by a Benedictine of Stanbrook Abbey (New York: P. J. Kenedy and Sons, 1948), p. 457.

141. Ibid., p. 97.

142. Ibid., p. 104.

143. Ibid.

144. Ibid., pp. 105-106.

145. Ibid., p. 119.

146. Céline joined her three sisters — Pauline, Marie, and Thérèse — in the Carmelite convent at Lisieux within two months of her father's death. Léonie then joined the same convent within two years of Thérèse's death. All five surviving daughters became Carmelite nuns.

147. Lorene Hanley Duquin, *They Called Her the Baroness: The Life of Catherine de Hueck Doherty* (Staten Island, N.Y.: Alba House, 1995), p. 51.

148. Ibid., p. 82.

149. Ibid., p. 83.

150. Ibid., p. 113.

151. Ibid., p. 116.

152. Ibid.

153. Ibid.

154. Ibid., p. 115.

155. Ibid., p. 117.

156. Ibid., pp. 117-118.

157. Thérèse of Lisieux, *The Autobiography of St. Thérèse of Lisieux: The Story of a Soul*, tr. by John Beevers (Garden City, N.Y.: Doubleday and Co., Inc., 1957), p. 120.

158. John Clarke, tr., *St. Thérèse of Lisieux: Her Last Conversations* (Washington, D.C.: Institute of Carmelite Studies, 1977), p. 205.

159. Ibid., p. 27.

160. Ibid., p. 29.

161. Patrick Ahern, *Maurice and Thérèse: The Story of a Love* (New York: Doubleday and Co., Inc., 1998), p. 69.

162. Ibid.

163. Ibid., p. 87.

164. Thérèse of Lisieux, p. 116.

165. Ibid., p. 117.

166. Ibid., p. 118.

167. Ahern, p. 10.

168. Ibid., p. 53.

169. Ibid., p. 9.

170. Clarke, p. 204.

171. Ibid.

172. Ibid.

173. Ibid., p. 206.

PART 2

Family and Friends

St. Gregory Nazianzen

Gregory Nazianzen (329-389) and Basil the Great epitomized friendship. Together they grew up in Athens, studied at the same schools, chose the same hermits' lifestyle, became priests, and were ordained bishops. Gregory describes their relationship: "We seemed to be two bodies with the same spirit."[1]

When Gregory was forty-three, Basil asked Gregory to transfer his bishopric from Nazianzus to Sasima. Archbishop Basil had created this see as a political maneuver. Emperor Justinian, who supported the heretical Arians, was attempting to divide Basil's power in the capital city by dividing the municipality in half. Basil countered by creating a new see in the new municipality. Basil then appointed his best friend, Gregory, as the bishop there, thus undercutting the emperor's shift of power.

Gregory agreed to this plan. The new see, however, was a hotbed of controversy. Gregory had second thoughts about going to Sasima. But Basil pressured and rebuked him. As the tension increased, Gregory's confidence decreased. He remained at Nazianzus and never moved to the new assignment. Gregory resented that Basil, who knew Gregory's timid temperament, had even asked him to take this difficult assignment. Gregory preached in 374 the following excerpt during his father's funeral oration, at which Basil was present:

> Once I got a taste of trouble, disaster followed disaster. Basil, the closest of our friends, came to visit us. . . . He was to prove another father to me, and a far more burdensome one. My real father, even though he tyrannized over me, I must shelter; but no such duty holds in his case, where friendship actually brought injury instead of deliverance from trouble. I cannot know whether I should lay more blame on my own sins, which often indeed have tortured me, or on the highhanded style you acquired with the throne, O best of men [i.e., Basil].
>
> . . . What came over you? How was it that you suddenly cast me off? Any style of friendship that so deals with friends should perish from the earth. We were lions yesterday and today I am an ape. But of course even a lion is trifling in your eyes. And even if you took this view of your friends generally, I did not deserve this, the man you set

above your friends. That was before you climbed so high you thought everything beneath you.

Again my narrative turns toward its goal. In other respects the soul of integrity, that man was falsity itself to me. . . . Had my enemies deliberated long about a means to dishonor me, I don't think they would have found a better one than this one.[2]

Gregory was timid, not disloyal. He lacked confidence, not convictions. His battleground was theological treatises, not public confrontations and political machinations. He had fought many fights: he was stoned at Constantinople; he confronted the heretical Arians and Apollinarists at Nicaea; he succeeded his father as bishop at Nazianzus; he experienced near death at sea in a storm that lasted twenty days and nights. But Basil had asked too much of him. Gregory suffered a nervous breakdown in 375. He left the active ministry for five years and retired to the countryside. After Basil died in 379, Gregory came out of retirement. One year later, he agreed to serve as the archbishop of Constantinople. But he lasted just eight months in that position before retiring for good.

St. Martin de Porres

Martin (1579-1639) was born to Juan de Porres and Ana Velazquez. Juan was a Spanish nobleman who traveled to the New World as a conquistador. Ana was a black Panamanian woman, a former slave. Juan met her on the isthmus, loved her, and took her to his post in Peru. This liaison satisfied them both, for a while.

When Martin was born, the parish priest wrote in the baptismal records: "On Wednesday, December 9th, 1579, I baptized Martin — father, unknown — mother, Ana Velazquez, a free woman."[3] The father had refused to acknowledge Martin as his son. The infant possessed a complexion that reflected the mother's color more than the father's. Approximately two years later, this same couple gave birth to a girl, Martin's sister Juana. After this birth, the father deserted the family. It is said that the father was unwilling to accept his black mistress and mulatto children. The parents never married, and Juan eventually moved to Guayaquil in Ecuador.

"Little Martin endured all the pangs and sorrows of being an unwanted child."[4] Since "nature and nurture" are the twin influences in everyone's life, the absence of the father impacted this boy. The depriva-

72

tion of a father seemed to sensitize Martin to other people's deprivations. As a child, he literally could not pass beggars without sharing the food that he purchased on errands for his mother. As a child, he found consolation in the church where he regularly assisted at Mass, prayed devotions, and contemplated Jesus on the cross.

When Martin was eight, his father visited Lima. He embraced the two children as his own and sought permission from their mother to take them with him to Guayaquil. There he saw to their education. Four years later, he was transferred to Panama, where he had been appointed governor. He returned Martin to his mother and left his daughter in the care of her granduncle in Guayaquil.

> He gave funds for her support until she should reach a marriageable age. Martin he took with him to Lima, returning him to his mother and charging her to have him finish his studies and then to learn the trade of a barber. It is interesting to note that before leaving for Panama Don Juan saw to it that the boy received the sacrament of confirmation.[5]

We hear no more about Martin de Porres's father. Martin became a barber, a profession in those times and places that included the skills of surgeon, physician, and pharmacist. He applied these skills in caring for slaves brought in from Africa and infants and children abandoned in the streets.

ABANDONMENT BY MANY FRIENDS

St. Elizabeth Ann Seton

Immediately after Elizabeth Ann Bayley Seton (1774-1821) converted from her family's Episcopalian religion to the Roman Catholic religion, she was "abandoned by practically all her friends and relatives, deprived of even the necessities of life, and prevented because of prejudice from earning a livelihood."[6]

Elizabeth had been born into a wealthy family "of colonial stock and distinguished family background."[7] At nineteen, she married William Seton, whose family owned an international shipping company. After nine years of marriage, however, her husband's business fortunes plummeted. He lost the family's wealth and his health in the process.

In the hope of experiencing a medical recovery, William, Elizabeth, and their eldest daughter traveled to Italy. Within six weeks, however, William died. Elizabeth and her daughter continued to receive hospitality in the home of William's business associate Antonio Felicchi and his wife for another four months until warmer weather permitted their return voyage to New York City. Elizabeth remained forever grateful to the Felicchis for their kindness and the inspiration of their Catholic faith.

Two years after her return to New York City, Elizabeth converted to the Roman Catholic faith. She had always been a faith-filled woman. Because of her extensive charitable works, she had been called "the Protestant Sister of Charity."[8] When she converted, however, her family and friends turned against her. They refused to speak to her. They disowned this widow and her five young children. Elizabeth writes to her friend Antonio in early April 1805:

> Saturday last I had a very painful conversation (certainly for the last time with Mr. H. [Episcopal minister Dr. Henry Hobart]), but was repaid fully and a thousand times on Sunday morning by my dear Master at Communion, and my faith, if possible, more strengthened and decided than if it had not been attacked. My Mrs. Duplex goes on very fast — every day some one of the kind ladies sheds tears to her for the poor deluded Mrs. Seton, and she always tells them how happy she is that anything in this world can comfort and console me. . . .
>
> John Wilkes has made me some sharp yet gentle reproaches for my "imprudence in offending my uncle and other friends" — he said nothing of my religion but that he knew the "evidences of the Christian religion were all on that side" and my sentiments made no difference to him. Sister says, "tell me candidly if you go to our church or not." I answered, "since the first day of Lent I have been to St. Peter's [the only Catholic Church in New York City at that time]."[9]

In May, she comments in a letter about seeking financial assistance: "Mr. Post and Mr. Wilkes give their cool assent — and I am satisfied that my situation cannot be worse than to be dependent on such philosophic spirits."[10] In October, she writes to Antonio regarding her loneliness: "It is very painful to be so separated from all."[11] And in August 1806, she comments about the animosity she encounters:

> The anger and violence of the Setons, Farquhars, Wilkes etc. when they found Cecilia was not only a Catholic but as firm as the rock she builds on, cannot be described. They threatened that she should be sent from the country, I should be turned out a beggar with

my children, and many other nonsenses (as you call them) not worth naming, assembled a family meeting and resolved if she persevered that they would consider themselves individually bound never to speak to either of us again or suffer her to enter the house of either of them. . . . But Almighty God always provides, and to Him I commit my cause.[12]

Bl. Magdalene di Canossa

Magdalene (1774-1835) was born into a noble family that traced its lineage back seven hundred years to Emperor Henry IV, who at Canossa had knelt in the snow to receive the forgiveness of Pope St. Gregory VII. Magdalene's father died when he was thirty-nine. Her mother remarried two years later, but in doing so she abandoned her five children.

> Her mother married again and went to live with her new husband, the Marquis Zanetti, in Mantua, leaving her children to the care of their uncles. Magdalene, who was now eight, with her elder sister Laura, was put in the charge of a governess, a woman who "took out" on Magdalene a spite she had for someone who had criticized her inadequate religious instruction of the children. It was six years before Uncle Jerome found out how badly his second niece was being treated, and dismissed the governess. Apparently Magdalene had never said a word, and would not let her sisters do so. Perhaps these years of domestic tyranny had something to do with the period of painful sickness that followed them, during which Magdalene "took stock" with herself: she was definite that she did not wish to marry, but was not sure that she wanted to be a nun. [13]

As a young woman, Magdalene entered the Carmelite community but discovered that cloistered life was not her vocation. She returned home. In 1806, when Napoleon visited the family mansion, she requested his permission to use an unoccupied convent to educate poor and neglected girls. Many women offered to assist Magdalene in this work. In 1808, she founded the religious community of the Canossian Daughters of Charity. In 1831, she founded a male counterpart to educate poor and neglected boys. She opened many schools in the major cities of her native region.

St. Patrick

When Patrick (c. 389-c. 461) was fifteen, he confided his worst sin to a friend. Three decades later this friend reported publicly what Patrick had shared privately. Patrick was crushed by this breach of confidence.

At fifteen, Patrick was not yet a Christian. At sixteen, he was captured by pirates and taken from his native Britain to Ireland, where he was enslaved as a shepherd. After six years, he escaped and sailed to France and on to Britain. In 412, he pursued studies at Lérins and Auxerre, where he was ordained a priest in 417 and a bishop in 432. Patrick was assigned to Ireland to succeed the country's first bishop, who had just died. Patrick traversed the whole of Ireland preaching God's word and winning converts. His reputation spread beyond his adopted country to Britain and the continent. And then his erstwhile friend betrayed Patrick's confidence. Patrick writes about the incident:

> As cause for proceeding against me they found — after thirty years! — a confession I had made before I was a deacon. In the anxiety of my troubled mind I confided to my dearest friend what I had done in my boyhood one day, nay, in one hour, because I was not yet strong. I know not, God knoweth — whether I was fifteen years old; and I did not believe in the living God, nor did I so from my childhood, but lived in death and unbelief until I was severely chastised and really humiliated, by hunger and nakedness, and that daily. . . .
>
> And so I say boldly, my conscience does not blame me now or in the future: God is my witness that I have not lied in the account which I have given you.
>
> But the more am I sorry for my dearest friend that we had to hear what he said. To him I had confided my very soul! And I was told by some of the brethren before that defence — at which I was not present, nor was I in Britain, nor was it suggested by me — that he would stand up for me in my absence. He had even said to me in person: "Look, you should be raised to the rank of bishop!" — of which I was not worthy. But whence did it come to him afterwards that he left me down before all, good and evil, and publicly.[14]

St. Marguerite d'Youville

At nineteen, Marguerite Lajemmerais (1701-1771) became engaged to Monsieur de Langloiserie. They seemed like the perfect aristocratic couple. "They had much in common: family prestige and noble traditions; high ideals; culture, refinement, and similarity in tastes. To these people a good name was indeed better than great riches."[15]

When she was seven her father died, and because Marguerite was the firstborn she ended up helping her mother raise the five younger children. At age eleven, she traveled from home at Varennes to the Ursuline Sisters school in Quebec City, where she studied for two years.

She possessed a very pleasant manner. "Serious and reserved by nature, Marguerite was also endowed with a sweetness of personality that made her a delightful companion in a group. She could enter into the joys of others as well as into their sorrows. She sincerely liked everyone."[16] Her appearance is described as "above average in height, of perfect form and features. Soft, dark brown hair framed a clear, rosy countenance. . . . Her movements were graceful; her manners, gracious."[17] She smiled easily. Her eyes sparkled. "Her inner qualities as well as her physical appearance made her one of the truly beautiful persons of her time."[18]

Abruptly and without explanation or communication, Langloiserie broke off their engagement. Although she was brokenhearted and her dreams were dashed, Marguerite needed no explanation. Langloiserie's about-face had been precipitated by her mother's social sin of marrying beneath one's social class. For class-conscious eighteenth-century Quebec, Marie Renée Gaultier-Lajemmerais's action was unpardonable.

Marie Lajemmerais married Timothy Sullivan, who had changed his name to Sylvain to try to accommodate himself, albeit unsuccessfully, to the French environment. He presented himself as a medical doctor, even though he possessed no medical license; despite that, the corrupt governor De Vaudreil implored the king to eventually award Sylvain an honorary practitioner's license in 1724. "His aggressive manner and his violent temper had already embroiled him in unpleasant legal proceedings."[19] Court records indicate he frequently appeared in court. After the marriage, "all Varennes was shaken in surprise and shock. To think that Marie Renée Gaultier, respected widow of Captain Lajemmerais, would entrust her life, her family, and her name to a foreigner of doubtful reputation!"[20]

Shortly after her mother's remarriage and Marguerite's broken engagement, the new stepfamily moved to Montreal. Within less than one year, Marguerite met and married a fur-trader named François d'Youville. Marguerite discovered shortly that her husband was despised by church-men, Native Americans, and honest traders. She experienced firsthand the reasons for others' rejection of her husband. Her eight-year marriage to François is described in this section under the title "Self-indulgent hus-band."

St. Margaret of Cortona

Margaret of Cortona (1247-1297) eloped with a young nobleman when she was about twelve. Her mother had died when she was seven and her father remarried when she was nine. Her stepmother "had little sympa-thy with the high-spirited, pleasure-loving child."[21] Margaret lived with her lover for nine years and bore him a son. The family traveled in style and without shame, but Margaret was the subject of much gossip and slander.

One day her companion set out to collect rents that were due him. By nightfall, he had not returned. After the master's dog returned home alone, it led Margaret back to a wooded area where her lover's body lay buried. He had been beaten to death and thrown into a pit. She was dev-astated and decided to depart from the region. She turned over to her lover's family all his belongings. Then she set out for her father's home. Upon arriving home, Margaret asked her father to allow her inside. He refused, urged on by Margaret's spiteful stepmother. Where, Margaret wondered, would she go?

Margaret walked to the nearby town of Cortona, where the Friars Minor had a reputation for assisting persons in need. Before she encoun-tered the friars, she met two older women to whom she told her story and who welcomed her and her son to live in their home. They then intro-duced her to the friars, two of whom, in particular, guided her spiritually for many years. She struggled spiritually, emotionally, and physically. The transition from common-law wife to widow was difficult for her. She chose to perform severe physical austerities, which the friars advised her to mod-erate. She insisted, however, on doing penances. She explained to one of the priests, "Father, do not ask me to come to terms with this body of mine, for I cannot afford it. Between me and my body there must needs be a struggle till death."[22]

For three years, she prayed and performed harsh forms of self-discipline. Confident of her conversion, she founded a house and soon a hospital to care for the sick poor. Many women followed her. Some women pledged themselves to the religious community that Margaret founded but never entered. Other women pledged themselves as nonreligious tertiaries to aid the poor in material and monetary ways.

She advanced in conversion, contemplation, and service to the poor, but the townspeople could never forget the sin of her youth. Gossips created a storm of suspicion about her relationship with the friars in general and one Fra Giunta, in particular. He was transferred to Siena in order to assuage suspicion. Years later, he returned to administer to her the sacrament of the sick and dying. She spent the last three decades of her life in penance for her youthful sin.

COHABITATION ON MORE THAN ONE OCCASION

St. Augustine of Hippo

Augustine (354-430) developed his teachings on the morality of sexuality based on considerable personal experience. He writes explicitly about the sexual hungers he felt. In his famous *Confessions* he addresses the Lord:

> For in my youth I burned to get my fill of hellish things. I dared to run wild in different darksome ways of love. . . . I could not distinguish the calm light of chaste love from the fog of lust. Both kinds of affection burned confusedly within me and swept my feeble youth over the crags of desire and plunged me into a whirlpool of shameful deeds. . . . I was tossed about and spilt out in my fornications; I flowed out and boiled over in them, but you kept silent. Ah! my late-found joy, you kept silent at that time, and farther and farther I went from you, into more and more fruitless seedings of sorrow, with a profound dejection and a weariness without rest.
>
> . . . But I, poor wretch, foamed over: I followed after the sweeping tide of passions and I departed from you. I broke all your laws but I did not escape your scourges. . . . For you fashion sorrow into a lesson to us. You smite so that you might heal. You slay us so that we might not die apart from you.
>
> Where was I in that sixteenth year of my body's age, and how long was I exiled from the joys of your house? Then it was that the

madness of lust, licensed by human shamelessness but forbidden by your laws, took me completely under its scepter, and I clutched it with both hands. My parents took no care to save me by marriage from plunging into ruin. Their only care was that I should make the finest orations and become a persuasive speaker.[23]

After having lived some twelve years with a mistress, by whom he fathered his only child, Adeodatus, Augustine was persuaded by his mother, Monica, to send his consort back to Carthage in North Africa. Monica wanted Augustine to marry someone of his social class. Although he loved dearly this anonymous woman, he sent her home, but he missed her terribly. While waiting to find someone suitable for marriage, he took another mistress. He had no intention of marrying her, but in her he hoped to find temporary comfort. He writes:

> In the meantime my sins were multiplied. The woman with whom I was wont to share my bed was torn from my side as an impediment to marriage. My heart still clung to her: it was pierced and wounded within me, and the wound drew blood from it. She returned to Africa, vowing that she would never know another man, and leaving with me our natural son. But unhappy man that I was, no imitator of a woman and impatient of delay, since it would be two years before I could have her whose hand I sought, and since I was not so much a lover of marriage as a slave to lust, I procured another woman, but not, of course, as a wife. By her my soul's disease would be fostered and brought safe, as it were, either unchanged or in a more intense form, under the convoy of continued use into the kingdom of marriage. Not yet healed within me was that wound which had been made by the cutting away of that former companion. After intense fever and pain, it festered, and it still caused me pain, although in a chilling and more desperate way.[24]

DISAPPOINTMENT

St. Catherine of Siena

Catherine of Siena (1347-1380) and Raymond of Capua were soul friends. When she suffered public criticism and official investigation from Church leaders and her religious community, he was appointed her confessor, and became her public defender, best friend, and biographer.[25] When he was struggling with responding to theological and political controversies, she provided him with intellectual and moral support. Unfortunately, Raymond caused her one of her greatest sufferings.

Catherine exhorted Raymond to travel from Siena to Avignon to urge the pope to return to and reside at Rome. He traveled by foot the one hundred fifty miles from Siena to Genoa, where he was to sail to Marseilles, which would leave him some fifty miles from Avignon. At Genoa, sailors warned him that enemies at Marseilles were lying in wait to murder him. Raymond was more cautious than courageous. He decided to enjoy life on Italian soil rather than risk death on French shores.

After Catherine heard about Raymond's aborted mission, she wrote him in a playful and affectionate manner. She addressed him, "Oh my naughty father."[26] She commented, "How blessed your soul and mine would have been could you have sealed with your blood a stone in Holy Church! I do wish I could see you risen above your childishness — see you shed your milk teeth and eat bread, the mustier the better!"[27]

Raymond responded that he hoped that she did not love him less because of his lack of courage in facing probable martyrdom. Catherine responded in a tone markedly different from the first letter. She states unequivocally that her love for him was not diminished but heightened in his moment of weakness. She charged, however, that he reveals the diminution of his love for her by the mere suggestion that she might love him less. She writes in her second letter to Raymond:

> You did not seem to yourself strong enough for me to measure you with my measure, and on this account you were in doubt lest my affection and love to you were diminished. But you did not see aright, and it was you who showed that I had grown to love more, and you less; for with the love with which I love myself, with that I love you. . . . Yes, yes, I show you a love increased in me toward you, and not waning. But what shall you say? How could your ignorance give place to one of the least of those thoughts? Could you ever believe that I wished anything else than the life of your soul? Where is the faith that you always used to have and ought to have, and the certainty that you have had, that before a thing is done, it is seen and determined in the sight of God — not only this, which is so great a deed, but every least thing? Had you been faithful, you would not have gone about vacillating so, nor fallen into fear toward God and toward me; but like a faithful son, ready for obedience, you would have gone and done what you could.[28]

Catherine resigned herself to the providence of God. She had not expected Raymond's failure, but she believed the scriptural exhortation "that in everything God works for good with those who love him."[29] Her final words of the letter repeat her love for him. "I beg you to pardon me whatever I might have said that was not honor to God and due reverence to yourself: let love excuse it. I say no more to you. Remain in the holy and sweet grace of God. I ask your benediction."[30]

DIVORCE

St. Helena of Constantinople

Helena (c. 250-c. 330) is famous throughout history as the mother of Constantine the Great, as a Christian philanthropist, and as the discoverer of the Holy Cross. Her husband divorced her after twenty years of marriage, but her son always admired and supported her.

Helena grew up in the small town of Drepanum, near Istanbul, Turkey. Her father owned a tavern and inn where she allegedly worked as a barmaid. Helena fell in love with the soldier Constantius Chlorus. They married, but did so according to the classical morganatic system whereby "a man of high rank marries a woman of inferior social status with the stipulation that, although the children, if any, will be legitimate, neither they nor the wife may lay claim to his rank or property."[31]

Their love brought forth one child who was born about the year 273 at Naissus, a military outpost located south of the Danube River between the Adriatic and Black Seas. This child grew to become Constantine the Great. Twenty years later, Helena and Constantius divorced. He saw it as a career move. The once-promising soldier was offered the position of Caesar of the Western Empire if he would divorce the innkeeper's daughter and marry the emperor's stepdaughter, Theodora. Constantius accepted. "There is no record . . . of Helena's personal reaction to her dismissal."[32]

Two questions are raised about Helena's divorce: had she truly married in the first place, and did she convert to Christianity before or after her divorce?

> The claim has frequently been made that Constantius and Helena were not truly married, and that in fact she lived with him in legal concubinage, rather more than a mistress but much less than a wife. It has also been suggested that the fiction of a legal marriage between

them was invented by their enemies late in her life, so that the story of Constantius' having divorced her in order to marry Theodora could be used to denigrate both her and Constantine in Christian eyes. However, rejection by one's husband was no sin, whereas to the Christians prostitution and concubinage were. The attack would have been more telling if it could have been argued that Constantine was the illegitimate son of an immoral woman. The fact that this charge was not made is a strong argument for the validity of the marriage. On the other hand, there is no documentary proof that the marriage ever took place, although Victor writes of Constantius "taking as his wife Theodora, the step-daughter of Herculius Maximianus, divorcing his first wife," using the legal terms usually reserved for legitimate marriages in both instances.[33]

When Constantius married Theodora at Rome, he ordered Helena and Constantine to travel to and reside at the imperial court in the Eastern Empire. The political machinations of the day posed a real threat to the life of his son. In 305, the son escaped from his guard and fled to fight beside his father. One year later, the father was killed in a battle at York, England. The troops then declared Constantine the new Caesar. He earned his title by fighting a series of rivals. Six years later, these battles culminated at the Milvian Bridge in Milan, where Constantine, in response to a vision received the previous night, ordered his soldiers to paint on their shields the sign of Christ's cross.

Victorious, Constantine bestowed upon his mother the title Augusta and ordered that full honors be given to her as empress. One year later, 312, Constantine and his co-emperor, Licinius, promulgated the Edict of Milan, which eliminated the worship of pagan gods as the official state religion and tolerated all religions. Not until 393 did Christianity become the state religion.

Around the time of the Edict of Milan, when she was sixty-three years old, Helena converted to the Christian religion. Her son and she moved to Istanbul, which he renamed Constantinople. Helena dedicated herself to works of charity for the poor and the construction of churches throughout Rome, Constantinople, and Palestine. Authoritative sources report that she searched for and discovered the True Cross on which Jesus had been crucified.

St. Fabiola

The Roman patrician Fabiola (d. 399) won a civil divorce from her first husband on the grounds of his dissolute living. When she married a second time, the Christian community in Rome regarded the remarriage as a great scandal. After both husbands died, she asked for readmission to the Church. The pope himself performed the rite of reconciliation after she performed the customary penances.

Until her divorce, Fabiola possessed a reputation for prayerfulness and philanthropy. She had chosen Jerome as her spiritual director. She participated in his prayer group, which included the saintly Marcella, Paula, and Eustochium Julia. Because "Fabiola was of a lively, passionate and headstrong disposition,"[34] the prayer group did not fit her style. She was an activist more than a contemplative. She founded the first Christian hospital in the Western world, where she personally tended the sick. She financed the construction of many churches, and numerous individuals and institutions benefited from her generosity. "She needed company and activity, and St. Jerome remarks that her idea of the solitude of the stable of Bethlehem was that it should not be cut off from the crowded inn."[35]

About 394, the priest Amandus from Bourdeaux asked Jerome, with obvious reference to Fabiola, "Can a woman who has divorced her first husband on account of his vices and who has during his lifetime under compulsion married again, communicate with the Church without first doing penance?"[36] Jerome scoffed at the suggestion of coercion. He writes:

> Therefore if your sister, who, as she says, has been forced into a second union, wishes to receive the body of Christ and not to be accounted an adulteress, let her do penance; so far at least as from the time she begins to repent to have no further intercourse with that second husband who ought be called not a husband but an adulterer.[37]

Jerome reviewed many popular secular reasons offered in support of divorce and remarriage. Basing himself on the Scriptures, however, he rejected them all as excuses. He writes:

> The apostle has thus cut away every plea and has clearly declared that, if a woman marries again while her husband is still living,

she is an adulteress. You must not speak to me of the violence of a ravisher, a mother's pleading, a father's bidding, the influence of the relatives, the insolence and the intrigues of servants, household losses. A husband may be an adulterer or a sodomite, he may be sustained with every crime and may have been left by his wife because of his sins: yet he is still her husband and, so long as he lives, she may not marry another. The apostle does not promulgate this decree on his own authority but on that of Christ who speaks in him.[38]

The next year, Fabiola visited Jerome at Bethlehem. She remained with him a few months while weighing whether or not to spend the rest of her life in his prayer community. She decided instead to return to Rome, to continue her charitable activities.

When Fabiola died, Jerome preached the eulogy. He praised her praying, fasting, and almsgiving. He addressed head-on the issue of her divorce and remarriage. His viewpoint, however, had mellowed. Although he did not excuse her divorce and remarriage, he did not condemn her or her second husband as adulterers. The content and tone of his words differ vastly between the letter of 394 cited above and the eulogy of 399 excerpted below:

> So terrible then were the faults imputed to her former husband that not even a prostitute or a common slave could have put up with them. If I were to recount them, I should undo the heroism of the wife who chose to bear the blame of a separation rather than to blacken the character and expose the stains of him who was one body with her. . . .
>
> If however it is made a charge against her that after repudiating her husband she did not continue unmarried, I readily admit this to have been a fault, but at the same time declare that it may have been a case of necessity. "It is better," the apostle tells us, "to marry than to burn." She was quite a young woman, she was not able to continue in widowhood. . . . Fabiola therefore was fully persuaded in her own mind in putting away her husband, and that when she had done so she was free to marry again.[39]

St. Dymphna

The story of Dymphna (d.c. 650) appears to be popular legend rather than historical fact. The story of seventh-century Dymphna originated only in the thirteenth century.

We are told that Dymphna's parents were Celts: a pagan prince and a Christian princess. The mother raised her daughter in the faith until the mother died at a young age. As the daughter matured, she developed a striking resemblance in appearance and manner to her beautiful mother. The father perceived this similarity and developed an unholy attraction to his daughter. Dymphna confided this situation to her priest-confessor. The priest, Gerebernus, urged her to flee from home in order to avoid the incestuous advances of her widowed father.

The priest assisted the young woman and two of her aides in their flight. The foursome sailed from Ireland to Belgium, where they made their way from the coastal city of Antwerp overland on horseback twenty-five miles southeast to Gheel. There they lived as hermits and constructed an oratory in the solitude of the forest.

The father was furious when he learned of his daughter's flight. He gathered a few henchmen and pursued her. According to legend, the foreign coins used by the escaping foursome left a trail along their route. The determined father tracked down his daughter and surprised her in the oratory. The priest came to her defense and refused the father's order to release her. The father ordered his mercenaries to kill the priest and the two court aides. Nevertheless, the daughter refused to return with her father. He begged and cajoled her. She resisted him. The father knew that he could not persuade his determined daughter. "Thereupon the unnatural father struck off his daughter's head with his own sword."[40]

A commentator provides this overview: "The true history of these saints is probably lost, but popular belief, reaching back to the date of the finding of their relics, has attached to them a story which, with local variations, is to be found in the folk-lore of many European countries."[41]

St. Margaret Mary Alacoque

Margaret (1647-1690) was eight years old when her father died. Her mother sent her to a boarding school administered by the Poor Clares, where she enjoyed everything except good health. At eleven, she became chronically bedridden with rheumatism. At fifteen, the nuns sent her home for recuperation because of her deteriorating health.

Meanwhile, her father's relatives had moved in. Her father's brother had drawn up a new lease on the family property, but in his name and not that of Margaret's mother. The father's side of the family were hardworking farmers who ridiculed Madame Alacoque's family for being educated and cultured. The uncle chose not to live with Margaret's family, but as agent of the property and legal guardian of the children, he allowed his widowed mother, widowed aunt, and unmarried sister to live in the home. This trio assumed charge of the home and took away the joyful atmosphere that used to pervade there. So deep was the oppression that many years later Margaret titled the first chapter of her autobiography, "Tyrannical Home-Life."[42] She tells us:

> It was when mother ceased to have any authority in her own house. . . . She'd been forced to hand it over to others. With the reins in their hands, we were neither of us little better than prisoners. (However, I don't want it to appear — from what I am going to say — that I blame them; I don't think they were wicked to make me suffer as I did. God never let this idea enter my head; I saw them only as instruments of his will.) Well, we hadn't any further say in the running of the house, and we didn't dare do anything without permission. It was one long fight. Everything was under lock and key; often I couldn't even find anything to wear to Mass. I was even obliged to borrow clothes. I felt this slavery keenly, I must acknowledge.[43]

Margaret turned to prayer: "It was at this time that with all my strength I sought my consolation in the Most Blessed Sacrament of the Altar. But being in a country-house far from church, I could not go there without the consent of these same persons; and it so happened that the permission granted by one was often withheld by the other. When my tears showed the pain I felt, they accused me of having made an appointment with someone, saying that I concealed it under the pretext of going to Mass or Benediction. This was most unjust."[44]

When Margaret could not flee to church, she prayed at home.

> I hid myself in a retired corner of the garden, in the stable, or in some other out-of-the-way place where I could, unobserved, kneel and pour out my heart in tears before God. This I always did through my good Mother, the most Blessed Virgin, in whom I had placed all my confidence. I remained there entire days without eating or drinking. Sometimes the poor villagers, pitying my condition, gave me in the evening a little fruit or milk. When I ventured to return to the house, it was with such fear and trembling as, it seems to me, a poor criminal endures when about to receive sentence of condemnation.[45]

Margaret was pained especially by the mistreatment directed at her mother: "The rudest cross I had to bear was my inability to alleviate my mother's trials. They were a thousand times harder for me than my own."[46] She writes about her mother: "Necessary nourishment was withheld from her by our jailers, and I was forced to beg from the villagers eggs and other things suitable for the sick. This was a special torment to me, for I was naturally timid, and I was frequently received very rudely."[47]

At twenty, Margaret first experienced Christ in revelations that lasted one-and-a-half years. He instructed her to institute the feast of the Sacred Heart and the practice of praying a Holy Hour on nine consecutive First Fridays. After ten years of investigation, the most reputable theologians and Church leaders decreed the validity of the revelations.

LONELINESS

St. Rose Philippine Duchesne

Rose Philippine (1769-1852) was an indefatigable worker, but she lacked friends. Four years after she had entered the community of the Visitation Sisters, the leaders of the French Revolution disbanded her community and virtually all religious houses. Back at home, she continued caring for the sick, teaching children, and sheltering priests during the bloody revolution.

As soon as the revolution ended, she attempted to regroup the nuns of the Visitation order. A few returned. In 1804, these few joined the Society of the Sacred Heart, which St. Madeleine Sophie Barat had just founded in 1800. Philippine made a novitiate with the younger, inexperienced women, even though she was thirty-four, not twenty, as they were. In 1818, she and four other sisters sailed for the United States to establish the first free school west of the Mississippi. In the next ten years she founded convents, parish schools, boarding schools, and a school for American Indian children. At seventy-two, she received her wish of being missioned to Kansas to live and work with Native Americans. They named her the "woman who prays always."[48]

The external aspects of life — climate, diet, and language — were difficult for Philippine. More difficult, however, were the internal aspects — communications and relations with people. Because of her hard work, self-sacrifice, and obvious holiness, she was appointed superior of houses in which she lived and principal of schools in which she taught. But she was never popular. And she knew it. It became necessary for her general superiors to remove her as local superior. St. Madeleine Sophie Barat writes:

> I sent you a letter quite recently, dear Philippine, answering one from you, but I had not then read all the mail that has since come from you, from your companions, and from the newly arrived religious. From the ensemble of details given me I cannot help being worried about the present condition of your house. . . .
>
> I must then, for the sake of the general good, submit a plan to you. You will, of course, consult the Bishop Rosati, to whose judgment I refer it for final decision, and I beg you to follow his advice. This is what I suggest: let Mother Thiefry take your place in St. Louis and give her, as assistant, Mother de Kersaint, and perhaps Mother Regis as mistress general. Do your utmost to build a separate orphanage first of all, then little by little on a well constructed plan erect the other buildings necessary as the academy grows and additions can be undertaken prudently. You, dear Mother, may go either to Florissant or to St. Charles, whichever you think better.
>
> I realize, my dear daughter, that at your age and after all you have suffered, the foundation of an American academy, which calls for so much care and perfection along all lines, quite surpasses your strength. For several years all those who have been at the St. Louis convent have complained of the lack of order, the shabbiness, even the uncultivated condition of the property. Now God forbid that I should blame you, dear Mother. I know only too well all that you have done and suffered. But times change and we must change, too, and modify our views. I realize from experience that it is unwise to leave

superiors for long years in the same house. Good government requires a change of superiors once in a while.[49]

St. Madeleine Sophie Barat did not answer mail from St. Rose Philippine Duchesne for the last two years of the elderly sister's life.[50]

Bl. Frederic Ozanam

Frederic Ozanam (1813-1853) was very purposeful. By eighteen, he discerned that his life's work was to demonstrate intellectually the role of Christianity, in general, and Catholicism, in particular, in guiding civilization. Truth and faith were the guideposts of his life. He found support among family, friends, and members of what he eventually named the Society of St. Vincent de Paul. He delighted in discussions with unbelievers who were genuine truth-seekers. He was bored, however, by superficial people who were not interested in the pursuit of historical truth and the practice of religious faith.

Young Frederic writes in an autobiographical sketch that he did not have friends outside of the family home. The recurrent revolutions of the day kept interrupting his and others' education. He grew up without the socialization that school provides. When school reopened, he writes, "I must confess that I exchanged a great number of blows with my companions."[51]

At sixteen, he studied philosophy with an open-mindedness that created in him a short-lived crisis of faith.

> "He made a promise that if he could see the truth, he would devote his entire life to its defense."[52] He emerged from his studies with an intellectual foundation for his faith. He published an article critiquing, from a Catholic perspective, contemporary social teachings. This article won him accolades from leading Catholic thinkers. He then left Lyons for Paris, where he studied at the Sorbonne. It was at this time that Frederic's attraction to history took on the dimension of a life's task: as apologist, to write a literary history of the Middle Ages from the fifth to the thirteenth centuries with a focus on the role of Christianity in guiding the progress of civilization. His aim was to help restore Catholicism to France where materialism and rationalism, irreligion, and anticlericalism prevailed.[53]

Frederic had gone cheerfully to Paris. By early November, however, he was lonely. He writes to his mother, "Who bothers about me? My young acquaintances are too far away from my lodgings to see them often. To confide in, I have but you, mother . . . and God."[54] His mother requested that a family friend in Paris might find another boarding house. The woman searched and found a lodging that was not to Frederic's liking. He writes to his mother:

> At the table are old and young ladies, forward, noisy, frivolous, vulgar, even gross. The young men are still worse; loose conversations about indecent representations and Parisian scandals. Barrack-room talk repeated word for word. After supper giddy groups are formed at the card-tables; shouts and vacant laughter penetrate to his room. "I have been pressed," he said, "to join in those amusements; you can readily understand how I refused. Yet these people are neither Christians nor Turks. I am the only one who keeps the fasts, which has made me the butt for many a gibe. It is very annoying to me to find myself in such society."[55]

Five days later Frederic wrote to his father that alternative housing had been found. A neighbor in Lyons had offered lodging with a relative in Paris; the relative was the renowned electrical scientist André Ampère. Frederic and Ampère were two of a kind: they had similar values regarding faith and similar discipline in seeking knowledge.[56] They became best friends.

Frederic and like-minded students, guided by a former professor, established a study group that discussed and defended the faith. They occasionally debated students critical of Christianity and the Catholic Church. In one of the heated exchanges, a student grew weary of Frederic's esoteric defenses from history and shouted to Frederic, "What is your church doing now? What is she doing for the poor of Paris? Show us your work and we will believe in you!"[57] Frederic accepted the challenge. He replied, "Yes, let us go to the poor."[58] The group changed its *modus operandi* from discussion-and-debate to faith-in-action. Frederic and his group went on to found the "Society of St. Vincent de Paul."

Frederic continued his research and studies at the same time as his charitable works. He passed the bar exam in 1834 and within the next five years he received two doctoral degrees, in law and foreign literature. He was offered an assistantship and three years later he was promoted to the university rank of full professor at the Sorbonne.

St. Louise de Marillac

The adage says, "Children learn what they live." Louise (1591-1660) learned that she was unwanted and unloved by her entire stepfamily except her father, who had begotten her out of wedlock. And she never knew her birth mother. The author of the definitive study of Louise writes: "Is it any wonder that she was nervous, withdrawn, and timid throughout the first half of her life?"[59]

Louise wondered if she even should have married. At age twenty, her application to become a nun was rejected on the grounds of poor health. A priest consoled her with the prophetic words, "God has other designs on you."[60] Two years later, she married Antoine le Gras. They enjoyed the first seven years of marriage until he became ill, which adversely affected his disposition. As secretary to the queen, he had always been gentle, but in poor health he became very demanding. "She (Louise) took his anger personally and blamed herself for all of his distress."[61] Two years after her husband became ill and two years before he died, she writes, "I was very disturbed because of the doubt I had as to whether I should leave my husband, as I greatly wanted to do."[62]

Louise's relationship with her son was marked by even greater insecurity. She thought that Michel, who was born nine months after Louise married, ought to become a priest. She pushed him to pursue what was obviously the mother's vocation. He had no desire for the priesthood. She pleaded repeatedly with her spiritual director, Vincent de Paul, to help gain Michel's acceptance into a seminary. Michel entered and left three seminaries. Finally, Vincent urged her to yield to God's will. Vincent writes to Louise in 1636:

> I have never seen such a woman as you are for taking certain things tragically. You say your son's choice is a manifestation of God's justice on you. You really did wrong to entertain such ideas, and still worse to give expression to them. I have often begged you before not to talk like that. In the name of God, Mademoiselle, correct this fault and learn, once and for all, that bitter thoughts proceed from the Evil One, and sweet and gentle thoughts from our Lord.
>
> Remember, too, that the faults of our children are not always imputed to their parents, especially when they have had them instructed and given good example, as, thank God, you have done.

Moreover, our Lord, in his wondrous Providence, allows children to break the hearts of devout fathers and mothers. Abraham's was broken by Ishmael, Isaac's by Esau, Jacob's by most of his children, David's by Absalom, Solomon's by Roboam, and the Son of God's by Judas.

I may tell you that your son told Fr. de la Salle that he was embracing this state of life [priesthood] only because it was your wish, that he would rather die than do so, and that he would take Minor Orders to please you. Now, is that a vocation? I think he would rather die himself than desire your death. However that may be, whether this comes from nature or the devil, his will is not free in its choice of such an important matter, and you ought not to desire it. Some time ago a good youth of this city took the subdiaconate in a similar state of mind, and he has not been able to go on to the other Orders; do you wish to expose your son to the same danger? Let him be guided by God; He is his Father, more than you are his mother; and He loves him more than you do. Leave him to settle it.[63]

After Michel failed at becoming a priest, he tried other professions and succeeded in none of them. He borrowed but failed to pay back money loaned by his wealthy Marillac relatives. When he disappeared overnight, his mother prayed publicly in the Cathedral of Chartres for his safety. As the absence grew longer, parishioners winked knowingly at each other. After three months, it was discovered that Michel "had been consorting with a girl who had been arrested and forcibly constrained in the convent of the Magdalens."[64] Eventually, Michel and his consort settled down and married, when their little girl was already nine.

Louise had constantly implored persons of influence to intercede on behalf of her son. They did. But Michel never completed his part of the arrangement. When Louise lay dying, Michel, his wife, and their daughter gathered at the bedside. Louise blessed the trio and urged them simply "to live like good Christians."[65]

PARENTAL OBJECTION TO VOCATION

St. Teresa Benedicta of the Cross (Edith Stein)

Although Edith Stein (1891-1942) grew up in a devout Jewish family, she gave up the faith of her fathers during her teen years. She pursued instead the abstract truth of philosophy. This brilliant student was selected as the University of Göttingen's teacher's assistant to the world-renowned professor of phenomenology Edmund Husserl.

One of Husserl's students first introduced Edith to Catholicism. Years later, another classmate inspired and intrigued Edith by manifesting much faith-based peace when the classmate's young husband died. While visiting the home of a Lutheran classmate, Edith picked up a biography of St. Teresa of Ávila. Edith borrowed the book and read it overnight. The next morning, she asked a priest to baptize her. He explained that sufficient time had to be given to study. She challenged him to quiz her. He did. And he baptized her immediately. She was thirty years old.

After her baptism, Edith left Husserl and joined the faculty of an all-girls' Catholic school in the Rhineland. Besides teaching, she translated Thomas Aquinas's work *On Truth* and reconciled traditional Catholic teaching with the language of philosophical phenomenology. She remained at the school for ten years until her reputation for scholarship and lectures, especially on the topics of education and women's studies, required her to leave the girls' school in order to have a broader forum. In 1932, she became lecturer at the Educational Institute at Münster; but one year later, she left that post because of anti-Semitic Nazi legislation.

This transition occasioned Edith's entrance into the religious life of the cloistered community of the Carmelites. She went home to prepare her mother. From home, Edith wrote that her mother's reaction was a "desperate resistance" and "she still hopes that I will not be able to manage to carry out what for her is the worst thing imaginable."[66] On October 9, she writes to a friend, "Your letter made me very happy. It is so good for me during these very difficult last days [at home] to receive something from people who understand my path — in contrast to the great pain I must be causing her [mother] and have before my eyes daily. You will help me, won't you, to beg that my mother will be given the strength to bear the leave-taking, and the light to understand it?"[67]

On October 17 she writes to another friend:

> I have never told my mother about you. It was not possible to give any of your writings to her because she declines anything that is beyond her Jewish faith. For that reason, too, it was impossible at this time to say anything to her that might have somewhat explained the step I have taken. She particularly rejects conversions. Everyone ought to live and die in the faith in which they were born. She imagined atrocious things about Catholicism and life in a convent. At the moment it is difficult to know what is causing her more pain: whether it is the separation from her youngest child to whom she has ever been

attached with a particular love, or her horror of the completely foreign and inaccessible world into which that child is disappearing, or the qualms of conscience that she herself is at fault because she was not strict enough in raising me as a Jew. The only point at which I believe you might make contact with her is in the very strong and genuine love for God that my mother has, and the love for me that nothing can shake.[68]

Just after Edith's conversion, her sister Rosa also wished to convert. The two sisters and their siblings never told their mother, but two weeks after the mother died in mid-October 1936, Rosa joined Edith in the convent and there received baptism.

When the Nazis intensified their persecution of Jews, the Carmelite superiors rushed Edith and Rosa from Germany to the Netherlands on December 31, 1938. Eight months later, the Gestapo burst into the convent where Edith and Rosa were living. The Nazis were rounding up priests and religious of Jewish origin in reprisal for the Dutch bishops' letter condemning anti-Semitic activity. Edith and Rosa were transported by train to Auschwitz, where they were exterminated within the week.[69] Edith's name in religious life was Sister Teresa Benedicta of the Cross.

PARENTAL OBJECTION TO VOCATION CAUSES FLIGHT FROM HOME

St. Stanislaus Kostka

Stanislaus (1550-1568) ran away from home when he was seventeen. He wanted to become a Jesuit, but his father refused to discuss the topic. The father even pressured the Jesuit provincial at Vienna not to accept Stanislaus. The provincial bowed to the father's power and prestige and complied "for fear of incurring the wrath of the father."[70] The father was an aristocrat whose family had served for centuries in the Senate, which was comprised of bishops and elite lay leaders.[71]

In order to fulfill his vocation, Stanislaus knew that he had to flee from home. Early along his escape route, Stanislaus encountered a Jesuit traveling from Vienna to Dilligen in Upper Germany, a distance of three hundred fifty miles. Stanislaus explained his situation, and the two agreed to travel together. At Dilligen, the local provincial, Peter Canisius, listened carefully as Stanislaus expressed his desire to become a Jesuit. Peter offered the young man hospitality, and after three weeks' observation, Peter recommended that Stanislaus travel to Rome to request formal admission as a novice. Peter had already recommended to the superior general, Francis Borgia, that Stanislaus be accepted.

Stanislaus's father became furious when he learned of his son's flight. The father threatened to "procure the banishment of the Jesuits out of Poland."[72] He ridiculed his son's vocation for its "contemptible dress and following a profession unworthy of his birth."[73] Stanislaus replied kindly but firmly that he would remain where he was. The father then ordered his elder son to travel to Rome "to bring back Stanislaus to Poland at all costs."[74] When the elder son arrived at Rome, he discovered that his younger brother had died one month previously.

In a letter to a friend Stanislaus recounts his narrow escape when he ran away from home. Stanislaus had disguised himself as a peasant. His costume and demeanor were so convincing that even his brother failed to recognize him. Stanislaus writes:

> Close to Vienna two of my servants (*aulici mei*) overtook me. As soon as I recognized them, I hid myself in a wood hard by, and thus escaped their onset. After climbing a number of hills, and passing through many a wood, when I was refreshing my wearied body with some bread by the side of a clear stream, I heard the tramp of a horse. I got up and looked at the rider. It was [his brother] Paul! His steed was covered with foam, and his face was hotter than the sun. You can fancy, Ernest, how frightened I was.
>
> All chance of flight was gone because of the rate at which he was riding. So I stood still. And plucking up courage, I went to the horseman, and just like a pilgrim begged respectfully for an alms. He asked about his brother, described his dress and his height to me, and said he was very like myself in appearance. I replied that in the early morning he had gone along this road. Without waiting a moment he put spurs to his horse, threw me some money, and went off with a gallop. As soon as I had thanked the Holy Virgin, my Mother Mary, I betook myself to a cave nearby to avoid being pursued. After staying there a short time, I resumed my journey.
>
> Let me tell you another misfortune and of what crosses Jesus my Lord made me a present, and learn from this to join me in praising Him. My brother had paid the guards at the gates of the towns and villages to look out for his runaway Stanislaus, to cross-question and examine me, and he had given them a full description of me. This was a great trouble to me, but I chanced to meet one of the Society of Jesus, who was on his way, by order of his superiors, from Vienna to Dilligen. He recognized me, and I told him the reason of my journey,

of my disguise, and of my brother's pursuit, and I explained to him the difficulties I had to encounter at the gates of various towns. Accordingly . . . he took me in a carriage.[75]

Pope John XXIII

Angelo Giuseppe Roncalli (1881-1963) was born and raised poor in the town of Sotto il Monte, located in the foothills of the Apennine Mountains. Most of the twelve hundred inhabitants worked as sharecroppers for a landlord who provided a home and land on which families lived and worked, and in turn shared their produce with the landowner. His parents and their thirteen children shared the home with their paternal cousin and his ten children plus Angelo's great-uncle and other uncles, aunts, and cousins. Altogether thirty-two family members lived in the home, which was a "two-story, log-beamed structure [which] . . . had no running water, no fireplace, and in winter the animals were kept on the lower floor."[76]

> We were poor, but happy with our lot and confident in the help of Providence. There was never any bread on our table, only *polenta*; no wine for the children and young people; only at Christmas and Easter did we have a slice of home-made cake. Clothes, and shoes for going to church, had to last for years and years. . . . And yet when a beggar appeared at the door of our kitchen, when the children — twenty of them — were waiting impatiently for their bowl of *minestra* [vegetable soup], there was always room for him, and my mother would hasten to seat this stranger alongside us.[77]

The main crop consisted of kale to feed the animals. Cows yielded milk and veal. Pigs provided pork and bacon. The vineyards produced a potable although nonexportable wine. The family worked from sunrise to sunset except when winter made farming impossible.

Angelo began his education at age six in a schoolhouse that consisted of three benches: one bench for each class. Promotion at the end of each year meant moving from one bench to another. By law, education was universal, but in reality few students completed all three years. Angelo advanced beyond this village school to a neighboring parish school.

Continuing to progress in the classroom, Angelo received the opportunity to study at the Episcopal College at Celana, where his relatives happily provided him lodging. The experience, however, proved to be unpleasant. Angelo was a country bumpkin compared to the students from the larger town. "They made fun of his clothing and rustic mountain dialect."[78] His peers ridiculed him also for being so short and stocky in build. After a family feud over an inheritance, his mother kept him at home. Now he had to walk to school, five miles each way, morning and night. The mistreatment by his peers continued. His grades fell. After one year at Celana, he stayed home, where the local priest tutored him privately.

At ten, he left home and entered the junior seminary at Bergamo. Although the tuition was paid by the landlord's brother, Angelo's mother knew that her son would need some spending money. She went from door to door, visiting the relatives in the village to take up a collection for her son. The alms amounted to forty cents. The mother wept. The son accepted his poverty. He commented later: "We were very poor, but so was everyone so we didn't realize that we lacked anything."[79]

After some years in the seminary, Angelo wrote to his parents that while he had learned much in the classroom, there was nothing more important than what they had already taught him at home: "Ever since I left home, towards the age of ten, I have read many books and learned many things that you could not have taught me. But what I learned from you remains the most precious and important, and it sustains and gives life to the many other things I learned later in so many years of study and teaching."[80]

RAPE, ATTEMPTED

St. Maria Goretti

"No" means "no." But eighteen-year-old Alessandro was not taking "no" for an answer. He attacked Maria Goretti (1890-1902) when she was sitting at home alone, babysitting an infant while her widowed mother and siblings plus Alessandro's father and his children were working on the farm. At midday Alessandro ran home, retrieved a knife that he had sharpened recently, and called Maria to come inside the house. The documented conversation and events follow:

> "What do you want?" she asked. "I tell you to come inside," he repeated. "No," she responded. "I won't unless you tell me what you

want." Without further words Alessandro ran from the kitchen to the porch, grabbed Maria by the arms, forcibly dragged her inside the house and then locked the doors. He lunged at her dress, ripping it in half. She screamed, "What are you doing?" He continued coming at her. "No! No! Do not touch me. It is a sin! You will go to hell!" Alessandro stopped at nothing. He lunged at her with the knife raised. He stabbed her thirteen times. She lay moaning, saying "My God, my God! I am dying. Mamma! Oh, Mamma!"[81]

The baby in the home cried out in terror. Alessandro fled to his room. Maria's mother heard the cries and raced home. She found her daughter lying in a pool of blood. Maria exhaled whispers, saying that Alessandro had tried to rape her. An ambulance rushed Maria to the hospital.

At the hospital, doctors worked feverishly for two hours. Maria had been stabbed through the lungs, intestines, and heart. Her condition was fatal. Standing at her bedside were her mother and the parish priest, who had administered her First Communion a few months previously. He asked Maria if she was willing to forgive her attacker. She replied, "Yes, I, too, for the love of Jesus, forgive him. Poor Alessandro. And I want him to be with me in paradise. May God forgive him, because I have already forgiven him."[82] Maria died within twenty-four hours of the attack.

In court, when Alessandro was asked if he was guilty, he replied only that he had a headache. Impenitent, he received a sentence of thirty years in jail. Shortly before his release, he received a vision of Maria offering lilies to him as a sign of forgiveness. He lost his remorselessness overnight. He wrote to the bishop: "I am deeply sorry for depriving an innocent person of life, one who, to the very end, was intent on safeguarding her honor, sacrificing her life rather than yielding to my sinful desires. I wish to make public my detestation of my crime and ask pardon of God and the distressed family of my victim."[83]

Three years after his release, Alessandro wrote to Maria's mother to ask for forgiveness. They agreed to meet at the rectory where she worked as a housekeeper. On Christmas Eve, Maria's mother answered the rectory door, and Alessandro fell to his knees. He wept profusely and asked, "Assunta, will you forgive me?"[84] Assunta, with tears streaming down her face, replied, "Maria has forgiven you. Must I not also forgive you?"[85] The parish priest invited Alessandro to stay for dinner and Christmas Eve Mass. Assunta served Alessandro the dinner she had prepared. Assunta and Alessandro attended Mass together, kneeling side by side, conveying a message that no words can describe adequately.

The mother was present at her daughter's beatification in 1947 and canonization in 1950. The crowds of four hundred thousand and five hundred thousand respectively represented the largest gatherings ever held at St. Peter's Basilica. Alessandro attended neither ceremony. He worked as a gardener in a monastery until he died.

Bl. Kateri Tekakwitha

Family, friends, and fellow villagers ridiculed Kateri Tekakwitha (1656-1680) because she stood alone in her desire to pray, do penance, and remain a virgin. People whom she expected to support her ostracized her.

Kateri's village of Ossernenon, forty miles west of Albany, New York, had been visited by Jesuit missionaries ten years before Kateri was born. In 1646, Isaac Jogues, René Goupil, and John Lalande had been brutally martyred there by the Iroquois. By the time of Kateri's birth, eighty of the four hundred villagers were already Christians. Kateri asked to be baptized even though her uncle, the chief of the village, discouraged her from converting to "the Prayer." He and two of Kateri's aunts had adopted her at four years of age after her parents had died in a smallpox epidemic. Kateri possessed a deeply religious spirit even as a child. Daily she knelt before the Blessed Sacrament and performed her ritual of prayers. She practiced austerities that would be discouraged nowadays.[86] While other villagers passed their time at powwows, extra work, or gossip, Kateri passed her time at prayer. For this singular behavior, adults ridiculed her and children spat at her, contemptuously calling her "Christian."[87]

Since all eligible young women were expected to marry,[88] family members encouraged Kateri to marry, but she ignored their requests. As an eight-year-old, she chose not to confirm a "betrothal" customarily made in infancy, and as a teenager she twice ran and hid outside her home when her uncle and aunts arranged visits by potential husbands. One time, her uncle invited a group of drunken men to molest his niece to introduce her to sexual experiences. Another time, her aunt denounced her to the priest, suggesting that Kateri kept running to the woods not to pray but to enjoy sex with a secret lover. Kateri's "firmness of will stood unshakable; but her relatives called it the height of insanity, unbearable stubbornness, a thing unheard of in all Iroquois history. Thenceforth she had to put up with all sorts of inconvenience in the cabin, for she was treated as an enemy and a slave."[89]

At twenty, Kateri fled from the village, risking her life as her uncle chased her with a loaded gun. By prearranged plan, two lay Native American catechists from Quebec led her three hundred miles to safety to the Catholic village of Sault St. Louis, located four miles from Montreal. A Jesuit in Ossernenon wrote a letter to his counterpart in Sault St. Louis to introduce Kateri: "You will soon know what a treasure we have sent you."[90] At Montreal, she saw nuns working in the hospital "waiting on the sick with admirable charity and modesty."[91] The example of these nuns confirmed Kateri in her dedication to virginity.

Even in Sault St. Louis, however, Kateri's stepsister and the best friend of Kateri's deceased mother tried to manipulate Kateri into marrying. The stepsister quizzed Kateri:

> Have you thought seriously of what you are doing? Have you ever seen or heard tell of such a thing among the Iroquois girls? Where did you get this strange idea? Can you not see that you expose yourself to the derision of men and the temptations of the devil? Can you expect to accomplish what no girl among us has ever done? Forget these thoughts, my dear sister; do not trust your own strength, but follow the custom of the other girls.[92]

Kateri was upset by people's continuous efforts to have her act contrary to her commitment to God. Exasperated, she sought out the priest to receive his approval for her actions. The priest urged Kateri to ponder her commitment. He advised her to think and pray about this matter for three days. Kateri listened. She left, but returned in ten minutes. She replied: "I have thought it over long enough; I have already decided what I am going to do; I cannot put it off any longer. I have dedicated my whole self to Jesus, Son of Mary; I have him for my spouse and only He shall have me as a spouse."[93]

Kateri was no misfit. She did not seek religion as an escape from reality. Instead, she sought religion to join herself to the divine reality, committing her body, mind, heart, and soul to God.

SEDUCTION, SEXUAL

St. Thomas Aquinas

In 1231, the parents of Thomas Aquinas (1225-1274) brought their ninth and youngest child to the Benedictines at Monte Cassino. The parents hoped that Thomas might one day become abbot of the prestigious monastery. The monks educated him and in 1243 sent him to continue his studies at the University of Naples, where he met the Dominicans for the first time. He was attracted by the Dominicans' dedication to poverty and study, and their avoidance of civil and ecclesiastical privileges. The next year, he sought and received formal admission into the nascent mendicant community. His family was aghast, since their political and financial ambitions were tied to the Benedictines.

In early May 1244, Thomas and other Dominicans were traveling on foot from Naples through Rome on to Bologna, where an annual meeting of the friars was being conducted. Outside of Rome, one of Thomas's brothers kidnapped Thomas and sent him home under military escort. Thomas's mother had devised this abduction.

At home, Thomas was kept for at least fifteen months, and perhaps as long as twenty-four months, in a tower of the castle. He was treated severely but was not tortured. He received food and drink, and wood for the fireplace. But during this confinement, his family tried to persuade him to change his commitment from the Dominicans to the Benedictines. Two of his five sisters, including Marotta, whom he persuaded to become a Benedictine in the process, spent a great deal of time and effort in conversations trying to change his mind.

> They were their mother's representatives. They presented the arguments for the entire family. Why did Thomas insist on keeping the Dominican habit? They were not asking him to give up the religious state, only to remain faithful to the Order of his childhood. This was only a question of color, a black robe in place of an entirely white one. The tradition and prosperity of the family depended on his making this sacrifice.[94]

Two of his three brothers kept harassing him. They tore off his Dominican garb and left him only a Benedictine habit with which to clothe himself. After all else had failed, the determined family sent a woman of loose virtue to seduce Thomas. His confidant and chief biographer reports at the investigation for canonization one year after Thomas's death the following incident:

> While he [Thomas] was alone in the room which he customarily slept in under custody, they sent in a very attractive girl decked out like a prostitute. She tempted him to sin, using all the devices at her disposal, glances, caresses, and gestures. The fighter [Thomas] had taken God's wisdom as his spouse and beloved, and he was not overcome by

her appearance. Yet when he began to feel fleshly desire rise within him, which he always had kept under rational control (this exception was allowed by consent of divine providence, so he might rise to a more glorious triumph from this test), he snatched a burning stick from the fireplace, and indignantly chased the girl out of his room.

Internally raging, he strode to a corner of the room, made the sign of the cross on the wall with the point of the burning stick and, prostrating himself tearfully on the floor, prayerfully begged God for the girdle of perpetual virginity to keep himself immaculate in temptation. While praying and in tears, he suddenly fell asleep. Behold, two angels were sent to him from heaven; they told him that he had been heard by God and that he had gained a triumph in a very difficult struggle.[95]

By the summer of 1245, the mother exhausted her attempts to influence her son's thinking. In the same summer, the Council of Lyons deposed Frederick as the Holy Roman Emperor. Because Thomas's family was suspected of cooperation with the enemy papal forces, the family fled northward. The mother apparently gave permission to let Thomas escape. He descended the wall of the tower by the use of a rope. His sisters aided his escape past his sleeping brothers.

Historians have argued for many centuries about the veracity of the seduction and its details.[96] Some reject the story outright, insisting, "There seems to be no historical truth to the legends of an attempt to seduce Thomas with prostitutes."[97] Others take a middle course and argue about details, suggesting that perhaps the women were not prostitutes but Thomas's sisters trying to dissuade him rationally. Still others accept the story as originally told, strange as it is to twentieth-century readers, but not strange at all to those familiar with the wiles of noble families of medieval Italy.

SELF-INDULGENT HUSBAND

St. Marguerite d'Youville

Marguerite d'Youville (1701-1771), born and raised near Montreal, is Canada's first native-born saint. She married François d'Youville in an arranged marriage in 1722. It was said then of Marguerite that "her inner qualities, as well as her physical appearance, made her truly one of the beautiful persons of her time."[98]

Within days of moving into the home of François and his mother, Marguerite discovered that her mother-in-law was domineering and that her husband tolerated this abuse against his wife. The mother-in-law allowed no guests inside her home and if someone dropped by unexpectedly, no refreshments were served. The d'Youville home had lots of money, but little love. Marguerite's husband was absent most of the time, including for the births of their first three children. He was present for the fourth and fifth deliveries because he had "retired" already from working. When he died in 1730, Marguerite was pregnant with their sixth child. Four of the six children died between two months and one year of age.

François had inherited his father's privileged position as the governor-general's agent in fur trading. François and a small band of soldiers positioned themselves on Tourtes Island on the western outskirts of Montreal, where they intercepted the fur-laden canoes of the American Indians. François prohibited the natives' travel to the marketplace and exchanged liquor for their furs. This action was contrary to Church and civil laws. The governor-general, however, permitted this abuse because he received a commission on furs bought and sold by d'Youville. As early as 1723, the Indians complained formally about d'Youville. The local bishop and pastor, who had married François and Marguerite, added their voices to the natives' plea. The Indians' message to the corrupt governor-general was:

> O Father, we come to tell you that we cannot pray to God because Youville, who has set up trade on the island of Tourtes, gets us drunk every day, and makes us drink up the value of all our furs, so that we are miserable and naked, without even shirts or clothes of any kind to cover us, or firearms to hunt with. Every morning he comes into our cabins with wine and brandy, saying, with reference to the Marquis de Vaudreuil, "You have a good father; he wants you to drink his milk," and he always gets us drunk to the full value of the pelts, so that the good missionary, who makes us pray to God, always finding us then senseless, told us that he would not teach us any more. So we make this strong appeal to you, O Father, to tell you that we want to pray to God, and that if you do not send Youville away from the island of Tourtes, we do not want to go there any more.[99]

When the governor-general died in September 1725, François lost his protector and position at the island of Tourtes.

> Now he entered into a worse phase of his life. Free from the necessity of making money, thoroughly indifferent to his home ex-

cept as a place where his material needs were satisfied, he gave himself up to the excesses of an utterly dissipated life. Using his wealth as an opening wedge, he now entered into gay social circles only too glad to profit by his prodigality. Drinking, gambling, and dancing filled his wretched days while he remained in Montreal. Occasionally he interrupted his revelries to pursue his not entirely abandoned fur-trading interests.

For his wife he now had no concern whatever. He was as indifferent to her sufferings as if she were a person totally unknown to him. If she had hoped that after his mother's death he would take a normal, manly interest in his home and family, she was cruelly mistaken. He did not even provide for them. For his own selfish pleasures he squandered all his inheritance and every cent that he could take from their common fund. The time came when the poor mother had to resort to difficult and constant work in order to provide the necessities for her little ones. This was the very depth of her sorrowful life.

Yet it was not even her husband's utter indifference to the needs of his children that hurt her personally the most. It was the intangible violation of her finest feelings, the careless rejection of those delicate gifts of the heart that can not be described with the frail substance of words. The recognition of a lack of sympathy was hard enough to bear; but almost intolerable was the final realization that in his soul there was nothing akin to hers, that between them there could never be that spiritual union which is the essence of perfect wedlock. Nevertheless, she accepted this painful disillusionment, protecting in faith, hope, and charity the integrity of her own marriage promise.[100]

Marguerite suffered scornful looks and abusive comments in the village of three thousand people. Yet she was as powerless as her neighbors to persuade her incorrigible husband. Despite the indifference with which he treated her and the children, despite the poor living he provided and the massive debts he accumulated, one of her two priest-sons writes, "So great was the goodness of her heart that all her indifference and harshness towards him could not keep her from extreme grief at his death. She mourned him most sincerely, and for a long time she wept for him."[101]

After François died, Marguerite opened a small shop where she sold her handmade crafts. She paid off the enormous debt left by her husband. She always found money and time to take care of the hungry and sick who found their way to her doorstep. Her faith-in-action attracted other women to spend their lives like her. They consecrated themselves to God to serve the poor. This group became known officially as the Sisters of Charity of Montreal, and known popularly as "the Grey Nuns."

St. Elizabeth Ann Seton

Elizabeth Ann Bayley (1774-1821) and her husband, William Seton, came from prominent New York City families. Elizabeth's father taught medicine at the prestigious Kings College, now known as Columbia University.[102] William's family founded the Bank of New York and owned an international shipping company.

Elizabeth and William married in 1794. Nine years later he died, leaving her with five children. Her two sons, second-born William and third-born Richard, caused her much heartache throughout her life. After the family converted, Elizabeth sent the boys to study at Catholic institutions. Her husband's former business associate Antonio Felicchi of Leghorn, Italy, and Archbishop John Carroll of Baltimore arranged and financed the boys' education.

The boys also traveled to Italy to perform an internship with Antonio. Unfortunately, neither boy manifested any extraordinary gifts. Elizabeth writes to Antonio in 1814 about her teenage sons: "They have no striking talents, no remarkable qualifications, nor are their dispositions even unfolded, in many points they can never be brought to express any decided wish, but they only desire to please Mother and do what she thinks best."[103]

William was committed to the open sea. He rarely communicated with his family. He showed no interest in starting his own family. His mother worried about his physical and spiritual safety. She writes to William in 1818:

> I miss you to such a degree that it seems my own self is gone — greatest comfort I can find is to be begging our God with every affection of my soul to bless you continually, and calculate every night laying down where you may possibly be — your first letter is so longed for — Just now I have one from sweet Kit mentioning your safe arrival in Philadelphia and kind reception — but that you were to go on next day, and then I suppose but half a day in New York. Of course, what fatigue — mind you, tell me every thing about it, and who you saw, and how it has all passed from the time you left Philadelphia — last

night I had you ever so long drawing the life nourishment where you fed so long, where lies the heart that loves you so dearly.[104]

Two years later, she writes again:

> William, William, William, is it possible the cry of my heart don't (sic) reach yours? I carry your beloved name before the tabernacle and repeat it there as my prayers, in torrents of tears which Our God alone understands.
>
> Childish weakness, fond partiality, you would say half-pained, if you could see from your present scene the agonized heart of your mother. But its agony is not for our present separation, my beloved one; it is our long, eternal years which press on it beyond all expression. To lose you here a few years of so embittered a life is but the common lot; but to love as I love you and lose you forever — oh, unutterable anguish! A whole eternity miserable, a whole eternity the enemy of God, and such a God as he is to us! Dreading so much your faith is quite lost, having every thing to extinguish and nothing to nourish it. My William, William, William, if I did not see your doting Bec and Nina above, what would save my heart from breaking?[105]

These two sons never achieved much. William was described as a restless, "hollow self-centered seeker after his own."[106] In midlife he eventually became a Navy captain. Richard was described as thoughtless, irresponsible, and profligate. He attended but never completed Georgetown College in Washington, D.C., and Mount St. Mary's College in Emmitsburg, Maryland.

ILLEGITIMATE CHILD

St. Louise de Marillac

Louise de Marillac (1591-1660) was born out of wedlock. Her father recognized her as his child, but she never knew her birth mother. No historian questions her status. "Louise's illegitimacy is evident from a number of incontrovertible facts."[107]

> Absolutely nothing, therefore, is known of Louise's mother. This fact alone makes it probable that the mother was low-born, perhaps a servant. Had she been more gently born, it would have been hard to con-

ceal her identity and, of more significance, Marillac could have married her. As it was, society decreed rigidly whom a nobleman might and might not marry. It was an age when family honor had to be jealously guarded, whatever the cost. Louise was to be a victim of this hypocritical code, caught between a grudging acceptance by the proud Marillacs and their resultant disapproval and coldness. Is it any wonder that she was nervous, withdrawn, and timid throughout the first half of her life?

Her father, then, is responsible for placing her in this half-world between honor and shame, for despite her origin, he chose to recognize her as his daughter. This was, indeed, to his credit and to our gain. Had he not acknowledged her, she would have been a foundling, outside the orbit of respectable society, or perhaps a serving maid in some Marillac household: in either circumstance, her life's work would have been virtually impossible. But her father did acknowledge her and, illegitimate or not, she was a Marillac before the world; the only legal penalty attached to her birth was that she had no title of inheritance to her father's lands and moneys.[108]

Louise suffered mistreatment and emotional scars on account of her inferior social status. Except for the love she received from her father, who died when she was thirteen, she felt generally unwanted, unaccepted, and unloved. She perceived herself as an accident born of a moment's passion. One biographer imagines how Louise might describe her feelings:

> These are the years I'd like to skip over because they are so painful for me. You know I have no idea who my mother was. Some say that she might have been a maid in my father's house. His first wife died [in 1588], and I was born in 1591 before his second marriage in 1595. The Marillacs were a well-known family in France; my uncles held important positions in the court of the king. There was no way they could hide my birth, and I always got the feeling that they were ashamed of me. I think my father was too, because when I was three he remarried and sent me away to a convent school at Poissy. I never went home again. Although I did see my father now and then, I missed growing up with a mother.[109]

At thirteen, she was transferred to the Dominican sisters' boarding school, where "Louise received a solid education in philosophy, theology, Latin, Greek, and literature" and a practical education that included cooking, housekeeping, and sewing.[110]

Louise was treated as a second-class citizen by her family. Her stepmother kept her four children from her first marriage physically distant from her husband's illegitimate child. At meals, Louise was served only after all the others had eaten. On her wedding day, the Marillac family attended, but "denied their kinship by signing the marriage register as 'friends' rather than family."[111]

St. Catherine of Genoa

At age sixteen, Catherine of Genoa (1447-1510) married Giuliano Adorno in a wedding arranged for financial and political reasons. She was refined and sensitive. He was coarse and self-indulgent. During Catherine's first five years of married life, her husband philandered regularly. One of his numerous affairs begot him an illegitimate daughter for whom he, and Catherine after her husband's death, accepted financial responsibility. Lonely and depressed, "she withdrew from the social life of her class for the first five years of her marriage."[112]

During the second five years, Catherine tried to compensate for the first five years. She distracted herself day and night with mundane parties and idle conversation. After ten years of married life, "her inner depression deepened to desperation."[113]

> Having gone into the church of that saint [St. Benedict], in her grief she exclaimed: "Pray to God for me, Oh, St. Benedict, that for three months he may keep me sick in bed." This she said almost in desperation, not knowing what to do, so great was her distress of mind; for during the three months before her conversion she was overwhelmed with mental suffering, and filled with deep disgust for all things belonging to the world; wherefore, she shunned the society of every one. She was oppressed with a melancholy quite insupportable to herself, and took no interest in anything.[114]

Three months later, while going to confession, "she felt herself suddenly overwhelmed by the immense love of God, lifted above her miseries, enlightened by grace, and radically changed."[115] "In her heart she said, 'No more world for me! No more sin.' "[116]

Meanwhile, her husband's dissolute living had affected adversely not only his marital relationship but also his business endeavors. He lost so much money that the couple had to move to a poorer section of the city.

These developments culminated in a conversion for both husband and wife. They agreed to live a continent and frugal life, dedicated to the service of God and God's sick and poor people. He became a Franciscan tertiary. She volunteered in a local hospital, at first as a nurse and eventually as an administrator. She possessed the unusual ability to be both a mystic and administrator, a spiritual leader and business person.

Bl. Seraphina Sforza

Seraphina (c. 1432-1478), whose baptismal name is Sueva, married Alexander Sforza, a widow with two children, when she was sixteen. Everyone appeared happy in this young family for the first few years of marriage. Then her husband was called away to fight for and alongside his brother, the duke of Milan.

As soon as Alexander returned from his prolonged absence, he began a public affair with the wife of a local physician. "Sueva used all the means at her disposal to win her husband back, but with so little success that he added physical cruelty and insult to unfaithfulness."[117] Finally, he tried to poison her. From then on, Sueva stopped trying to hold on to him. She turned to prayer to sustain herself. "This served only to irritate Alexander and he at last drove her from the house with violence, telling her to take herself off to some convent."[118] She was twenty-three.

Sueva found refuge with the Poor Clares, the community she later joined and there took as her religious name, Seraphina. Meanwhile her former husband and his mistress paraded around town shamelessly. The mistress even visited the convent from time to time, wearing what had been Seraphina's jewelry. Seraphina continued to pray for her husband's conversion, which took place just before he died in 1473.

The story does not end there. "Unfortunately, further research in contemporary evidence suggests that at the time of her leaving the world she was not so entirely an innocent victim as has been assumed."[119] While no evidence has been discovered to support her husband's charge of Seraphina's infidelity, evidence exists that she was plotting to have him killed. Such were the machinations practiced in Renaissance Italy. For the last twenty years of her life, Seraphina lived in exemplary fashion. She gave herself faithfully to the rigors of the convent. She put behind herself the attitudes and actions of her previous situation. She forsook worldly ways and dedicated herself completely to religious life.

St. Monica

Monica (c. 331-387) married Patricius, who had a reputation for "disso-lute habits and ill temper."[120] Whereas she had been raised by Christian parents, he had been raised in a pagan home. She prayed continuously for his conversion, which was achieved one year before he died. Monica and Patricius raised three children, the firstborn among whom became known as St. Augustine of Hippo, whose story is told in more detail else-where in this book. In his autobiography, Augustine describes his father's verbal abusiveness and his mother's response. Augustine addresses his confession to God.

Brought up modestly and soberly in this manner, and made subject by you to her parents rather than by her parents to you, when she arrived at a marriageable age, she was given to a husband and served "him as her lord." She strove to win him to you, speaking to him about you through her conduct, by which you made her beauti-ful, an object of reverent love, and a source of admiration to her hus-band. She endured offenses against her marriage bed in such wise that she never had a quarrel with her husband over this matter. She looked forward to seeing your mercy upon him, so that he would be-lieve in you and be made chaste. But in addition to this, just as he was remarkable for kindness, so also was he given to violent anger. How-ever, she had learned to avoid resisting her husband when he was angry, not only by deeds but even by words. When she saw that he had curbed his anger and become calm and that the time was oppor-tune, then she explained what she had done, if he happened to have been inadvertently disturbed.

In the end, when many wives, who had better-tempered hus-bands but yet bore upon their faces signs of disgraceful beatings, in the course of friendly conversation criticized their husbands' con-duct she would blame it all on their tongues. Thus she would give them serious advice in the guise of a joke. From the time, she said, they heard what are termed marriage contracts read to them, they should regard those documents as legal instruments making them slaves. Hence, being mindful of their condition, they should not rise up in pride against their lords. Women who knew what a sharp-tem-pered husband she had to put up with marveled that it was never reported or revealed by any sign that Patricius had beaten his wife or that they had differed with one another in a family quarrel, even for a single day. When they asked her confidentially why this was so, she told them of her policy, which I have described above. Those who acted upon it, found it to be good advice and were thankful for it; those who did not act upon it, were kept down and abused.[121]

Augustine writes movingly about his mother, Monica. He expresses gratitude that, after Patricius' death, Monica pursued her son from their native Tagaste in North Africa to Rome, where he ended, at his mother's suggestion, the twelve-year affair with his mistress. Then Augustine and Monica moved to Milan, where Augustine, having regularly listened to the sermons of St. Ambrose, converted to the Christian faith on Easter Sunday, 387. Less than one year later, Monica died. Augustine reveals in his *Confessions* that he wept profusely at his mother's death. He loved her deeply.

St. Francis Borgia

Francis (1510-1572) was the great-grandson of a pope and a king, and cousin to the reigning emperor. While still a young man, he was promoted in quick succession to employment as the marquis of Lombay, adviser to the emperor, viceroy of Catalonia, and duke of Gandía.

In spring 1543, Francis and his wife, Eleanor, were promised employment as master and mistress of the household of the Spanish prince and his fiancée. This job seemed like the perfect situation: not only was Francis a cousin to the prince and Eleanor was Portuguese like the princess, but also the engaged couple stood next in line to become king and queen of Spain. Expectations and excitement rose for Francis and his wife.

Confirmation of the appointment, however, was delayed. The spring ended and summer arrived. Autumn came and so did winter. Almost a year went by before the prince informed Francis that he would not be hired. The reason given was that protocol had not been followed: the emperor had spoken with Francis before speaking with the prince.[122] Shortly thereafter, the prince and princess married, but within the year, she died in childbirth. The prince arranged to marry another princess, but she died just before the wedding. Francis and Eleanor kept waiting for another royal appointment, but none came.

Eleanor's health, which had never been strong after a miscarriage in

1540, deteriorated rapidly under the stress of no employment. Her health periodically recovered and relapsed until she died in April 1546.

Endnotes

1. *Liturgy of the Hours*, vol. 1 (New York: Catholic Book Publishing Co., 1975), p. 1286.
2. Gregory Nazianzen, *Four Funeral Orations*, tr. by Leo P. McCauley. In *Funeral Orations by Saint Gregory Nazianzen and Saint Ambrose*, tr. by Leo P. McCauley and others. Vol. 22, pp. 88-89. *The Fathers of the Church* (New York: Fathers of the Church, Inc., 1953).
3. J. C. Kearns, *The Life of Martin de Porres: Saintly American Negro and Patron of Social Justice* (New York: P. J. Kenedy and Sons, 1937), p. 13.
4. Ibid., p. 13.
5. Ibid., pp. 14-15.
6. Joseph Bernard Code, "Seton, Elizabeth Ann, St.," in *New Catholic Encyclopedia*, vol. 13, p. 136.
7. Ibid.
8. Ibid.
9. Ellin Kelly and Annabelle Melville, eds., *Elizabeth Seton: Selected Writings* (New York: Paulist Press, 1987), p. 174.
10. Ibid., p. 180.
11. Ibid., p. 186.
12. Ibid., pp. 192-193.
13. *Butler's Lives of the Saints,* ed. by Herbert Thurston and Donald Attwater, four volumes (Westminster, Md.: Christian Classics, 1990), vol. II, p. 310.
14. Patrick of Ireland, *The Works of St. Patrick: St. Secundinus Hymn on St. Patrick*, tr. by Ludwig Bieler, no. 17 of *Ancient Christian Writers* series (Westminster, Md.: The Newman Press, 1953), pp. 29-30.
15. Mary Pauline Fitts, *Hands to the Needy. Blessed Marguerite d'Youville: Apostle to the Poor* (Garden City, N.Y.: Doubleday and Co., Inc., 1971), pp. 37-38.
16. Ibid., p. 37.
17. Ibid.
18. Marie Cecilia Lefevre and Rose Alma Lemire, *A Journey of Love: The Life Story of Marguerite d'Youville* (Buffalo: D'Youville College, 1990), p. 8.
19. Fitts, p. 38.
20. Ibid.
21. Butler, vol. I, p. 396.

22. Ibid., p. 397.

23. Augustine of Hippo, *The Confessions of St. Augustine*, tr. by John K. Ryan. Book 2, chapters 1 and 2 (New York: Doubleday and Co., Inc., 1960), pp. 65-67.

24. Ibid., Book 6, chapter 15, pp. 153-154.

25. Beginning at six years of age, she experienced throughout her life visions of Jesus, Mary, and the saints. Most people thought she was a fraud. After her vindication at a general chapter of the Dominicans, Raymond of Capua was appointed her confessor. Two successive popes then involved her in the major politico-ecclesiastical struggles of the day: reconciling Florence and Rome, ending the seventy-year long Avignon Papacy, and trying to avert the Great Western Schism. At her death it was discovered that she had been a stigmatist, unbeknown to everyone including Raymond.

26. Catherine of Siena, *Saint Catherine of Siena, As Seen in Her Letters*, tr. by Vida D. Scudder (New York: E. P. Dutton and Co., 1911), p. 324.

27. Ibid.

28. Ibid., pp. 327-328.

29. Romans 8:28.

30. Catherine of Siena, p. 332.

31. Definition of "morganatic," as found in *Webster's New World Dictionary of the American Language* (Cleveland: The World Publishing Co., 1960), p. 957.

32. John Holland Smith, *Constantine the Great* (New York: Charles Scribner's Sons, 1971), p. 22.

33. Ibid., pp. 16-17.

34. Butler, vol. IV, p. 623.

35. Ibid., p. 624.

36. Jerome, *The Principal Works of St. Jerome*, tr. by W. H. Fremantle, G. Lewis, and W. G. Martley. Letter LV in vol. VI in the series of *Nicene and Post-Nicene Fathers of the Christian Church* (Grand Rapids, Mich.: Wm. B. Eerdmans Publishing Co., 1961), p. 109.

37. Ibid.

38. Ibid., p. 110.

39. Jerome, Letter LXXVII, pp. 158-159.

40. Butler, vol. II, p. 321.

41. Ibid.

42. Ibid., vol. IV, p. 135.

43. Margaret Mary Alacoque, *The Autobiography of Saint Margaret Mary*, tr. by Vincent Kerns (Westminster, Md.: The Newman Press, 1961), pp. 5-6.

44. Ibid., p. 48.

45. Ibid., pp. 48-49.

46. Ibid., p. 49.

47. Ibid.

48. Louise Callan, "Duchesne, Rose Philippine, Bl.," in *New Catholic Encyclopedia*, vol. 4, p. 1089.

49. Louise Callan, *Philippine Duchesne: Frontier Missionary of the Sacred Heart* (Westminster, Md.: The Newman Press, 1965), p. 361.

50. Butler, vol. IV, p. 380.

51. Shaun McCarty, "Frederic Ozanam: Lay Evangelizer," *Vincentian Heritage*, vol. 17, no. 1, p. 6.

52. Ibid.

53. Ibid., p. 7.

54. Msgr. Baunard, *Ozanam in His Correspondence*, tr. by a member of the council of Ireland of the Society of St. Vincent de Paul (Dublin: Catholic Truth Society of Ireland, 1925), p. 27.

55. Ibid., p. 28.

56. Ibid., pp. 28-29.

57. McCarty, pp. 7-8.

58. Ibid., p. 8.

59. Joseph Dirvin, *Louise de Marillac: Of the Ladies and Daughters of Charity* (New York: Farrar, Straus and Giroux, 1970), p. 6.

60. Audrey Gibson and Kieran Kneaves, *Praying with Louise de Marillac*, in *Companions for the Journey* series (Winona, Minn.: St. Mary's Press, 1995), p. 15.

61. Ibid., p. 16.

62. Louise de Marillac, *Spiritual Writings of Saint Louise de Marillac*, tr. by Louise Sullivan (Albany, N.Y.: De Paul Provincial House, 1984), pp. 3-4.

63. A Benedictine monk of Stanbrook Abbey, ed., *Letters from the Saints* (New York: Hawthorne Books, Inc., 1964), pp. 143-144.

64. Dirvin, *Louise de Marillac*, pp. 234-235.

65. Ibid., p. 386.

66. Edith Stein, *Self-Portrait in Letters: 1916-1942*, vol. V, letter no. 146a, in *The Collected Works of Edith Stein*, ed. by L. Gelber and Romaeus Leuven, and tr. by Josephine Koeppel (Washington, D.C.: ICS Publications, 1993), p. 147.

67. Ibid., letter no. 156, p. 158.

68. Ibid., letter no. 158, p. 160.

69. Ibid., p. 352.

70. Butler, vol. IV, p. 335.

71. Edward Healey Thompson, *The Life of St. Stanislaus Kostka, Of the Society of Jesus* (New York: P. J. Kenedy and Sons, n.d.), p. 21.

72. Ibid., p. 336.

73. Ibid.

74. Ibid.

75. A Benedictine monk, pp. 137-138.

76. Lawrence Elliott, *I Will Be Called John: A Biography of Pope John XXIII* (New York: E. P. Dutton and Co., Inc., 1973), p. 14.

77. Peter Hebblethwaite, *Pope John XXIII: Shepherd of the Modern World* (Garden City, N.Y.: Doubleday and Co., Inc., 1985), p. 8.

78. Elliott, p. 16.

79. Ibid., p. 14.

80. Hebbletwaithe, p. 15.

81. Alicia Von Stamwitz, *Women of Valor: The Trials and Triumphs of Seven Saints* (Liguori, Mo.: Liguori Publications, 1986), pp. 33-34.

82. Ibid., p. 35.

83. Ibid., p. 37.

84. Ibid., p. 38.

85. Ibid.

86. She fasted until she fainted; she slept on thorns four consecutive nights in imitation of young St. Alphonsus Liguori who had just been canonized and who had thrown himself naked into a brier patch to punish his flesh.

87. *The Positio of the Historical Section of the Sacred Congregation of Rites on the Introduction of the Cause for Beatification and Canonization and on the Virtues of the Servant of God: Katharine Tekakwitha, The Lily of the Mohawks* (New York: Fordham University Press, 1940), p. 139.

88. Lifelong chastity was unheard of among Kateri's tribal members. Neither her mother's Algonquin tribe nor her father's Mohawk tribe, in which she was raised, practiced lifelong chastity. On the contrary, young people were expected to satisfy sexual curiosities and desires. Not much was hidden from the eyes and ears of young people, since entire families slept together in separate sections of the longhouses; these rectangular longhouses measured twenty feet by one hundred twenty-five feet and were usually occupied by twenty families. Children discovered early where children came from! Marriage was normative for anyone capable of marriage; not to marry was abnormal. Kateri chose not to marry. She steadfastly held to her conviction.

89. *Positio*, p. 386.

90. Ibid., p. 69.

91. Ibid., p. 394.

92. Ibid., p. 277.

93. Ibid.

94. L. H. Petitot, *The Life and Spirit of Thomas Aquinas* (Chicago: The Priory Press, 1966), p. 39.

95. Vernon J. Bourke, *Aquinas' Search for Wisdom* (Milwaukee: The Bruce Publishing Co., 1965), p. 37.

96. All the witnesses agree that Thomas's entry into the Dominican order was a stormy one, marked by his family's abduction of him and their attempts to lure him into unchastity. It is stated that Catherine, his niece, was the prime source here; and there seem to be no grounds for doubting her. Though such events are still a part of the Southern Italian way of life, the story reflects no credit upon his family (even his mother, however reluctantly, had consented to the abduction), and William would hardly have risked offending them at a time when their good will was so much needed, had he not been satisfied that they knew the story to be true.

   The account of his temptation by the harlot, whom he drove out with a burning brand, was given appendix, which then became inalienable from it. William of Tocco said at the process that the previous year at Anagni he had been told by Robert of Sezze, O.P., who had been told by his uncle Stephen that after Thomas had thrown the woman out, Thomas prayed that he might never again be assailed by such a temptation, and so fell asleep. In a vision two angels appeared to tell him that God had heard his prayer. They pressed upon his loins and said: "Ecce ex parte dei cingimus te cingulo castitatis quod nulla possit temptatione dissolvi." He cried aloud with the pain and awoke, but refused to say what had made him shout. Edmund Colledge, *Saint Thomas Aquinas, Commemorative Studies: The Legend of Saint Thomas Aquinas* (Toronto: Pontifical Institute of Mediaeval Studies, 1974), p. 21.

97. William A. Wallace and James A. Weisheipl, "Thomas Aquinas, St.," in *New Catholic Encyclopedia*, vol. 14, p. 103.

98. Marie Cecilia Lefevre and Rose Alma Lemire, *A Journey of Love: The Life Story of Marguerite d'Youville* (Buffalo: D'Youville College, 1990), p. 8.

99. Ibid., pp. 57-58.

100. Ibid., pp. 62-63.

101. Ibid., p. 64.

102. Kings College was founded in 1754, became known as Columbia College in 1784, and Columbia University in 1912.

103. Fay Trombley, "Toward Eternity: Elizabeth's Experience of Suffering and Hope," *Vincentian Heritage*, vol. 14, no. 2, p. 349.

104. Kelly and Melville, p. 293.

105. Ibid., p. 294.

106. Joseph Dirvin, *Mrs. Seton, Foundress of the American Sisters of Charity* (New York: Farrar, Straus and Cudahy, 1962), p. 413.

107. Dirvin, *Louise de Marillac*, p. 4.

108. Ibid., p. 6.

109. Loretto Gettemeier, "Louise: A Life in Her Own Words," *Vincentian Heritage*, vol. 12, no. 2, p. 106.

110. Ibid.

111. Betty Anne McNeill, "Last Will and Testament of St. Louise de Marillac," *Vincentian Heritage*, vol. 15, no. 2, p. 97.

112. Ibid.

113. Pacific Lawrence Hug, "Catherine of Genoa, St.," in *New Catholic Encyclopedia*, vol. 3, p. 255.

114. Catherine of Genoa, *Life and Doctrine of Saint Catherine of Genoa*, ed. and tr. by Isaac Thomas Hecker (New York: Catholic Publication Society, 1874), pp. 22-23.

115. Hug, p. 255.

116. Catherine of Genoa, *The Spiritual Dialogue*, tr. by Serge Hughes, *Classics of Western Spirituality* (New York: Paulist Press, 1979), p. 3.

117. Butler, vol. III, p. 518.

118. Ibid.

119. Ibid.

120. John J. Delaney, *Dictionary of Saints* (New York: Doubleday and Co., Inc., 1980), p. 413.

121. Augustine of Hippo, *The Confessions of St. Augustine*, tr. by John K. Ryan (New York: Image Books, 1960), pp. 218-219.

122. Margaret Yeo, *The Greatest of the Borgias* (London: Sheed and Ward, 1936), p. 114.

PART 3

*Life
in the
Church*

St. Cyprian of Carthage

Cyprian (c. 200-258), the archbishop of Carthage, opposed Pope Stephen's position that baptism administered by heretics was valid. Cyprian argued for a more rational approach: "Nor must we prescribe this on the basis of custom alone, but prevail by reason. For Peter, whom the Lord chose first and on whom he built his Church, did not claim or usurp anything for himself insolently and arrogantly when Paul later argued with him about circumcision."[1]

In spring of 256, Cyprian convened at Carthage a council attended by seventy-one North African bishops. They resolved that "there is only one baptism, that of the catholic [i.e., universal] church. Those who come from other bodies are not, indeed, rebaptized, for what they have had is not baptism."[2] The council sent Stephen a letter that opened with the usual courtesies and expressions of affection for the pope but which concluded with the following confrontation:

> But we know that there are some who will not lightly drop what they have once accepted and who do not easily change their minds but retain certain peculiarities which they have adopted, while keeping the bond of peace and concord with their colleagues. Concerning this we neither use force nor impose a law on anyone, since each bishop has freedom to make up his own mind in the administration of the Church, remembering that he will have to give an account of his conduct to the Lord.[3]

Stephen responded, however, by threatening to excommunicate Cyprian and all those who rebaptized heretics. This threat sent shock waves through the Christian world. Firmilian, the bishop of Caesarea in Cappodocia, supported Cyprian and noted in a letter the irony that if Stephen excommunicated others, "that one bishop who excommunicates everyone else, would find that it was really himself who was excommunicated."[4]

In autumn of 256, Cyprian convened another council at which eighty-seven North African bishops were in attendance. Cyprian explained the council's purpose: "Our present business is to state individually our views on the particular subject before us, judging no one, and not excommunicating anyone who may hold different views from ourselves.

For no one of us sets himself up as a bishop of bishops, nor by autocratic intimidation compels his colleagues to a forced obedience."[5]

Although Cyprian had the deepest respect for Rome and the unity of the universal church, he did not perceive the primacy of Rome in doctrinal matters. A twentieth-century theologian comments:

> Actually, Cyprian recognized the Bishop of Rome's special position in the Church in many practical ways. But he never formulated this to himself as implying a real authority over the whole Church. Hence, though his practice repeatedly went further than his theory, it is not surprising that, at a moment of crisis, he should have refused to accept the ruling on heretical baptism notified to him by Stephen of Rome. His unwonted vehemence on receiving it shows that he was nonplussed. He had always taken for granted that Carthage and Rome would see eye to eye on any matter of importance: he now found himself in disagreement with Rome on a matter which involved the unity of the Church itself. His theory had, in fact, broken down, but he saw no way out of the impasse. For his instinctive regard for Rome prevented his even considering the only logical course open to him: to break off relations with Rome by excommunicating Stephen.[6]

In August 257, three significant events occurred: first, Emperor Valerian's anti-Christian persecution was enforced in North Africa, and Cyprian was captured; second, Stephen died of natural causes in Rome; and third, the new pope, Sixtus II, "upheld as firmly as Stephen the Roman view . . . but restored friendly relations with Cyprian . . . and quietly accepted the coexistence of divergent practices."[7] In August 258, another imperial edict decreed that all bishops, priests, and deacons were now to be killed. Cyprian in Carthage and Sixtus II in Rome were both beheaded. The threat of excommunication was never enacted. All three protagonists died.

BISHOPS' BURDENS — PASTORAL DILEMMA

St. Boniface of Canterbury

A famous historian judges that Boniface (c. 680-754) "had a deeper influence on the history of Europe than any Englishman who has ever lived."[8] Boniface earned this encomium by assisting in the integration of the Germanic tribes into the Roman system of civilization.

Boniface's efforts at evangelization won immediate success by his cutting down the ancient Oak Tree, in which the local god Thor was supposed to be living, but without Boniface's incurring any evil consequences. Onlookers waited aghast for Thor to strike Boniface dead. But when Boniface survived, Christianity thrived.

As metropolitan archbishop of Germany, Boniface discovered that one of his priests, although an effective pastor, was an adulterer. How ought he to deal with this complex situation? He wrote to a friend about this conundrum involving clerical celibacy.[9]

> Meanwhile, the greatest necessity forces us to seek your advice and judgment. For I have found a priest who long ago fell into adultery, and after repentance was restored again to his place by the Franks; now, dwelling in a vast district occupied by faithful but erring people, alone without other priests he administers baptism, and celebrates mass. If in accordance with the most binding canons I remove this man, infants will die without the sacred waters of regeneration, owing to the scarcity of priests — provided that I have none better to take the place of the fallen one. Judge therefore between me and an erring people, whether it is better, or, at least a smaller evil that such a man should discharge the ministry of the holy altar, or that a multitude should die in unbelief, because they could not obtain a minister of purer life. But if amidst all our priests I find one who has fallen into the same sin and through repentance has been restored to his former rank — in whom all the priests and people have had confidence begotten of favorable opinion — if he is degraded in this manner, his secret sin will be revealed, a multitude will be scandalized, through the scandal many souls will be lost and there will result a great hatred of the priests and a distrust of the ministers of the church, so that believing in none they will look down upon all as false. Wherefore, we boldly ventured to suffer him to remain in the holy ministry, thinking the danger to one man a lighter thing than the ruin and damnation of the souls of almost all the people. But in all these matters, I desire above all else to see in writing and to hear your holy counsels, as to what I must tolerate, forced by the necessity of avoiding scandal, or what I must reject.[10]

St. John Chrysostom

After John (c. 347-407) earned a reputation as a caring pastor and passionate preacher of practical Christianity, he was named the archbishop of Constantinople.

> Immediately he was plunged into a morass of ecclesiastical and political intrigue. [His predecessor] Nectarius had wasted church revenues; John curbed expenses, opened hospitals, and alleviated the misery of the poor. Since Nectarius had likewise permitted clerical laxity, John had to institute reforms. He ousted one deacon for murder, another for adultery. His clergy were forbidden to keep virgins and deaconesses in their houses, a practice which had occasioned much scandal. Monks who preferred aimless wandering to cenobitic discipline were confined to their monasteries. Worldly widows were ordered to remarry or show the decorum proper to their state.[11]

John was embraced by ordinary people, but was detested by recalcitrant clergy and some wealthy laity. He offended repeatedly the Empress Eudoxia, whom he criticized for her vanity in makeup and dresses and her entertainments at court. He alluded to her as an Old Testament Jezebel and New Testament Herodias. People who were stung by him wanted him either out of office, or better, out of Constantinople. Two assassination attempts were made.

Theophilus, the archbishop of Alexandria, had resented that John and not he had been appointed archbishop of the capital city of the world. In order to depose John, Theophilus convened at Constantinople the uncanonical Synod of the Oak. All thirty-six bishops in attendance were sworn enemies of John. In John's absence, the assembly found him guilty of forty-six charges, including "misuse of church funds, tyrannical treatment of his clergy, irregularities in ritual, invasion of jurisdiction, and even high treason."[12] The synod condemned and deposed John as patriarch. The civil authorities were responsible, because of the charge of treason, to enforce his exile. John describes for Pope Innocent the military action that followed the synod's illicit decision.

> How am I to relate the events which followed, transcending as they do every kind of tragedy? What language will set forth these

events? What kind of ear will receive them without shuddering? For when we were urging these things, as I said before, a dense troop of soldiers, on the great Sabbath itself, as the day was hastening towards eventide, having broken into the churches, violently drove out all the clergy who were with us, and surrounded the sanctuary with arms. And women from the oratories who had stripped themselves for baptism just at that time, fled unclothed, from terror at this grievous assault, not being permitted to put on the modest apparel which benefits women; indeed many received wounds before they were expelled, and the baptismal pools were filled with blood, and the sacred water reddened by it. Nor did the distress cease even at this point; but the soldiers, some of whom as we understand were unbaptized, having entered the place where the sacred vessels were stored, saw all the things which were inside it, and the most holy blood of Christ, as might happen in the midst of such confusion, was spilt upon the garments of the soldiers aforesaid: and every kind of outrage was committed as in a barbarian siege. And the common people were driven to the wilderness, and all the people tarried outside the city, and the churches became empty in the midst of this great Festival, and more than fifty bishops who associated with us were vainly and causelessly expelled together with the people and clergy.[13]

John was banished to Cucusus, Armenia, despite the pleas of the Christians in Constantinople, the pope in Rome, and bishops throughout the Western Empire. He continued his influence, however, in the city by copious correspondence. The emperor then ordered John's removal to even more remote Pityus, almost a thousand miles from Constantinople, at the eastern edge of the Black Sea. The sixty-year-old exile succumbed to the rigors of the forced march and died en route. He had served as patriarch of Constantinople for fewer than seven years.

FACULTIES SUSPENDED

St. Philip Neri

Almost all of Rome loved Philip Neri (1515-1595). He was welcoming and humorous. He invited conversation by asking passersby, "Well, brothers, when shall we begin to do good?"[14] People responded individually, in pairs, in small groups, and sometimes in large crowds. The masses were spiritually hungry for "soul food" in the malaise of post-Reformation, but not yet Counter-Reformation, Rome. Philip discovered that he possessed a gift for preaching God's word and making converts.

In 1548, he and other lay leaders formed a fraternity to assist pilgrims and to promote religious devotion. Three years later, he was ordained a priest. The primary venue for his ministry became the confessional, to which he attracted thousands of penitents. Numerous priests followed him and this group grew into the Congregation of the Oratory. Philip became known affectionately as "the Second Apostle of Rome," second only to St. Paul of Tarsus.

Rich and poor, powerful and powerless, clergy and laity flocked to see and hear Philip. Numerous popes and Charles Cardinal Borromeo were among his donors and promoters. "The whole College of Cardinals resorted to him for counsel and spiritual refreshment; and so great was his reputation that foreigners coming to Rome were eager to obtain an introduction."[15]

Not everyone, however, was enamored with Philip. The pope's nephew, the cardinal of Spoleto, was suspicious of him. The cardinal observed that Philip created an atmosphere of enthusiasm similar to Philip's fellow-Florentine Savanarola, whom the Inquisition had condemned and civil authorities had hanged and burned at the stake in 1498. After all, Philip was creating new devotions, namely, the visitation of the Seven Churches and the Forty Hours adoration. The cardinal was not a corrupt man. In fact, he "lived a blameless life, but he was a typical bureaucrat: narrow-minded and punctilious in carrying out all decrees."[16]

After months of observation, the cardinal officially charged Philip with starting a new sect. The cardinal forbade Philip to lead pilgrimages to the Seven Churches, to invite people to pray at the Oratory, and to hear confessions for fifteen days. Philip acceded in obedience, but he regarded this attack as a persecution. "He prayed without ceasing, and wept with compassion at the error of those who were persecuting him and at his inability to undeceive them."[17] A summary of the events follows:

> These rumors however increased, and at last came to the ear of the Pope's Vicar, who being misled by ill-natured information, summoned Philip before him, and rebuked him with great severity. "Are you not ashamed," said he, "you who make profession of despising the world, to collect together such a multitude of persons in order to court popular repute, and thus under pretence of sanctity to hunt for preferment?" And after bitterly reproving him with these and similar words, he commanded him to abstain from hearing confessions for a fortnight, not to continue the exercises without fresh leave, and not

to go about with any company of persons, threatening him with imprisonment if he should disobey, and furthermore obliging him to give security for his appearance at the first summons. Philip very modestly replied, that as he had begun these exercises for the glory of God, so for His glory he would leave them off; that he should always prefer the injunctions of his superiors to his own plans; and that his only object in introducing the pilgrimage to the Seven Churches had been to recreate the minds of his penitents, and to keep them out of the way of the sins so commonly committed during Carnival time. The Vicar replied, "You are an ambitious man, and what you do, you do not for the glory of God, but to make yourself head of a party." When Philip heard this, he turned to a crucifix which was there, and said, "Lord, Thou knowest if what I do is to make myself head of a party, or for Thy service"; and then went away.[18]

Shortly after the ban was imposed, the cardinal suffered a stroke and died. "When one of Philip's friends opined that the hand of God was visible in this, Philip put his hand over the man's mouth and said, 'Be still.' "[19] The pope, who was the cardinal's uncle, then lifted the ban. He sent to Philip the message that, while the pope would like to participate in Philip's pilgrimage, he was unable to do so, and would Philip remember to pray for the pope.

FAILURE — IN EVANGELIZATION

St. Francis Xavier

Commissioned as papal nuncio to the Far East, Francis Xavier (1506-1552) left European soil on his thirty-fifth birthday and died eleven years later in the harbor of Canton. Even though this exemplary missionary had converted hundreds of thousands of persons and evangelized the peoples at Mozambique, Goa, India, Ceylon, Malacca, Japan, and the many islands in between, "we are not without proofs, both internal and external, that to many at least of his contemporaries he was thought a failure."[20]

Time and again, Francis appeared to fail. Professionally, he dedicated himself to Ignatius of Loyola's burgeoning community rather than to offers of a prestigious ecclesiastical career or a distinguished professorship. Ministerially, this restless missionary received five different assignments in his first five years of the priesthood, and for years felt estranged from community members who preferred the educational apostolate. In community, he lacked the closeness that many members enjoyed because of his intensity and austerity, and even with Ignatius he shared a mutual respect rather than a heartfelt friendship. Apostolically, in India, his converts suffered persecution; in Japan, virtually all the religious leaders refused conversion, and while approaching China, he died in the harbor, six miles short of his goal of the mainland.

Perhaps his most poignant failure consisted in not establishing a seminary to develop native vocations to the priesthood. Because he knew that the American Indians needed native priests, he began at Goa a college seminary to which only native students were admitted. In response to Francis' request for someone to lead the school, Ignatius sent Antonio Gómez. Unfortunately, while Francis was busy in Malacca, Antonio imposed on this seminary in the East the spirit, structures, and studies found in the West. When Francis returned two years later, he discovered that the native students had left in droves. Francis confronted Antonio and demanded that he promote native vocations. Antonio listened politely, but ignored Francis' instructions. Francis wrote to his provincial in Portugal: "As you know well, the office is dangerous for one who is not perfect. I ask you, therefore, to send as rector and superior of the brethren in India one to whom this office will do no spiritual injury. Antonio Gómez does not possess the necessary qualifications."[21] Francis left two months later.

Antonio continued his policies, which drove away the few remaining native students. European students with no aspirations for the priesthood enrolled. These were the sons of Dutch and Portuguese business, military, and political leaders. They admired Antonio and his European school, transplanted into this colonial outpost.

After another two years' absence, Francis returned. Francis, who was now the provincial of the Indies, determined that "enough was enough." Francis transferred Antonio as far up the coast as possible. Seven months later, in August 1552, Francis departed for China, where he died in December 1552. Today, only the foundation remains of Francis' school.

Ven. Charles de Foucauld

Charles de Foucauld (1858-1916) founded a community called the Little Brothers of Jesus. He authored a book of common rules and built two large houses for confreres. Charles corresponded with numerous inquirers for many years with only one candidate visiting, and he already belonged to a religious community. After three months, however, this inquirer became ill and returned home. No one else came to see. No one joined the community Charles had founded.

Living in the desert on the border between Morocco and Algeria, Charles used the Muslim word *zaouia* to describe his cluster of huts. *Zaouia* means "a place where the members of a religious fraternity meet and live together."[22] After nine months of living alone, Charles changed the misnomer *zaouia* to *khaoua,* which means "house of brotherhood where visitors are welcomed."[23] His dream of a community of permanent members evolved into a desert shelter for passersby. "He never resigned himself to this solitude, but continued to do all he could to call others as co-laborers in what he considered the most barren corner of the Lord's vineyard."[24] He writes to a friend:

> As for companions, I shall, my very dear Father, from the bottom of my heart, be perfectly content with whatever may happen. If one day I have some, I shall be satisfied to see in that the accomplishment of God's will and His name glorified. If I have none . . . I shall say to myself that He is glorified in so many other ways, and that His beatitude so little needs our poor praises and hearts! If I could — but I cannot — do otherwise than lose myself totally in union with His divine will, I should prefer for myself total failure and perpetual solitude and defeats all round: *elegi abjectus esse* [I have chosen to be abject]. There we see the union with the abjection and the Cross of our divine Well-Beloved, which to me has always seemed most desirable of all. I do all I can to have companions; the means of getting them is, in my eyes, to sanctify myself in silence.[25]

Charles had joined the Trappists in 1896, but in search of greater austerity he left the order the next year. He traveled to the Holy Land, where he labored as a gardener for the Poor Clare nuns and studied for the priesthood. Ordained in 1901, he moved to Morocco. "By contemplation and action, he aimed to show himself as a man of God and as 'the universal brother.' "[26] In 1905, he moved deeper into the Sahara to Tamanrasset in the Hoggar (Ahaggar) Mountains, where robbers later killed him. Although Charles's institutional efforts failed, his personal efforts drew much admiration.

"In ten years in the desert, he had not made a single convert. . . . His plans for new orders had not been carried out."[27] Charles was revered, however, by all who met him: Muslims and Christians, soldiers and civilians, rich and poor, educated and illiterate. The Muslims described him by his demeanor and dress: "the *marabout* with the red cross." *Marabout* means "holy man" or "saint."

Ironically, seventeen years after Charles's death, his vision bore life. In 1933, the Little Brothers of Jesus, who regard Charles as their founder and René Voillaume as his successor, received formal approbation from Rome. In 1939, Voillaume helped to found a women's community: the Little Sisters of Jesus. These communities of vowed religious live in secular society, performing practical service. They proclaim "by their life the charity and truth of the Gospel as Father de Foucauld had wished it."[28] In 1933, a predominantly contemplative congregation was founded on the rule of Charles: the Little Sisters of the Sacred Heart. These communities continue, even though no one had chosen to live with the founder.

FAILURE — IN LEADING A RELIGIOUS COMMUNITY

St. Joseph Calasanctius

Joseph Calasanctius (1556-1648) succeeded in all endeavors until he founded a religious community. Having earned a doctoral degree in law, he was serving as vicar-general of his diocese when he experienced an interior call to leave Spain to minister at Rome. In the Eternal City, he became an adviser to a cardinal, which allowed Joseph time to pursue ad hoc ministries, namely, serving plague victims and teaching children through the newly founded Confraternity of Christian Doctrine. But Joseph discovered that "periodical instruction was utterly inadequate to cope with the situation."[29] In 1597, Joseph founded a community of teachers and "opened the first free public school in Europe."[30]

In 1621, Rome approved Joseph's new community of the Clerks Regular of Religious Schools, popularly called the Piarists. By the time he died, the community had expanded from three men to five hundred and from one school in Rome to thirty-seven houses in six countries. Expansion, however, lessened Joseph's personal impact on his community. Some Piarists questioned the ability and authority of the aging founder, and others complained that his vision of poverty was too strict. Dissension spread like a cancer. One nefarious protagonist named Mario Sozzi transferred into the nascent community.

Mario exposed, in 1639, a boarding house that had doubled as a brothel operated jointly by its madam and the cathedral chaplain. Mario became a self-proclaimed "defender of public morality and orthodoxy before the Holy Office in Florence and Rome."[31] Ingratiating himself to the Inquisitors, he looked everywhere for suspicious incidents to report, even among his own community members.

In August 1642, Mario informed the Inquisitors that Joseph had broken into Mario's room and had stolen certain documents. The chief assessor rushed to Joseph's residence, barged in, and barked to Joseph, "You are a prisoner of the Holy Office."[32] Joseph, despite being eighty-six years old, was force-marched by the police in the midday heat through the crowded streets of Rome, while the Inquisitors rode triumphantly in a carriage behind their captive. Joseph later referred to this humiliating event as his *via dolorosa*. A four-hour trial resulted in acquittal, thanks to the intervention of a cardinal, who admitted weeks later that he himself had stolen the documents in question.

In December 1642, officials of the Inquisition appointed Mario vicar-general of the Piarist community, and in January 1643, removed Joseph as superior general. Mario ruled well for the first few months, but then his manner changed. "Fr. Mario began to act like a dictator. His three assistants protested and tried to resign."[33] Joseph repeatedly urged the community members to obey Mario. An eyewitness reports a confrontation between Mario and Joseph, after Mario had intercepted Joseph's mail and discovered complaints from two local superiors against Mario.

> Fr. Mario went after the Superior General and began to shout at him: "Hi, you doddering old fool! These ones do not want to obey me and you have no power over them. I have brought the Order to ruin and I shall not rest until I tear it up by the roots." He even said more irascible words. Then the Superior General patiently answered him: "You have appointed these superiors; not I. Watch out for God's punishment because of the destruction you are causing to the Institute. Fear his wrath because it will catch up with you soon."[34]

Two weeks later, Mario, at age thirty-five, contracted a virulent case of leprosy. Two months later, he died. The Inquisitors then appointed Father Cherubini as vicar-general. The Piarists rose up in outrage. The Piarists, whose mission was to teach youth, knew that Cherubini was a twice-discovered pedophile.[35] Cherubini continued the arrogant spirit and oppressive policies of Mario.

Between 1643 and 1646, Inquisitors reviewed the status of Joseph and his community. When the commission recommended that Joseph be restored, some jubilant brothers threatened retribution against externs who had investigated the community, and against internal members who had cooperated with the investigation. This vindictive reaction prompted the commission to rescind its recommendation. It advised instead to dissolve the community. The Piarists were declared a society of secular priests subject to local bishops, without the right to accept novices or open new houses. With neither lifeblood through new members nor vitality through new ministries, the community would die. When Joseph received the decision, he "kept repeating the words of Job: 'The Lord has given it; the Lord has taken it away. Blessed be the name of the Lord.' "[36]

Cherubini soon contracted leprosy. He and Joseph reconciled just before both died in 1648. Even though the community was disbanded, some members attempted to regroup, and the community was eventually restored, partially in 1656 and fully in 1669. The Piarists flourish to this day.

FOUNDER — BETRAYED

St. Alphonsus Liguori

Sixteen years after Alphonsus Liguori (1696-1787) founded the Redemptorists, the pope, not the secular authority in Naples, approved the establishment of the community. The anticlerical governor in Naples and Alphonsus were already locked in a dispute that lasted almost Alphonsus' entire life.

When a new governor took office in 1780, the advisers of Alphonsus suggested that the timing was propitious to gain secular approval. Alphonsus' trusted aides prepared a document, which the governor and Alphonsus signed. While Alphonsus believed that the document was a harmless statement of mutual recognition, in reality the document was a radical rewriting of the constitution and rule that Rome had approved earlier. The four vows were reduced to an oath of chastity and obedience, and poverty and perseverance were eliminated altogether. All mention of community life was deleted. Authority over internal matters was transferred from the superior general to the consultors. Authority over external matters was relegated to the bishops. Alphonsus, eighty-four and nearly blind, signed a document he could not read: it was written illegibly, in small print, with many erasures, deletions, and marginal notes. Alphonsus had been betrayed.

Chaos erupted. Since Alphonsus had replaced the rule approved by the papacy, the papacy replaced Alphonsus. Rome appointed a new superior general over the local renegade Redemptorists. When Alphonsus discovered the deception, he was distraught.

"It isn't possible, it isn't possible!" Alphonsus repeated, looking over the fatal pages. Turning to Villani [his confessor] he said: "Don Andrea, I did not expect to be deceived like this by you." To the whole community he said: "I deserve to be dragged at the end of a horse's tail. As superior I should have read it, but you know that I have trouble reading more than a few lines."

He raised his eyes toward the Crucifix: "My Jesus Christ, I trusted my confessor; who else could I have trusted but my confessor!" Sobbing he repeated: "I have been deceived! I have been deceived! . . . Oh, Lord, do not punish the innocent but mortify him who is at fault for having ruined your Opera." Naturally he himself was the "culprit." He lost his appetite and his sleep over it.

Two days later he summoned Father Corrado from Ciorani for help, writing an urgent plea: "Don Bartolomeo, I am in danger of going mad. I find the new Regolaménto [rule] drawn up by Father Maione almost entirely in contrast with my views. All the young people here are in turmoil. I beg you to leave everything and come to see me if you do not want to see me stark raving mad and dead of apoplexy."[37]

The betrayal by his most trusted colleagues and the alienation from the papacy tormented Alphonsus. He frantically removed from office those who had deceived him, and he sent to Rome confreres to explain the deceit. The papacy, however, announced the dissolution of the Redemptorists in the kingdom of Naples. Receiving this news, Alphonsus declared, "God is abandoning the congregation because of my sins. Help me for I do not wish to offend God."[38] He resigned himself to the inevitable, saying, "The pope's will, God's will."[39] His colleagues were not so accepting; they rebuked him, stating, "You founded the congregation, and you have destroyed it."[40] For him, this ordeal began an eighteen-month "dark night of the soul," during which "he was assailed by temptations against every article of faith and against every virtue, prostrated by scruples and vain fears, and visited by diabolical illusions."[41]

Ironically the same pope who condemned Alphonsus in 1781 introduced his cause for sainthood in 1796. The proceedings moved swiftly: Alphonsus was beatified in 1816 and was canonized in 1839. He was declared a doctor of the church in 1871.

Bl. Thérèse de Soubiran

In 1854, Marie Thérèse de Soubiran (c. 1837-1889) founded a lay community of women, which ten years later, grew into a religious community called the Society of Our Lady Auxiliatrix. In 1874, however, the foundress, charged with fiscal mismanagement, was expelled from office and then from the community. After she died, community members discovered that the charges were false. Thérèse thus joined the company of many saintly founders who were expelled, or nearly so, from the communities they founded.[42]

Many candidates were attracted to Thérèse's ministry of providing a "home away from home" for working women. Among the new members was Mary Frances, who explained that she had been widowed recently. Intelligent and personable, Frances advanced rapidly within six years from being novice to counselor to assistant general to mother general. Even Thérèse observed that Frances could advance ideas by "the brilliance of her explanations, the force and clarity of her arguments, the justness of her estimates, her shrewdness, tact and skill in affairs . . . and the lively and warm faith that animated her."[43]

Frances maneuvered herself into a position to lead the community. Responsible for the community's finances, she fabricated a report showing that Thérèse's policies had led the community to the brink of ruin. Frances persuaded the community's spiritual director that Thérèse lacked the intelligence, integrity, and spirituality to be mother general. The spiritual director, without understanding the finances or complexity of community issues, asked Thérèse to step down. She did so humbly, despite her deep hurt.

Having ascended to the position vacated by Thérèse, Frances suggested to Thérèse that she might leave the motherhouse and live with the Sisters of Charity for "a few weeks' rest."[44] Those few weeks became seven months. Frances used the interim to manipulate the director and the community members to expel Thérèse.

After twenty years in the convent, Thérèse was homeless. Publicly disgraced, she was refused entrance into two communities. Finally, the Sisters of Charity accepted her. Wanting to expunge every memory of Thérèse, Frances expelled also Thérèse's sister.

Fifteen years later, Thérèse died. About that same time, Frances' control of the community was unraveling. The nuns had grown weary of

Frances' arbitrary rule. They resisted her interminable changes; for example, within five years, Frances closed several houses and moved the novitiate seven times. Finally resisted and rejected, Frances left office and the community in 1890, sixteen years after she had forced Thérèse's resignation.

The new mother general investigated the events of the previous years and discovered that Thérèse's alleged mismanagement was unfounded. She learned too that Frances had deserted her still-living husband. Frances was a fraud. All her actions, therefore, were declared invalid, including the expulsion of Thérèse.

FOUNDER — REJECTED

St. Francis of Assisi

Francis (c. 1181-1226) provided his followers with a rule on three occasions. Many of the friars, however, could never be satisfied. At least two factions developed: the charismatics, who wanted a rule with strict standards and evangelical foundation; and the educators, who wanted a rule with moderate demands and legal formulation. The struggle over the rule threatened to divide the nascent community.

While in Egypt during his third unsuccessful missionary trip to the Muslims, Francis received urgent word of internal unrest back home. When the friars lacked either Francis in person or a rule in hand, they lacked a source of authority to guide them. Francis rushed home to Assisi in 1219.

> The rapid development of the Order, which had grown within a few years from a dozen brothers to several thousand, as well as the admission of scholars into its ranks, had considerably altered its initial aspect. New needs had made themselves felt which the vicars general, in Francis' absence, had tried to meet. But they had done it rashly and unwisely, without sufficiently taking into account the legitimate susceptibilities of the first brothers, or even the deepest intentions of the founder himself. To more than one their innovations had appeared as a betrayal of Francis' ideal. The result had been dramatic crises in many a conscience, and in the Order at large a schism so real that it led to some defections. Two camps now tended to confront each other; on one side were the fervent advocates of evangelical life in its simplest and most improvised form, as Francis himself had lived and loved

it with his early companions in the most total stripping of self and the freedom of the children of God. On the other side were the champions of moderation, who wanted to tone down and codify the uninhibited spontaneity of this evangelical life by casting it into more traditional, better-tested molds, even at the risk of altering it. Each camp, of course, had its extremists, bent upon seeing their idea through, and ready to excommunicate those who did not share it.[45]

The original rule had been communicated orally to the friars and the pope, who approved it in 1209. Ongoing disagreements, however, required that the rule be written, a rule that was approved by a general assembly and became known as the First Rule of 1221. Complaints about the rule, however, did not cease.

Francis agreed to rewrite the rule with the assistance of Brothers Leo and Rufino. After months of praying and writing, Francis was visited by a contingent of friars led by his handpicked successor, Brother Elias. Elias said, "These ministers, hearing that you are making a new Rule, and fearing that you might make it too harsh, protest that they do not wish to be bound to observe it. And that you make it for yourself and not for them."[46] Francis handed the completed rule to Elias, who, "after a few days, asserted that it had been lost through carelessness."[47] Francis immediately recalled Leo and Rufino. The trio quickly rewrote the rule. This time, however, Francis delivered the rule not to Assisi, but to Rome; not to Brother Elias, but to the pope. The general chapter approved this Rule of 1223. These two rules were not new rules, but confirmations of the original rule.

Francis perceived that he was no longer able to lead the community that had grown to five thousand men over the space of seventeen years. Simply, many friars no longer wanted to follow him. Francis passed on the baton of leadership in 1221. Technically, he remained the superior general, but daily administration of the community was conducted by the vicars.

At his retirement in 1221, he said, "From now on I am dead to you."[48] He commented that he was retiring "for reason of illness and for the good of my soul and the souls of all the brothers."[49] Since his leadership had become divisive, he observed, "I'll become more truly their father by making myself more truly their brother."[50] His desire was to lead now by example.

At times a brother would suggest that he intervene in the affairs of the Order. His answer would be: "The brothers have their rule, and they have moreover sworn to uphold it. So that they might have no excuse, after it had pleased the Lord to place me over them as superior, I made the same oath in their presence, and it is my will to observe it to the end. Since the brothers know what they ought to do, and what they must refrain from doing, there is nothing left for me to do but teach them by my deeds.[51]

Francis' retirement consisted of prayer and short travels. He popularized the tradition of the Christmas crib at Grecchio, received the stigmata at Mount Alvernia, and composed the "Canticle of Brother Sun" while visiting St. Clare of Assisi at San Damiano. On his deathbed, "he called for bread and broke it and to each one present gave a piece in token of mutual love and peace saying, 'I have done my part; may Christ teach you to do yours.' "[52]

St. John of the Cross

John de Yepes took the religious name John of the Cross (1542-1591) when he transferred from the Calced to the Discalced (meaning shoeless, or barefooted) Carmelites in 1568, just one year after ordination. In 1571, he met Teresa of Ávila and shared with her the possibility of his transferring to the Carthusians because he was seeking a more prayerful community. She persuaded him instead to help her reform the Carmelites and to serve as spiritual director for herself and the community. For this, he sought and received permission from the papal nuncio, who assigned him to the position. In 1571, Teresa wrote to her sister, "The people take him for a saint; in my opinion he is one, and has been all his life."[53]

Not everybody appreciated John's sanctity. In 1577, his provincial ordered John to leave the ministry with the Carmelite nuns and return to his original friary. John refused because the papal nuncio, and not the provincial, had assigned him. The provincial responded to the rebuff from this young priest by sending armed men to break into his house, drag him out, and bring him not to Ávila, where people admired him, but to Toledo, where nobody knew him.

At Toledo, John refused to abandon the reform movement. Because authorities viewed him as obstinate and recalcitrant, he was thrown into a cell measuring six by ten feet. The cell had one window, which "was so small and high up that he had to stand on a stool to see to read his office."[54] He was oftentimes physically beaten privately in his cell and once publicly at a general assembly to dissuade him from the alleged error of his ways. He bore the marks from these beatings even to his dying days. The imprisonment and mistreatment continued for nine months.[55]

> In the intolerable atmosphere of the cell, stinking in the summer heat, the prior Maldonato visited Brother John on the eve of the Assumption, stirring him up with his foot as he lay prostrate. John apologized for the weakness that did not allow him to get up more promptly when his superior entered. "You were very absorbed," said Maldonato. "What were you thinking about?" "I was thinking," replied John, "that it is Our Lady's feast tomorrow, and what a happiness it would be to say Mass." "Not in my time," retorted the prior.[56]

Finally, he escaped, with the alleged assistance of the Blessed Virgin Mary, who showed him an escape route through a window in the monastery wall above the Tagus River.

John's troubles in community were not over. In 1582, a controversy swelled about the rigor with which the Carmelites should live. John sided with the moderates. Nicholas Doria led the immoderates, that is, the Discalced who rejected moderation and sought full separation of the Discalced from the Calced. The chapter elected as provincial a Discalced, and John as vicar for one of the six provinces. John implemented moderate reform, but discontent kept brewing. Doria removed John from all responsibilities as consultor and reduced him to the rank of simple friar. He was sent to a remote house where he spent months in contemplation, "for I have less to confess when I am among these rocks than when I am among men."[57]

Two men in particular, Fathers Diego and Francis, would not permit John to spend his last days in peace and prayer. John had once corrected these two friars. When Diego replaced John as consultor, Diego circulated rumors that he had sufficient evidence to expel John from the community. Other friars, because they feared the wrath of Diego, shunned John and tore up any letters they had received from him.

Then John's health broke. The provincial allowed John to choose which of two houses he preferred to be sent to. One house was led by a prior, who was a friend of John's; the other by Father Francis. John asked to be sent to Francis' house, where he suffered mistreatment until the day he died.

> The fatigue of his journey made him worse, he suffered great pain, and submitted cheerfully to several operations. But the unwor-

thy prior treated him with inhumanity, forbade any one to see him, changed the infirmarian because he served him with tenderness, and would not allow him any but the ordinary food, refusing him even what seculars sent in for him. The state of affairs was brought to the notice of the provincial who came to Ubeda, did all he could for the saint, and reprimanded Father Francis so sharply that he was brought to repentance for his malice. After suffering acutely for nearly three months, St. John died on December 14, 1591, still under the cloud which the ambition of Father Nicholas and the revengefulness of Father Diego had raised against him in the congregation of which he was co-founder and whose life he had been the first to take up.[58]

IMPRISONMENT — BY THE INQUISITION

St. Ignatius Loyola

Ignatius (1491-1556) was imprisoned twice in 1527 by members of the Inquisition: at Alcalá for forty-two days and at Salamanca for twenty-two days. In each case he was charged with teaching "dangerous doctrines," and after investigation was acquitted of all charges.[59] In the spiritual maelstrom of the post-Reformation, strange spiritual cults were surfacing throughout Spain. Admittedly, Ignatius, who was uneducated and unsophisticated about theology, brought to his teaching and convert-making more heart than head, more emotion than erudition.

In his autobiography, Ignatius relates the events surrounding both imprisonments. The autobiography is expressed in the third person, since it resulted from conversations between Ignatius and his secretary who refers to Ignatius as "the pilgrim."

The Inquisitors from Toledo visited Alcalá because they had heard rumors of certain "sack wearers" going barefoot and being robed in imitation of members of religious orders, pretending to be "enlightened ones."[60] The Inquisitors sought out Ignatius and his followers; "they were going to make mincemeat out of them."[61] After an investigation, it was resolved: "No error was found in their teaching, nor in their living habits, and thus they could continue doing what they were doing, and without any restrictions. But since they were not members of a religious Order, it did not seem proper for all of them to go about wearing a habit."[62]

Four months later, "a married woman of some prominence" and her daughter disappeared.[63] Because these two women had been seen in the company of Ignatius, he was arrested and jailed. He continued his ministry of preaching and teaching, since visitors were allowed. After seventeen days, during which time he had no idea of why he was in prison, Ignatius was visited by the vicar-general, who explained that as soon as the women returned home and corroborated his story, Ignatius would be released. After forty-two days' absence, the pair returned home and testified to Ignatius' innocence. He was released, but was advised not to dress like a religious and not to speak publicly on religious matters until he received the proper education. The vicar-general himself purchased garments for the pilgrim and his companions. Ignatius left Alcalá and traveled to Salamanca.

At Salamanca, Ignatius met up again with the Inquisitors. The Dominican friars invited Ignatius and his companions to Sunday dinner. After dinner, the group moved to the chapel. Friendly conversation turned to investigation. Ignatius admitted that he had more education than his colleagues, but that even his education was quite limited. That being said, his hosts asked:

> "Then, about what do you preach?" The pilgrim said: "We do not preach, we speak to a few in a friendly manner about the things of God, just as one does after dinner with those who invite us." "But," the friar asked, "of what godly things do you speak? That is precisely what we would like to know." The pilgrim answered: "Sometimes we speak about one virtue, then another, always with praise; sometimes we speak about one vice, then another, always condemning it." "You have no education," the friar spoke out, "and you talk about virtue and vice? No one can speak of these except in either of two ways: either because of having been educated, or by the Holy Spirit. Since you have had no education, then it is by the Holy Spirit." The pilgrim was now on his guard, for this way of arguing did not seem good to him. After a bit of silence, he said there was no further need to discuss these matters.[64]

The friars urged Ignatius to speak more. He refused. One friar insisted: "Remain here; we will easily get you to tell all."[65] The friars left and locked the doors behind them, preventing Ignatius and his two companions from leaving.

> At the end of three days a notary came and took them to jail. They were not put down below with the criminals but in an upper room where, because it was old and unused, there was much dirt. They were both bound with the same chain, each one by his foot. The

chain was attached to a post in the middle of the house and would be ten or thirteen palms long. Each time that one wanted to do something, the other had to accompany him. All that night they kept awake. The next day, when their imprisonment was known in the city, people sent to the jail something on which they could sleep and all that was needed, in abundance. Many people came continually to visit them, and the pilgrim kept up his practice of speaking about God, and so forth.[66]

A team of four Inquisitors intended to examine Ignatius on his teachings pertaining to these topics: the Spiritual Exercises, the Trinity, the Blessed Sacrament, and the First Commandment. Ignatius waxed so eloquently and correctly about the First Commandment that his challengers chose not to question him further about the other themes. During that night a jailbreak occurred. All the prisoners fled except Ignatius and his companions. "When they were found the next morning, all alone with the doors wide open, everyone was deeply edified, and this caused much talk in the city. Because of this they put all of them in a nearby mansion as their prison."[67]

> After twenty-two days of imprisonment, they were summoned
> to hear their sentence. No error was discovered either in their life-
> style or in their teaching; therefore they could continue as they had
> been doing, teaching doctrine and speaking about the things of God
> as long as they did not determine "This is a mortal sin" or "This is a
> venial sin," until they had completed four years of study.[68]

Although Ignatius and his companions were declared innocent of all charges, they were prohibited from teaching. Ignatius decided to leave Salamanca and go to Paris to study. After walking over the Pyrenees in the dead of winter, he arrived at Paris in February 1528. He studied there for the next seven years. At the College of St. Barbara, Ignatius met Peter Faber and Francis Xavier. Eventually seven men joined together and in 1534 at Venice vowed themselves to poverty, chastity, and either to preach the Gospel in Palestine or to offer their services to the pope.

Impeded by war in the Adriatic from traveling to Palestine, the band traveled to Rome, where they were ordained priests. They called themselves "the Society of Jesus" because they were "united to fight against falsehood and vice under the standard of Christ."[69]

Pope St. Gregory the Great

When Gregory I (c. 540-604) ascended the chair of St. Peter in 590, he felt unworthy and incapable of responding to the task. The Roman Empire and its capital city had already collapsed.[70] Rome had lost its power, prestige, and pride; the Eternal City was depressed economically, politically, socially, and spiritually.[71]

Gregory was serving as political prefect of Rome in 574, when he felt called to the monastic life. He established monasteries at his home in Rome and on his estates in Sicily. Four years later, the pope appointed him one of seven papal deacons and assigned him as diplomat to the imperial court at Constantinople. In 586, he retired from his diplomatic position to become abbot at his home monastery. A few years later, he evangelized the Angles and Saxons in England. Recalled by the pope when a plague broke out in Rome, he busied himself assisting the poor and sick. When the pope himself died of the plague, Gregory was elected pope.

Gregory provided great leadership to the Church. His focus was to serve the people, and he called upon political and religious leaders to assist him. He ransomed Romans who had been captured by invading barbarians, and he protected Jews who were victims of oppression. To aid the hungry, sick, and dying, he created a citywide organization. He would not tolerate the customary interference into Roman affairs by Byzantine political and religious leaders. To convert the Angles, he sent missionaries to England. He wrote treatises on doctrinal and moral issues and penned hundreds of letters and sermons. Even though history has named him "Gregory the Great," he calls himself "servant of the servants of God." He preaches about himself in the following sermon.

> "Son of man, I have made you a watchman for the house of Israel." Note that a man whom the Lord sends forth as a preacher is called a watchman. A watchman always stands on a height so that he can see from afar what is coming. Anyone appointed to be a watchman for the people must stand on a height for all his life to help them by his foresight.
>
> How hard it is for me to say this, for by these very words I denounce myself. I cannot preach with any competence, and yet insofar as I do succeed, still I myself do not live my life according to my own preaching.

I do not deny my responsibility; I recognize that I am slothful and negligent, but perhaps the acknowledgment of my fault will win me pardon from my just judge. Indeed when I was in the monastery I could curb my idle talk and usually be absorbed in my prayers. Since I assumed the burden of pastoral care, my mind can no longer be collected; it is concerned with so many matters.

I am forced to consider the affairs of the Church and of the monasteries. I must weigh the lives and acts of individuals. I am responsible for the concerns of our citizens. I must worry about the invasions of roving bands of barbarians, and beware of the wolves who lie in wait for my flock. I must become an administrator lest the religious go in want. I must put up with certain robbers without losing patience and at times I must deal with them in all charity.

With my mind divided and torn to pieces by so many problems, how can I meditate or preach wholeheartedly without neglecting the ministry of proclaiming the Gospel? Moreover, in my position I must often communicate with worldly men. At times I let my tongue run, for if I am always severe in my judgments, the worldly will avoid me, and I can never attack them as I would. As a result I often listen patiently to chatter. And because I too am weak, I find myself drawn little by little into idle conversation, and I begin to talk freely about matters which once I would have avoided. What once I found tedious I now enjoy.

So who am I to be a watchman, for I do not stand on the mountain of action but lie down in the valley of weakness? Truly the all-powerful Creator and Redeemer of mankind can give me in spite of my weaknesses a higher life and effective speech; because I love him, I do not spare myself in speaking of him.[72]

Mother Teresa of Calcutta

The author of the definitive biography of Mother Teresa (1910-1997) writes: "She has asserted many times that to leave the Sisters of Our Lady of Loretto was the most difficult step of her whole life and the greatest sacrifice."[73] This same author quotes the nun: "It was much harder to leave Loretto than to leave my family and my country to enter religious life. Loretto meant everything to me."[74] Sister Teresa left home in 1928 to join the Sisters of Our Lady of Loretto. In 1948, she left the Sisters of Loretto to follow God's "call within a call."

Sister Teresa was a vowed nun; these vows would continue to shape her life no matter where the new call led. Entry into a religious order, when a young woman forswears the world for a lifetime of poverty, chastity, and obedience, is a dramatic event. . . . Leaving a religious order, especially before the Second Vatican Council, might be just as dramatic for the person concerned, but it would be a drama hidden in the heart — long drawn-out and painful.[75]

Agnes Gonxha Bojaxhiu had been born into a Catholic family of Albanian ancestry in the Protestant-dominated part of Serbia. Her parents were a wealthy merchant and a successful businesswoman. Ever since age twelve, Agnes felt called to be a missionary sister to India. For that reason, she joined the Loretto Sisters, who had been ministering in India since 1841. Arriving in India in 1929, Agnes worked within a large compound that housed two schools: Loretto Entally for those who could afford the tuition and St. Mary's for those of lesser means. Teresa taught also in a third school: St. Teresa's, which she reached by walking through the noisy, dirty, cluttered city streets of Calcutta.

She received a providential "call within a call" on September 10, 1946: " 'I was going to Darjeeling to make my retreat,' she related. 'It was on that train that I heard the call to give all and follow Him into the slums — to serve Him in the poorest of the poor. I knew it was His will and I had to follow Him. There was no doubt it was to be His work.' . . . 'The message was quite clear. I was to leave the convent and work with the poor while living among them. It was an order. I knew where I belonged, but I did not know how to get there.' "[76]

One month later, she returned to Calcutta. She shared with her superiors and sisters the experience of grace. She explained that she felt called to leave Loretto to serve the poorest of the poor. The change would not be easy. After twenty years of friendships and shared ministries, Teresa gathered the strength to leave her known and comfortable life in order to venture into the unknown and uncomfortable. Her community members were shocked: "We never had any idea that she would ever leave Loretto."[77] Teresa admits that it was more difficult to discern God's continuing call than to continue teaching in her existing call, more difficult to leave Loretto than to remain there. In leaving Loretto, she trusted that God would guide her.

She shared her call with the archbishop of Calcutta. He adamantly opposed her. He insisted that the work Teresa wanted to do was being done already by the Daughters of St. Anne. Teresa pointed out that the Daughters returned to their homes at night, whereas Teresa wanted to live among the poor day and night. The archbishop finally permitted her to depart from Loretto, but insisted that the departure would be done his way, not her way. She was requesting "exclaustration" so that she could live as a vowed sister outside of a community house, but he was insisting upon "secularization" with its concomitant "laicization."

> She [Sister Teresa] asked simply for exclaustration, the freedom from strict enclosure and the life of Loretto, to take up work directly with the poor. Exclaustration meant that Sister Teresa wanted to continue to live by her vows, but in a new setting. When the archbishop read the letter, he insisted on a crucial alteration. He wanted the word "exclaustration" changed to "secularization." This would mean that Sister Teresa would no longer be a vowed nun, but would become a laywoman. To both Van Exem [her spiritual director] and Sister Teresa this was a severe blow, and Van Exem remonstrated with the archbishop, pointing out that if Sister Teresa were without vows, it would not be easy to have young women join her. The archbishop's reply was, "She must trust God fully."[78]

The mother general of the sisters granted permission for the request for "exclaustration" even though the archbishop insisted on "secularization." Teresa, following the mother general's lead, sent the request directly to Rome. A biographer writes:

> My correspondence with the Loretto Motherhouse in Rathfarnham revealed that the Mother General at that time was Mother Gertrude M. Kennedy, but no copies of the letters exchanged would be released to me. The reply of Mother Gertrude also came through the intermediary of the archbishop, and Fr. Van Exem described it as "one of the nicest letters I have ever read in all my life." The letter was written by Mother Gertrude in her own hand. It was dated February 2, 1948, Van Exam remembered, and he recalled its contents: "Since this is manifestly the will of God, I hereby give you permission to write to the Congregation in Rome. My consent is sufficient. Do not speak to your provincial or to your superiors in India. I did not speak to my Consultors on this. I can give you permission for this. Write to Rome and ask for the indult of exclaustration."[79]

Sister Teresa wrote to Pope Pius XII. She explains, "I wrote that God was calling me to give up all and to surrender myself to Him in the service of the poorest of the poor in the slums."[80] The pope granted permission in April 1948.

St. Robert Bellarmine

Robert Bellarmine (1542-1621) studied at the best universities in Florence, Mondovi, Padua, and Louvain. He taught himself Hebrew to understand better the Old Testament. He wrote the four-volume *Disputations on the Controversies of the Christian Faith Against the Heretics of the Times*, which was so prodigious that Protestant opponents suggested it had been authored, not by Robert alone, but by "a syndicate of learned and wily Jesuits."[81] He produced *About Papal Authority* in response to King James I of England's attack. He oversaw the revision of the Latin Vulgate, which still bears his preface four hundred years later. He wrote two catechisms that remained in vogue until Vatican II. Robert was also an outstanding administrator, having served as the papal legate to Paris, the Jesuit provincial of Naples, the archbishop of Capua, a cardinal of the Church, and an adviser to Pope Clementine VIII.

Robert's preaching and teaching style was to present the truth as simply as possible. He did this whether he was criticizing the pope for exceeding his authority in temporal matters, or in advising his friend Galileo to present his teachings as theory and not incontrovertible fact.

The preaching style in Robert's day, however, suggested that the preacher try to impress more than instruct or inspire the congregation. Sermons were embellished to exhibit the preacher's virtuosity. Robert envisioned, though, that the sermon ought to communicate profound thoughts in simple ways, or in other words, to preach as Jesus preached. Robert prepared his homilies in the light of his sanctity, simplicity, and scholarship. He wrote a letter to Cardinal Antoniano in 1603 about the silly content of an overzealous and imprecise preacher.

> My preacher, in a sermon of his on the text, *Super Cathedram Moysis*, etc., so exalted priests that he made them out to be greater and higher in dignity than the Virgin Mother, than Christ, than God Himself. His proofs were very wonderful. A priest, he said, blesses the consecrated Host in which is Christ, but he whose dignity is less is blessed by him whose dignity is greater, *ergo* a priest is greater than Christ. Again, God creates creatures but a priest creates God Himself, *ergo* a priest is greater than God, and if he is greater than Christ and God, much greater must he be than the Blessed Virgin!
>
> I was very much afraid that I would have to put a stop to his

preaching after his exploit, but, when I pointed out to him in my room what unheard-of nonsense he had been talking, he edified me by his humility and obedience, expressing himself ready to do whatever I should bid him. So I told him that, on the following day, he must go into the pulpit and declare that the statements which he had made in his sermon were slips of the tongue due to rhetorical exaggeration. This he did most thoroughly, and I took the opportunity to give him a good, brotherly reproof, putting him in mind of the rule of St. Francis about simplicity in preaching. Then to sweeten the medicine, I sent him some trout. I must not detain your Lordship any longer. Enough to have made known to you something of our weal and our woe.[82]

Robert was a truth-seeker, a truth-speaker. He was a brilliant defender and expositor of the faith. He respected the truth more than any particular person. And he wished all preachers and teachers to do the same.

MISTREATMENT

St. Bernadette Soubirous

Bernadette Soubirous (1844-1879) experienced fourteen apparitions of the Blessed Virgin Mary at Lourdes between February 11 and April 7, 1858, and a final apparition on July 16. The Blessed Mother had warned Bernadette throughout the series of apparitions that she would suffer: "I do not promise to make you happy in this world, but in the next."[83]

Six years after the apparitions, Bernadette entered the convent of the Sisters of Notre Dame at Nevers. She was a twenty-two-year-old peasant, uneducated and unsophisticated. She left her native Pyrenees and traveled three hundred miles north to the region of Burgundy. Separated from family, friends, and familiar surroundings, including the grotto at Lourdes, she became homesick. The ordinary restrictions of convent life imposed unexpected hardships on her. And her religious superiors — namely, the superior general of the order, Mother Josephine Imbert, and the mistress of novices, Mother Marie Thérèse Vauzou — treated her unkindly and coldly.

On one occasion, when the novices were returning from a trip to Rome, the superior general embraced warmly and spoke fondly to each novice, except Bernadette. Some witnesses at Bernadette's canonization process tried to justify the superior general's behavior by saying, "She humiliated Bernadette and treated her coolly for fear that she herself might treat her with favoritism."[84] A bishop testified that the superior general treated Bernadette as a "useless person" and as "a little fool."[85] The only words that Bernadette spoke about the superior general are: "Mother Josephine! Oh, I'm scared of her!"[86]

The relationship between the mistress of novices and Bernadette was no better. Before Bernadette arrived at the convent in 1866, the mistress rejoiced that all the nuns would be "highly favored to be able to contemplate the eyes that had seen the holy Virgin."[87] Mother Vazzou soon became disappointed in Bernadette. Mother commented, "Oh! she was a little peasant girl. . . . If the holy Virgin wanted to appear somewhere on earth, why would she choose a common, illiterate peasant instead of some virtuous and well-instructed nun?"[88] "I do not understand why the holy Virgin should reveal herself to Bernadette. There are so many other souls more lofty and refined! Really!"[89] Mother summed up her condescending treatment of Bernadette: "Every time that I had something to say to Bernadette, I had the urge to speak harshly. . . . In the novitiate there were other novices to whom I would have gone down on my knees before I would have done the same to Bernadette."[90]

Four months after Bernadette entered the convent, she lay dying and received the last rites. As soon as Bernadette recovered, "Mother Vazzou told Bernadette that the period of testing for her was to begin."[91] Mother Vazzou spoke so disparagingly about Bernadette because "she is just an ordinary nun."[92] When Mother was asked to contribute words to the canonization process of the recently deceased Bernadette, Mother responded with a negative wave of her hand and said, "Oh! to lend my voice to the canonization of Bernadette. . . . Wait until after I'm dead."[93] Two months before her death, Mother Vazzou rationalized her behavior, "God deigned to let Mother Josephine Imbert and me be severe for Sister Marie-Bernard in order to keep her in the ways of humility."[94]

MISUNDERSTANDINGS

Ven. John Cardinal Newman

John Henry Newman (1801-1890) suffered at the hands of both Anglican and Roman Catholic Church authorities. "All through his long life, Newman was mostly misunderstood by the authorities."[95]

Bishops of the Church of England misunderstood Newman's involvement in the Oxford Movement, which reacted against Parliament's political designs to disestablish the Anglican Church in England. The pope and bishops of the Roman Catholic Church misunderstood Newman's refusal to offer public support for papal infallibility. After his essay, *On Consulting the Faithful in Matters of Doctrine*, Rome removed him in 1858 as editor of a periodical and refused for ten years to exonerate him. When the pope personally invited Newman to attend Vatican Council I, Newman, who disliked pomp, chose not to attend. The pope and many hierarchy interpreted this response as a snub and a sign of disloyalty.

Even at the local level, Newman failed to win the support of many people. For seven years, he delivered lectures and then produced his famous book, *The Idea of a University*, in order to establish a Catholic university in Dublin, but churchmen refused to support him. Because of his preaching against a former Dominican priest who was promoting antipopery activities in England, the law courts found him guilty and fined him today's equivalent of sixty thousand dollars. Even his best friend and fellow convert Frederick Faber imagined that Newman was trying to end their friendship when Newman suggested that Faber work in London and Newman in Birmingham. Newman simply intended to double and not to duplicate their activities. Newman writes in 1860:

> I have now been exerting myself, labouring, toiling, ever since I was a Catholic, not I trust ultimately for any person on earth, but for God above, but still with a great desire to please those who put me to labour. After the Supreme Judgment of God, I have desired, though in a different order, their praise. But not only have I not got it, but I have been treated, in various ways, only with slight and unkindness. Because I have not pushed myself forward, because I have not dreamed of saying "See what I am doing and have done" — because I have not retailed gossip, flattered great people, and sided with this or that party, I am nobody, I have no friend at Rome, I have laboured . . . to be misrepresented, backbitten, and scorned. I have laboured in Ireland, with a door ever shut in my face. I seem to have had many failures and what I did well was not understood.[96]

He writes three years later:

> What is the good of living for nothing? . . . O how forlorn and dreary has been my course since I have been a Catholic! Here has been the contrast — as a Protestant, I felt my religion dreary, but not my life — but, as a Catholic, my life dreary, not my religion. . . . It began when I set my face towards Rome; and, since I made the great

149

sacrifice, to which God called me, He has rewarded me in ten thousand ways. O how many! But He has marked my course with almost unintermittent mortification. Few indeed successes has it been His blessed will to give me through life. I doubt whether I can point to any joyful event of this world besides my scholarship at Trinity and my fellowship at Oriel — but since I have been a Catholic, I seem to myself to have nothing but failure, personally.[97]

In 1878, Newman, weary and almost worn out, was named a cardinal of the Church.

Sts. Cyril and Methodius

Duke Rastislav of Moravia, which is located in the present-day Czech Republic, desired independence from Western influences. He requested pastoral assistance from the Holy Roman Emperor at Byzantium. In 862, the emperor sent the brothers whom we know as Cyril (c. 826-869) and Methodius (c. 825-885). Moravia had been Christianized two hundred years previously by Celtic monks, and at this time German priests were ministering there. Western culture, however, lacked deep roots among the Slavs.

A clarification about the saints' names is necessary: Cyril and Methodius are religious names taken when the brothers became monks. Cyril's baptismal name was Constantine. He was already a deacon, probably a priest, and became a monk only fifty days before his death. Methodius's baptismal name is unknown. He was a former governor of a Slav colony and was already a monk as early as 861.

The brothers were familiar with the Slavic language because they had lived until their adolescent years among the Slavs in Macedonia, where their father served in the Byzantine army. Before departing for Moravia, the brothers created a Slavonic alphabet and translated the four Gospels. After arriving there, they introduced the Slavonic language into the liturgy.

Their mission soon led to conflict with the German clergy. The Westerners, believing that the liturgical languages consisted only of Hebrew, Greek, and Latin, disapproved of using Slavonic in the liturgy. Constantine referred to the Westerners as "trilinguists" and "Pilatians," noting that their choices of languages coincided with Pilate's choices used in the inscription on Jesus' crucifix.

News of the dispute reached Rome. Pope Nicholas I requested that Constantine and Methodius travel there to explain themselves. By the time the brothers arrived months later, Pope Nicholas I had died and Pope Adrian II succeeded him. The attitude at Rome was no longer one of investigation, but celebration. The new pope solemnly approved the Slavonic liturgy, ordained deacon Constantine and three of his disciples to the priesthood, and celebrated the Slavonic liturgy with the brothers at the most illustrious churches in Rome. Constantine's weak health prohibited him from traveling farther. He entered a monastery in Rome, where he took vows and the religious name of Cyril, and died.

Pope Adrian appointed Methodius the papal legate for all Slavic peoples, with the condition that the epistle and Gospel be proclaimed at Mass first in Latin and then in Slavonic. In 869, Methodius was ordained bishop. He was assigned to the newly restored ancient see of Sirmium, which was carved from the jurisdiction of the German bishops. This action infuriated the German king and bishops, who convened a synod at which they claimed the authority to depose Methodius. They arrested, imprisoned, and exiled him to Swabia, present-day Switzerland, where he remained for three years. He was released through the intervention of the new pope, John VIII.

Methodius's return to active ministry met opposition from Westerners and Easterners. Because Methodius had criticized the conduct of the Eastern political leaders, these complained to Rome against him. In 879, the pope called Archbishop Methodius to Rome to answer two allegations: unorthodoxy in teaching and use of the vernacular in the liturgy. After Methodius responded satisfactorily, the pope published a document in which he "unreservedly praised both the orthodoxy and conduct of Methodius, confirmed the privilege of his independence in jurisdiction from all except the Holy See itself, and expressly authorized the Mass in Slavonic."[98] The pope then made a political decision. To appease Methodius's critics, he appointed as the successor bishop one of Methodius's most vocal critics, Bishop Wiching. Wiching kept undermining the good that Methodius was performing. The archbishop threatened his suffragan bishop with excommunication.

In his final years, Methodius coordinated the translation into Slavonic of the remainder of the Bible.[99] He codified Slavic civil and canon law. He translated numerous works of the Fathers.

Methodius's administrative achievements, however, were short-lived. Within a year of his death, the political opponents of Methodius expelled his disciples from Pannonia and Greater Moravia. Within two decades, the entire Moravian Empire was overrun by the Hungarians. The good achieved by Methodius was thrown into chaos and the seeds of faith were scattered to flower again at a later time.

St. Hildegard of Bingen

When Hildegard (1098-1179) was eight, her parents entrusted her to her father's sister Jutta, who administered a convent school next door to the priests' monastery at Diessenberg. This monastery was founded allegedly by the seventh-century Irish missionary St. Disibod. Many pilgrims flocked to Jutta in order to receive her wisdom and to request her prayers. After Jutta died, pilgrims continued to visit the monastery to venerate her relics.

Jutta's protégée Hildegard had intercessory powers and miracles attributed to her too. Young women were attracted to her and her lifestyle. The convent of a few nuns grew into thirty women.

> Measured in purely external terms her achievements are staggering. Although she did not begin to write until her forty-third year, Hildegard was the author of a massive trilogy that combines Christian doctrine and ethics with cosmology; an encyclopedia of medicine and natural science; a correspondence comprising several hundred letters to people in every stratum of society; two saints' lives; several occasional writings; and not least, a body of exquisite music that includes seventy liturgical songs and the first known morality play.[100]

Hildegard decided to move to a more remote and less accessible location. She preferred to leave the valley of Diessenberg in favor of the nearby mountaintop of Rupertsberg.

Her decision to move the convent aroused much opposition. Merchants feared the loss of revenue if hungry and tired pilgrims no longer visited Diessenberg. The monks feared the loss of prestige if the monastery no longer housed Jutta's relics. Some nuns preferred the comfortable living associated with St. Disibod's monastery. The monks tried their best to block Hildegard's move. She writes an unusually acerbic letter to her opponents.

> I came here [Rupertsberg] with the approval of my superiors and with God's aid I have freely taken possession of it for myself and

all of those who follow me. After that I went back at God's direction to Diessenberg, the community I had left with permission, and I presented before all who lived there this proposal — namely, that not only our place of residence, but all the real estate added to it as gifts, should not be attached to them but should be released. But in all of this practical business I had nothing else in mind but the salvation of souls alone and concern for the discipline commanded in our rule.

I then shared with the Abbot [Kuno], the superior at this site, what I had received in a true vision: "The bright streaming light speaks, 'You should be the father over the provost [Volmar] and over the spiritual care of this mystical plant-nursery for my daughters. The gifts made to them belong neither to you nor to your brothers. On the contrary, your monastery should be their shelter.' But if you want to grow stubborn in your opposition and gnash your teeth against us, you will be like the hated Amalekites in the Bible and like Antiochus, of whom it is written that he robbed the temple of the lord. (1 Maccabees 1:21) Some of you have said in your unworthiness, 'We want to diminish your possession.' Here is the response of the Divine: 'You are the worst thieves! But if you should try to take away the shepherd of the sisters' spiritual healing [Provost Volmar], then I further say to you: You are like the sons of Belial and you don't have the justice of God before your eyes. Therefore, God's judgment will destroy you!' "[101]

Hildegard succeeded in obtaining a legal contract recognizing the sisters' ownership of the convent and independence from the monks.

Ven. Catherine McAuley

Catherine McAuley (1778-1841) founded in Dublin, Ireland, the House of Mercy to educate poor children and shelter poor women. Many priests criticized her for opening this house for the poor in the exclusive section of Baggott Street, for venturing imprudently into the slums to find poor people, for attracting to her institute women who might otherwise join orders of nuns, and for their impersonating nuns by wearing uniforms. One priest thought she was acting like a man in founding a new ministry, therefore addressed a letter to her in the masculine form: C. McAuley, Esquire. Another priest lied to her, saying that the bishop said she ought to leave the work that she had founded. Inquiring of the bishop what he meant, he responded that he had neither said nor even imagined those thoughts.

> "However," he added, "I did not think founding a new order was part of your plan." As she made no comment on this, he continued in freezing tones, and with a cold, disdainful air, which he could well assume: "Really, Miss McAuley, I had no idea that a new Congregation would start up in this manner."[102]

Catherine wondered why this was happening to her. She held the clergy in the highest esteem. "Alas," said she, "how little did I think, when I tried to devise some way of assisting the neglected poor, that I should ever live to give offense to the least of God's ministers!"[103] Many clergy felt angry toward Catherine. "As soon as her Institute (the House of Mercy) began to assume a distinctive character, bishops, priests, religious and seculars assailed her; many even deemed it a good work to persecute her."[104]

While some clergy criticized Catherine, others complimented her. Gradually, Catherine began winning ecclesiastical support. At the dedication of the chapel in the House of Mercy in 1829, the priest conferring the blessing said:

> I look upon Miss McAuley as one selected by heaven for some great work. Her heart overflows with the charity of Jesus, whose all-consuming love burns within her. No woman has ever accomplished more for suffering, sorrowing humanity. She may well rejoice over those whom she has been instrumental in snatching from the enemy's grasp, and may confidently claim a blessing from heaven on her future labors. I will venture to say that her name is written in the Book of Life, and I feel convinced that any individual presuming, by word or deed, to injure her establishment, will draw down upon himself the lash, the scourge of the Almighty, even in this world.[105]

Catherine later developed an orphanage and an employment agency. In order to ensure stability for the ministry, she founded the Sisters of Mercy in 1831. When she was fifty-two, "Catherine, believing that God was directing her through the call of the Archbishop, overcame her prejudice against religious life, her disapproval of conventual customs, her dislike of taking vows and her private dismay at the thought of becoming a nun."[106]

Bl. Katharine Drexel

Katharine Drexel (1858-1955) grew up as the middle child of three daughters in an extraordinarily wealthy family in Philadelphia, Pennsylvania. Her father was Francis Drexel, whose father had founded a banking and investment company. Her mother died five weeks after Katharine was born, and sixteen months later, her father married Emma Bouvier, of the family whose descendant Jacqueline Bouvier was the wife of President John F. Kennedy.

When Katharine's stepmother died of cancer in 1883, "it was revealed that she had quietly been paying the rent for over 150 families, and that she had dispensed $500,000 in alms in the preceding 20 years."[107] The stepmother employed a woman to seek out poor families, who would receive a ticket and an invitation to come to the Drexel mansion for assistance. Katharine writes:

> About three times a week, my mother would go to the back room, and the people would come to her. They would crowd around the entrance on Moravian St. As soon as my mother opened the door, there would be a grand rush to be the first one in. I often think my mother had no human respect. She never seemed to wonder what the neighbors would think or say when they saw the crowd gathered day after day during the winter months. My mother remained in this room, and each one who came and presented a ticket was received and given all the time she wanted to tell her story. My mother knew the details beforehand, from the woman who had reported it. My mother would try to devise means of giving the needed help right then and there — a grocery order or an order for coal or rent, or shoes — poor things, they mostly needed shoes.[108]

Katharine grew up in a prayer-filled home. She writes: "My father would come home from the office and go right up to his room and kneel down beside a chair. . . . Prayer was like breathing . . . there was no compulsion, no obligation . . . it was natural to pray. . . . Night prayers were always said together."[109]

At twenty-four, Katharine experienced a turning point in life. Her stepmother's death put life into a new perspective. She began considering a life of active service to the poor as a nun.

Father James O'Connor, Katharine's spiritual director, had been serving as the family's chaplain since the girls were toddlers. Even after he was named the bishop of Omaha and vicar apostolic of Nebraska in 1876, he maintained frequent correspondence with and visits to the Drexel home.

In 1885, Katharine's father died. She felt his death deeply, and it affected her health. She and her sisters traveled to Europe for rest and recuperation. Midway through the yearlong trip, the women visited the pope. Katharine, who had been requested by O'Connor to invite religious to be missionaries to the Native Americans in the American West, asked the pope if missionaries might be sent. Pope Leo XIII heard the question, reflected on it, and responded, "Why not, my child, yourself become a missionary?"[110]

Katharine brought this question to O'Connor. They exchanged questions and answers for six months, and gentle probings about her vocation. In August 1885, he reached a decision:

> The conclusion to which I have come in our case is, that your vocation is not to enter a religious order. The only order to which I could have thought of recommending you, as I more than once told you, is the Sacred Heart; but you have not the health to enable you to discharge the duties that would devolve upon you as a member of that society. But, though God does not will you to a religious order, He has, I am persuaded, a special mission for you in the world. He wishes you, in my opinion, to be in the world, but not of it, and to labor there for your own salvation and the salvation of others, just as you are now doing.[111]

After the sisters returned from Europe, they traveled to frontier Omaha to visit with Bishop O'Connor and see firsthand the missions they were supporting so generously. Katharine discussed her vocational quest with O'Connor, who remained firm in his opposition because of her weak health and accustomed comfort. The bishop insisted that he knew her best and repeated that "in your spiritual direction, yourself, you are not to be trusted."[112] Katharine pondered the matter. On November 26, 1888, she wrote back forcefully:

> How I wish to spend my entire life entirely given to Him by the three vows which would consecrate me to Jesus Christ! This night I feel a sadness out of which it is difficult to rally. It appears to me that Our Lord gives me the right to choose the better part, and I shall try to

draw as near to His Heart as possible, that He may so fill me with His love, that all the pains I may endure in the religious life may be cheerfully endured for the love of Jesus, the Lord of Love. Do not, Reverend Father, I beseech you, say, "What is to become of your work?" What is to become of it when I give it all to Our Lord? Will Our Lord at the day of judgment condemn me for approaching as near to Him as possible by following Him and then leaving my yearly income to be distributed among the Missions, or for the Missions in some way that I am sure could be devised if only Our Lord will free me from all responsibility, save that of giving myself to Him? . . . Are you afraid to give me to Jesus Christ?[113]

The bishop replied immediately, on November 30. He relented of his former opposition: "This letter of yours, and your bearing under the long and severe tests to which I have subjected you, as well as your entire restoration to health, and the many spiritual dangers which surround you, make me withdraw all opposition to your entering religion."[114]

Within three months, O'Connor was advising Katharine to consider whether she might found a new community of nuns to serve the American Indians and Negroes (as blacks were then called), or whether she should join an established order and donate her monies to the Indians and Negroes. In 1890, she announced plans for a new congregation, which thirteen women joined immediately. Katharine took her vows as Sister Mary Katharine Drexel, first superior of the Sisters of the Blessed Sacrament for Indians and Colored People. The community grew to include hundreds of sisters and dozens of houses that expanded from the motherhouse near Philadelphia to the southern and southwestern United States.

St. Robert Bellarmine

Robert Bellarmine (1542-1621) served the Church at the height of the Counter-Reformation. He became a priest in 1570, a cardinal in 1594, archbishop of Capua in 1602, and a papal legate at large in 1605.

As a young priest-teacher, he lectured on the Scriptures, the Fathers, and Church history. He taught at Louvain and the Roman College. He organized his lectures into a Herculean systematic presentation that "put order into the chaotic argumentation of attack and defense waged between Reformers and Catholics."[115]

After he was named a cardinal of the Church, "Bellarmine served as a member of all the Roman Congregations and of many commissions. One of Bellarmine's continual concerns was the discipline of bishops, that is, their appointment, residency, and transfer."[116] In 1605, the pope appointed Robert the pope's representative in theological and political disputes involving kings and theologians. Working closely with the popes and cardinals, Robert lamented the dearth of suitable candidates for the papacy. He writes to his provincial:

> A Pope was elected who, as you have heard, was a very good man, a friend of our Society, and full of good intentions so excellent that if he could only have carried them into effect he would have proved himself a model shepherd of souls. I know this for certain because, on Palm Sunday, he chose to unveil his heart to me in a general confession, as he expressed it, not of sins but of good resolutions. On April 27 he died. Who can unriddle these judgments of God?
>
> Here we are, then, once more preparing to enter the conclave, and we need prayers more than ever because I do not see in the whole Sacred College one who possesses the qualities which you describe in your letter. What is worse, the electors make no effort to find such a person. It seems to me a very serious thing that, when the Vicar of God is to be chosen, they should cast their votes, not for one who knows the will of God, one versed in the Sacred Scriptures, but rather for one who knows the will of Justinian, and is versed in the authorities of the law. They look out for a good temporal ruler, not for a holy bishop who would really occupy himself with the salvation of souls. I, for my part, will do my best to give my vote to the worthiest man. The rest is in the hand of Providence for, after all, the care of the Church is more the business of God than ours.[117]

A clarification is needed. The popes of Robert's time are not to be confused with the corrupt popes of the previous century. The Late Renaissance popes were remembered not only for their support of humanist scholarship but also for their licentious living.[118] Admittedly, Robert's Tridentine-era popes were notorious for nepotism, but not for immorality.[119] As early as 1504, reform-minded popes had been making genuine progress. By 1585, the tide had turned from reform to revival. In 1605, when Robert sat in two conclaves, the Counter-Reformation was in full bloom.

St. Thomas More

Sir Thomas More (1478-1535) was an author, poet, historian, jurist, chancellor of the state, and eventual martyr for the Catholic faith. In England, he led the Christian humanist movement, which focused on a "break with the immediate past in favor of antiquity."[120] The humanists applied linguistics and literary criticism not only to classical literature but also to the Scriptures. The movement encouraged critical thinking in matters of faith. Unlike many of his contemporaries, More maintained the balance between scholarship and faith.

More's humanist friend Erasmus criticized the Church for an apparent emphasis on external ceremony rather than internal commitment. He chastised monks for performing pious acts without being personally pious. Erasmus refused, however, to support reformers in their rejection of the Church's teachings and authority. Unfortunately, much of his intellectual work was exploited by the reformers against the Church. After Erasmus criticized the early Fathers for linguistic errors and contemporary monks for lack of genuineness, one monk publicly criticized Erasmus. More wrote in defense of his friend.

> Do you deny that [the early Fathers] ever made mistakes? I put it to you — when Augustine thought that Jerome had mistranslated a passage, and Jerome defended what he had done, was not one of the two mistaken? When Augustine asserted that the Septuagint is to be taken as an indubitable faithful translation, and Jerome denied it, was not one of the two mistaken?[121]

More pointed out that the monks themselves were not above criticism. He admitted that the Church's critics had formed many factions, but, "into what factions, into how many sects, are [monks and friars] divided!"[122] Although More criticized the monks, he nonetheless respected them, pointing out: "Not only have I ever loved them, but intensely venerated them. . . . I desire, indeed, all men to honor you and your orders, and to regard you with the deepest charity, for your merits deserve it, and I know that by your prayers the misery of the world itself is somewhat diminished."[123]

More then writes about the extraordinary contribution of Erasmus. More urges the monks to respect Erasmus's quantity and quality of work and his willingness to risk life and limb in the travels necessary for his mission. More suggests that the monks ought to live their vocations as well as Erasmus lives his.

> If one looks at [Erasmus's] hard work, he sometimes does more work in one day than your people do in several months. If one judges the value of his work, he sometimes has done more for the whole Church in one month than you have in several years, unless you suppose that anybody's fasting and pious prayers have as deep and wide influence as his brilliant works, which are educating the entire world as to the meaning of true holiness; or unless you suppose he is enjoying himself as he defies stormy seas and savage skies and all the scourges of land travel, provided it furthers the common cause. . . . Farewell, and if you do not wish to be cloistered in vain, give yourself to the life of the spirit rather than to these squabbles.[124]

More wrote these words around 1520, two years after he had entered royal service. In 1529, he was appointed the chancellor of King Henry VIII. Five years later he was imprisoned in the Tower of London for refusing to sign the Oath of Succession, which recognized as heirs Henry's offspring by his second wife. Thomas remained imprisoned for fifteen months before being beheaded.

SEMINARY STUDIES — POOR STUDENT

St. John Vianney

John Vianney's (1786-1859) report card from the conclusion of his college studies in 1813 indicates his weak academic performance:

Application	Good
General Knowledge	Very Weak
Conduct	Good
Character	Good[125]

Having grown up on his family's farm near Lyons, France, John attended school for only a few months before the French Revolution interrupted his education. At eighteen, he renewed his studies under the tutelage of a priest from nearby Ecully. John found all studies, but especially

Latin, difficult. Unfortunately, Latin was the language of the seminarian's textbooks for philosophy and theology.

Discouraged in his studies, John made a pilgrimage in 1806 on foot to the shrine of St. John Francis Regis, which lay sixty miles from his home. He prayed for the grace to know whether God and the Blessed Mother wished him to persevere in the call to the priesthood. John returned, renewed in spirit. He continued his studies with his usual lack of success, but with a new attitude. He believed that it was God's will that he be a priest.

His studies were suspended in 1809, when John was drafted erroneously into Napoleon's army. John's pastor had failed to include John's name on a list of exempt clerical students. After reporting to the military, he soon went AWOL, hiding out at a farm. One year later, Napoleon decreed amnesty for all deserters.

Returning to the seminary, John completed his studies in philosophy and began studies in theology. After one semester, he was academically dismissed. His classmates observed that he possessed common sense, but not an academician's ability.

Returning home to his priest-tutor, the Abbé Balley, John wept on the priest's shoulder. The priest renewed his tutoring of John. Three months later, John again tried, but failed to pass the examinations. The Abbé Balley traveled to Lyons to meet his friend, the secretary general of the archdiocese. These two implored the examiner, who was also the vicar-general, to visit Ecully and quiz John in a less threatening and more familiar atmosphere. The next day the makeup exam was administered and John passed. John was ready to be ordained.

The ordaining cardinal, however, was Napoleon's uncle, who had just fled the country after Napoleon abdicated and taken flight. In the cardinal's absence the highest-ranking ecclesiastical official was the vicar-general who had just administered the test. The vicar now asked: "Is the Abbé Vianney pious? Has he a devotion to our Lady? Does he know how to say the rosary?"[126] All responses were affirmative. The vicar replied, "A model of piety! Very well, I summon him to come up for ordination. The grace of God will do the rest."[127] "Thus at the age of 29 years and three months, after so many uncertainties, failures and tears, Jean-Marie was at last a priest."[128]

After ordination in 1815, John was assigned as curate to his tutor. When the abbé died two years later, John was transferred to the remote parish of Ars, where two hundred thirty persons lived. The simple "Curé of Ars" developed a reputation for the ability to read the hearts of people, even before they spoke. Eventually, people came by the thousands to see, pray with, and confess to John. In the last ten years of his life, he spent each day in the confessional from midnight until the following evening, that is, up to eighteen hours daily, with time away only for meals, Mass, and recitation of the Divine Office.[129]

St. John Neumann

John Nepomucene Neumann (1811-1860) relates in his autobiography that he possessed since his youngest years "a decided passion for reading" and "as a result the time that others spent in sports or bird catching I spent in reading all the books I could get hold of."[130] His mother nicknamed him "the little Bookworm."[131]

John encountered many teachers poorly suited for the profession. From Budweis, where he received the equivalent of a high school education, he writes critically about his priest-teachers.

> Since we got a professor who, because of his advanced age and easy-going ways, was also given to drink, we did not make progress in our studies. Actually, I even forgot a great deal of what I had formerly known. In our third year this unfortunate priest appeared drunk at the examinations in the presence of the Head Master and was dismissed. Shortly after that he shot himself to death.
>
> His successor was just as unlearned, and [he was] strict. In half a year he wanted to cover again the subjects of [the past] two and a half years. Considering the lax ways we had taken on under his predecessor, this was too much for most of the students. As a result, many dropped out. I was even more dissatisfied with the religion professor who was dryness and dullness personified. He had an obsession for every word and I did not have a good word-for-word memory. As a result, to me the two classes in religion were most boring.[132]

When he completed his course of studies in 1827, he writes, "I was very disgusted with my studies and during the vacation I even thought about giving them up."[133] He credits his mother and sister with encouraging him to persevere in school.

At college, he took a liberal arts curriculum with a major in philosophy. He delighted in this experience. "Added to this, there was the good and blameless conduct of our professors, the revered Cistercians, who were in charge of the Institute of Philosophy. With them everyone felt a very friendly welcome and complete satisfaction despite the fact that they were mercilessly strict when they discovered deceit or bad will."[134]

At the end of college John had to choose a professional field. He was inclined to study medicine, a choice his father supported, but his mother "was not too happy with this."[135] She suggested that he apply for the school of theology. He did and was accepted.

John enjoyed the first two years of theology. He writes, "I studied *con amore* Sacred Scripture (Old Testament), Hebrew and Church History."[136] He claims his teachers "had a good spirit and with great ease taught us in a short time a great deal of useful material."[137] Next, he studied the New Testament in Latin and Greek plus scriptural exegesis and canon law.

For the third year of theology, John transferred to the University of Prague to study French and English. Shortly after he arrived, however, the archbishop prohibited the seminarians from studying French, and the university no longer offered the English course. Even worse, however, was the quality of the professors.

> At Prague I was likewise displeased with the professors of Dogmatic and Moral Theology as well as of Pastoral Theology. The first was more against the Pope than for him, but he raised so many ridiculous difficulties that he was too little regarded to do any harm. The second was far too philosophical for a single one of us to understand him. The third was an out and out Josephinist. It cost me a great deal of effort and self-conquest to study subjects and opinions, the foolishness of which I had already learned to see through. It is a pity that, in institutions like this, so much [more] is done to keep up the appearance of learning than to spread good Catholic and useful knowledge. I was, obviously, genuinely happy when I could return to Budweis in August 1835, after having passed the examination successfully.[138]

Meanwhile, the bishop of Philadelphia was seeking missionaries for the New World. John volunteered. In February 1836, he left Bohemia and arrived four months later in New York City. After making a retreat, he was ordained subdeacon, deacon, and priest, all within a space of six days, at the original St. Patrick's Cathedral.

John applied his zeal for studies to zeal for the ministry. He became fluent in five languages besides his native Czech. This brick-and-mortar bishop built over one hundred churches and eighty schools in his diocese of Philadelphia, which stretched over the eastern third of Pennsylvania, the southern third of New Jersey, and all of Delaware.[139] Insisting that each parish have its own school, he transferred the funds that were budgeted for his welcoming parade and used this money instead to build another school.[140] He wanted his students to have an excellent opportunity to learn.

St. Catherine Labouré

Catherine Labouré (1806-1876) grew up taking care of others. As the ninth of seventeen children and the second eldest daughter, she inherited at age twelve, after her mother died and her elder sister joined the convent, the responsibility of caring for her father and siblings.

Four days after entering in April 1830 the novitiate of the Daughters of Charity of St. Vincent de Paul, she experienced visions and voices that continued until she died. The visions began with the heart of Jesus appearing to her for nine consecutive days and an inner voice saying, "The heart of St. Vincent is deeply afflicted at the sorrows that will befall France."[141] She writes that she "saw Our Lord in the Most Holy Sacrament," and that "I saw Him during the whole time of my (nine-month-long) seminary, except when I doubted."[142] In June, she received a vision of Christ the King, whose sudden dropping of his garments, royal accoutrements, and the cross, symbolized the sudden loss of the French monarchy.

Then the Blessed Mother appeared to Catherine. On the evening of July 18, beginning just before midnight, the two conversed for two hours. Mary wept as she prophesied: "The cross will be treated with contempt; they will hurl it to the ground. Blood will flow; they will open up again the side of Our Lord. The streets will stream with blood. Monseigneur the Archbishop will be stripped of his garments."[143] One week later, the "glorious three days" of the July 1830 revolution took place, during which "bishops and priests, members of religious orders, guilty and innocent alike, were imprisoned, beaten, and killed. Godlessness ran wild, desecrating churches, pulling down statues, trampling the cross under foot."[144] On November 27, Catherine experienced the first of six visions of the medal, which bears the inscription "O Mary, conceived without sin, pray for us who have recourse to you."[145] Catherine's spiritual director instructed her to write down the details of her visions, which she did in 1841, 1856, and 1876.

The news of these visions, Catherine insisted, must be kept secret between herself and her spiritual director. She maintained this secret for forty-six years until eight months before she died. She did ask her spiritual director to fulfill two requests the Blessed Mother had expressed: that he have a medal struck and a statue made. Regarding the medal, the director received ecclesiastical approval and an engraver produced the medal by 1832. Within a few years, millions of medals were distributed and thousands of miracles were attributed to its use, hence the name "Miraculous Medal." Church authorities investigated the alleged visions and in 1836 declared them authentic. Rumors spread, trying to identity the visionary. Even though people knew that the visionary was a member of Catherine's novitiate class, few suspected her. Lacking formal education and coming from a farming village of some one hundred fifty persons, Catherine impressed few people. Even her superiors speak of her as "rather insignificant," "matter of fact and unexcitable," and "cold, almost apathetic."[146] A younger nun, doubting that Catherine was the privileged sister, said: "I told myself then, 'No, it could not be her.' I did not find her mystical enough."[147] Even Catherine's own niece doubted that her aunt could have been the famous "Sister L." — and explained in a matter-of-fact fashion to her friends, "There are other sisters whose last name begins with L."[148]

Upon completion of the novitiate, Catherine was assigned to an old men's hospice at Enghien, near Paris. There she prepared meals, cleaned the laundry, fed the chickens, and milked the cows until age thirty, when she was appointed administrator of the home. She dedicated herself wholeheartedly to this hidden service. Occasionally she traveled to Paris for religious conferences, but she regularly refused invitations for social gatherings at other convents, saying, "I have to care for my old men."[149]

> Catherine's day changed very little over forty years; the faces of her charges changed as new inmates came to take the places of those who had died. Her order of day was substantially the same in 1876 as it was in 1836. The story of how she cared for her beloved old men is, exteriorly, the story of her life: serving their meals, mending their clothes, supervising their recreations, providing them with snuff and tobacco, bringing them into line when they broke her wise regulations, curing them in their illnesses, watching at their deathbeds. Select any year of the forty, and the results are plain to see: her old men were perfectly cared for in body and soul. Catherine was completely devoted to them, even jealously so. She was rarely off duty, and then only for the good of her own soul.[150]

At seventy, Catherine grew anxious about Mary's second request: that "a statue be erected depicting Mary holding the world in her hands."[151] Catherine had reported this request to her director back in 1830, but he had still not completed the task when he died in 1865. Eight months before she died, Catherine informed her superior that Catherine herself was the recipient of the apparitions, and that a new director ought to be found before it was too late to fulfill Mary's request. The job was undertaken immediately and the statue was completed just before Catherine passed away.

Hidden service pleased Catherine. It is said that "sanctity usually follows the pattern of personality."[152] She sought no celebrity status, no public acclaim. She had already seen the Lord, the Blessed Mother, and St. Vincent de Paul face-to-face.

St. Frances Cabrini

Frances (1850-1917) grew up in the comfort of a middle-class family. At twenty-four, she sought entrance to two religious communities, which rejected her on account of weak health. She then founded her own community, which burgeoned in less than four decades from the original eight nuns to more than a thousand, serving in sixty-seven orphanages, schools, and hospitals in eight countries.[153] She named her community the Missionary Sisters of the Sacred Heart. Contemporaries of both sexes criticized her because they thought that being a missionary was "inappropriate to women."[154]

She traveled extensively. She dreamed of going to China, but the pope requested instead that she go to New York City to serve the Italian immigrants. For thirty years, she sailed annually across the Atlantic Ocean and traversed the United States. She provides the itinerary for one trip: "Now I will have to go (from Chicago) to New York to attend to some important matter; then I will go to New Orleans and Scranton, after which I shall return to Colorado where the bishop wants us to have our own houses before I leave the country; then again to Chicago where there are some grand projects in the making."[155]

She served the poorest among her Italian compatriots. Two letters exemplify her ministry. She writes from Newark, Delaware: "Everything was lacking. There were no comforts of any kind, but there were their Italian sisters, who spoke their language. The children sensed they were loved by them and were happy and faithful to their poor classrooms. Soon attendance rose to 200, then 300, then 400. Many had no desks, no chairs, but it wasn't important, they were at the school of the Italian sisters and this was enough for them."[156]

A priest writes about the situation in Lower Manhattan: "With my own eyes I saw our immigrants being thrown out of church either because they weren't dressed well or because they were unable to pay the prescribed contribution. When our compatriots weren't accepted in the American churches, she (Cabrini) invited and zealously urged the immigrants to frequent the chapel of her community."[157]

She provides a glimpse of her mission in a newspaper interview:

> "Our object," she said, "is to rescue the Italian orphans of the city from the misery and dangers that threaten them and to make good men and women of them. At present we are especially anxious about the Italian girls who have no decent homes, but later on we shall look out for the boys also. We include under the title of orphans not only the fatherless and motherless, but also the children that are abandoned, or whose parents do not properly care for them. We have found that many parents do not properly care for them. We have found that many children are abandoned shortly after they reach this city. Their parents, who have come here expecting to be rich immediately, now learn their mistake, and being unprovided with money, they set the children adrift to care for themselves. . . .
>
> "Our mode of work is to go right down into the Italian quarters and go from house to house, from apartment to apartment. We are recognized by all Italians, and many of them are glad to see us. We try to learn about all the Italian children we meet, whether they have proper homes and proper schooling. I have said that we are especially anxious about the girls just now, and the reason must be apparent. The temptations that a big city like this offers to poor, ignorant girls of any nationality are very great, and to abandoned Italian girls, who have no means of livelihood and are ignorant even of the language of those around them, they are terrible."[158]

From Seattle she writes to one of her nuns about the success the local community enjoys.

> If you could see what a flourishing mission this is! How many Italians we are able to draw! By the hundreds they come and are moved by the ceremonies we have for them. Here in Seattle we celebrate the

feast of Our Lady of Montevergine who is venerated in Caserta, Italy. I have asked the bishop of Cosenza to send me a nice picture of that Madonna.

Here our mission will function as a parish and we will have baptisms, weddings, funerals, etc., as we have already begun to do. We started building the church but are going much faster than in Rome. . . . These are hard times, but we have the consolation of seeing many Italians coming to church. We are really touched by the great faith of some of them, who have been absent from church for twenty-eight, thirty, forty or fifty years.[159]

Mother Cabrini became in 1909 an American citizen, and in 1946 the first American citizen to be named a saint.

St. Paul

Paul (c. 10-65) provides seven lists of his sufferings. To the Corinthians he writes, "We have become, and are now, as the refuse of the world, the outscouring of all things."[160] "We are afflicted in every way, but not crushed."[161] "We are treated . . . as having nothing, and yet possessing everything."[162] "Three times I besought the Lord about this [thorn in the flesh], that it should leave me."[163] To the Philippians, he writes, "I know how to be abased, . . . in any and all circumstances I have learned the secret of facing plenty and hunger, abundance and want."[164] Rhetorically, he asks the Romans, "Who shall separate us from the love of Christ?"[165] Again to the Corinthians, he writes:

Are they servants of Christ? I am a better one — I am talking like a madman — with far greater labors, far more imprisonments, with countless beatings, and often near death. Five times I have received at the hands of the Jews the forty lashes less one. Three times I have been beaten with rods; once I was stoned. Three times I have been shipwrecked; a night and a day I have been adrift at sea; on frequent journeys, in danger from rivers, danger from robbers, danger from my own people, danger from Gentiles, danger in the city, danger in the wilderness, danger at sea, danger from false brethren; in toil and hardship, through many a sleepless night, in hunger and thirst, often without food, in cold and exposure. And, apart from other things, there is the daily pressure upon me of my anxiety for all the churches.[166]

Paul's faith-related sufferings originated when the resurrected Lord Jesus appeared to him. According to the Acts of the Apostles, while Paul was riding on the road from Jerusalem to Damascus, he was blinded by a bright light and was knocked to the ground. A voice asked, "Saul, Saul, why do you persecute me? . . . I am Jesus, whom you are persecuting."[167] The Lord then sent Ananias to Saul, saying, "[Saul] is a chosen instrument of mine. . . . I will show him how much he must suffer for the sake of my name."[168] Then Saul was cured by Ananias and converted to Christianity, about which he proclaims, "I count everything as loss."[169]

For the next three years, Saul retreated in the Arabian desert, probably at Petra. Traveling to Damascus, he preached to the Jews, who threatened to kill him. Continuing on to Jerusalem, he found there the Christians fearful of accepting him. Returning home to Tarsus, he remained there a few years, idle and discouraged. Finally at Antioch, Barnabas assigned Saul as a teacher, especially for those who had not yet heard the Gospel preached to them.

His first missionary journey took him from Antioch to Asia Minor through Cyprus, where Saul is from now on commonly called Paul.[170] While preaching to the Jews first and then to the Gentiles, Paul was chased from Lycaonia and stoned at Lystra. Setting out for Perga, Paul's colleague John Mark quit the mission team. At Antioch, Paul and Peter disputed about whether or not Gentiles needed to obey Jewish dietary rules and rites of circumcision.

As the second journey was beginning, Barnabas and Paul argued whether or not John Mark should accompany them. The dispute ended in division, with Barnabas taking his cousin John Mark, and Paul taking Silas. At Philippi, the Judaizers imprisoned and scourged Paul. At Athens, only a few listeners converted. At Corinth, the Judaizers brought official charges against Paul, but the proconsul dismissed the case because it was a religious and not a civil matter. This Roman indifference protected Paul for two more years at Corinth.

The third journey saw Paul imprisoned in four cities. At Ephesus, after preaching for two years, he was jailed when the silversmiths rioted because of Paul's condemnation of their statues of the goddess Artemis. At Jerusalem, after he and a Gentile companion entered the Temple's inner court, the Roman government placed him in protective custody because the Jews threatened to kill him. Having been transferred to Caesarea, he was confined for two years until the Roman procurators agreed to hear his case. And having appealed to Caesar, Paul was sent to Rome, where he remained under house arrest for another two years.

　While sailing for Rome, Paul was shipwrecked off the coast of Malta. At Rome, while under house arrest, he received visitors and encouraged believers. Finally freed, he traveled, according to tradition, to Spain and revisited Ephesus, Macedonia, Greece, and Crete, before being rearrested at Troas. Transported back to Rome, Nero ordered Paul's decapitation. All this Paul endured for the sake of the spread of the Gospel. He writes to the members of the early Christian community: "[Jesus] has now reconciled [you] in his body of flesh by his death, . . . provided that you continue in the faith, stable and steadfast, not shifting from the hope of the gospel which you heard, which has been preached to every creature under heaven, and of which I, Paul, became a minister."[171]

Endnotes

1. Peter Hinchliff, *Cyprian of Carthage and the Unity of the Christian Church* (London: Geoffrey Chapman Publishers, 1974), p. 90.
2. Ibid., p. 91.
3. Ibid., p. 92.
4. Ibid., p. 94.
5. Ibid., p. 96.
6. Cyprian of Carthage, *St. Cyprian: The Lapsed, and the Unity of the Catholic Church*, tr. by Maurice Bevenot. Vol. 25 of *Ancient Christian Writers* series (Westminster, Md.: The Newman Press, 1957), p. 7.
7. J.N.D. Kelly, *The Oxford Dictionary of Popes* (New York: Oxford University Press, 1986), p. 21.
8. Christopher Dawson, *The Making of Europe* (Cleveland: Meridian Books, 1968), p. 185.
9. Celibacy became required for the first time in any diocese at the Council of Elvira in Spain in 315. Around the year 800 the disciplinary rule was fairly widespread among the dioceses of western Europe. Only in 1054 did the Roman Catholic Church require celibacy of all its priests. Throughout the centuries, however, even though clerical celibacy was the law, clerical concubinage was oftentimes the practice.
10. Boniface, Archbishop of Mainz. *The English Correspondence of Saint Boniface*, tr. and ed. by Edward Kylie (New York: Cooper Square Publishers, Inc., 1966), p. 137.
11. Paul William Harkins, "John Chrysostom, St.," in *New Catholic Encyclopedia*, vol. 7, p. 1041.

12. Paul William Harkins, "Oak, Synod of the," in *New Catholic Encyclopedia*, vol. 10, p. 589.

13. Leo the Great, Pope, *The Letters and Sermons of Leo the Great, Bishop of Rome*, tr. by Charles Lett Feltoe. *Nicene and Post-Nicene Fathers of the Christian Church*. Second Series. Ed. by Philip Schaff and Henry Wace, 1956 (New York: The Christian Literature Co., 1889), vol. XII, p. 311.

14. *Butler's Lives of the Saints,* ed. by Herbert Thurston and Donald Attwater, four volumes (Westminster, Md.: Christian Classics, 1990), vol. II, p. 396.

15. Ibid., p. 398.

16. Paul Turks, *Philip Neri: The Fire of Joy*, tr. by Daniel Utrecht (New York: Alba House, 1995), p. 62.

17. Ibid., p. 64.

18. Bacci, *The Life of Saint Philip Neri: Apostle of Rome, and Founder of the Congregation of the Oratory*, ed. and rev. by Frederick Ignatius Antrobus (St. Louis: B. Herder, 1903), vol. I, p. 98.

19. Turks, p. 65.

20. Alban Goodier, *Saints for Sinners* (San Francisco: Ignatius Press, 1993), p. 62.

21. Ibid., p. 77.

22. Sergius C. Lorit, *Charles de Foucauld: The Silent Witness*, tr. by Ted Morrow (New York: New City Press, 1983), p. 105.

23. Ibid.

24. Ibid., p. 106.

25. René Bazin, *Charles de Foucauld, Hermit and Explorer* (New York: Benziger Brothers, 1923), p. 183.

26. Anthony Joseph Wouters, "Foucauld, Charles Eugene De," in *New Catholic Encyclopedia*, vol. 5, p. 1040.

27. Ann Ball, *Modern Saints: Their Lives and Faces* (Rockford, Ill.: Tan Books and Publishers, Inc., 1983), p. 239.

28. Michel Carrouges, *Soldier of the Spirit: The Life of Charles de Foucauld*, tr. by Marie-Christine Hellin (New York: G. P. Putnam's Sons, 1956), p. 298.

29. Butler, vol. III, p. 414.

30. Ladislaus Anthony Iranyi, "Joseph Calasanctius, St.," in *New Catholic Encyclopedia*, vol. 7, p. 1115.

31. Severino Giner Guerri, *Saint Joseph Calasanz*, tr. by S. Cudinach, Second Edition (Kochi, India: Argentinian Piarist Fathers, 1993), p. 190.

32. Ibid., p. 199.

33. Ibid., p. 211.

34. Ibid., p. 213.

35. Ibid., pp. 215-216.

36. Ibid., p. 228.

37. Theodule Rey-Mermet, *St. Alphonsus Liguori: Tireless Worker for the Most Abandoned*, tr. by Jeanne-Marie Marchesi (Brooklyn: New City Press, 1989), pp. 659-660.

38. Ibid., p. 665.

39. Ibid.

40. Ibid., p. 664.

41. Butler, vol. III, p. 248.

42. Ibid., vol. IV, p. 161. St. Alphonsus Liguori, St. Joseph Calasanctius, and Bl. Teresa Couderc were all expelled from their communities. St. Francis of Assisi, St. John of the Cross, and St. Benedict of Nursia were all mistreated but avoided expulsion.

43. Ibid., p. 159.

44. Ibid.

45. Eloi Leclerc, *Exile and Tenderness*, tr. by Germain Marc'hadour (Chicago: Franciscan Herald Press, 1965), pp. 149-150.

46. Maria Sticco, *The Peace of St. Francis*, tr. by Salvator Attanasio (New York: Hawthorn Books, Inc., 1961), p. 218.

47. Francis of Assisi, *The Writings of St. Francis of Assisi*, tr. by Benen Fahy (Chicago: Franciscan Herald Press, 1964), p. 54.

48. Thomas of Celano, *St. Francis of Assisi: First and Second Life of St. Francis, with Selections from Treatise on the Miracles of Blessed Francis*; *The Second Life*, Book Two, chapter CIV, no. 143 (Chicago: Franciscan Herald Press, 1962), p. 159.

49. Brothers Leo, Rufinus, and Angelus; *We Were With St. Francis*, tr. and ed. by Salvator Butler (Chicago: Franciscan Herald Press, 1976), p. 125.

50. Leclerc, p. 151.

51. Brothers Leo, Rufinus, and Angelus, p. 126.

52. Butler, vol. IV, p. 30.

53. Ibid., p. 414.

54. Ibid., p. 415.

55. While in prison, John wrote poems that he later used to introduce profound writings on spiritual theology. In prison, he wrote introductions to *Dark Night of the Soul* and the beginnings of *The Ascent of Mount Carmel* and *The Spiritual Canticle*.

56. Ibid.

57. Butler, vol. IV, p. 417.

58. Ibid.

59. Ibid., vol. III, p. 223.

60. Ignatius of Loyola, *A Pilgrim's Journey: The Autobiography of Ignatius of Loyola*, tr. by Joseph N. Tylenda (Collegeville, Minn.: The Liturgical Press, 1985), p. 67.

61. Ibid.

62. Ibid.

63. Ibid., p. 68.

64. Ibid., pp. 76-77.

65. Ibid., p. 78.

66. Ibid.

67. Ibid., p. 81.

68. Ibid.

69. Butler, vol. II, p. 224.

70. When historians try to pinpoint the collapse of the empire, the dates range widely. Common suggestions are 378, when the Visigoths swept across the Danube and killed the emperor; or 476, when the last Roman emperor abdicated and a barbarian ascended; or 565, when the Eastern emperor who had recaptured much of Italy, Spain, and North Africa died and these lands were redistributed among the barbarians. The Eternal City suffered a similar collapse: Rome, which was sacked by the Goths in 410, an event that "sent shock waves through the civilized world," was threatened again with destruction by Attila the Hun in 452, and succumbed to destruction three years later at the hands of Gaiseric and the Vandals. The inexorable waves of migrations kept coming: Vandals poured across the Rhine; Angles and Saxons moved southward into Britain; the Franks conquered Gaul; the Ostrogoths and Lombards invaded Italy. There was no holding back the barbarians.

71. As Chris Scarre tells us in *The Penguin Historical Atlas of Ancient Rome* (p. 135): "The transition from Roman province to Germanic kingdom did not mark an abrupt break with the past. In many areas the existing provincial aristocracy continued to hold land and power, to write and worship as before, only now as vassals of German elites. The new rulers needed these people to run their realms. Christianity remained the dominant religion and bishops took on a growing importance, save only in eastern Britain."

72. *Liturgy of the Hours*, vol. IV (New York: Catholic Book Publishing Co., 1975), pp. 1365-1366.

73. Roger Royle and Gary Woods, *Mother Teresa: A Life in Pictures* (San Francisco: Harper San Francisco, 1992), p. 25.

74. Eileen Egan, *Such a Vision of the Street: Mother Teresa — The Spirit*

and the Work (Garden City, N.Y.: Doubleday and Co., Inc., 1985), p. 31.

75. Ibid., p. 26.
76. Ibid., p. 25.
77. Royle and Woods, p. 17.
78. Egan, p. 29.
79. Ibid., pp. 29-30.
80. Ibid., p. 30.
81. Butler, vol. II, p. 294.
82. A Benedictine monk of Stanbrook Abbey, ed., *Letters from the Saints* (New York: Hawthorne Books, Inc.; 1964), p. 158.
83. René Laurentin, *Bernadette of Lourdes*, tr. by John Drury (Minneapolis: Winston Press, 1979), p. 193.
84. Ibid., p. 203.
85. Ibid.
86. Ibid.
87. Ibid.
88. Ibid., p. 204.
89. Ibid., p. 207.
90. Ibid., p. 208.
91. Ibid.
92. Ibid.
93. Ibid., p. 207.
94. Ibid., p. 209.
95. John Henry Newman, *Parochial and Plain Sermons* (San Francisco: Ignatius Press, 1987), in the Foreword by Louis Bouyer, p. xii.
96. John Henry Newman, *John Henry Newman: Autobiographical Writings*, ed. by Henry Tristram (New York: Sheed and Ward, 1957), p. 251.
97. Ibid., pp. 254-255.
98. Ibid.
99. Earlier Constantine and Methodius had translated the Psalms, Maccabees, the Gospels, and the Pauline letters.
100. Hildegard of Bingen, *Hildegard of Bingen: Scivias*, tr. by Mother Columba Hart and Jane Bishop; in the series *The Classics of Western Spirituality* (New York: Paulist Press, 1990), p. 9.
101. Hildegard of Bingen, *Hildegard of Bingen's Book of Divine Works with Letters and Songs*, ed. by Matthew Fox (Santa Fe, N.M.: Bear and Co., 1987), pp. 294-297.
102. Ibid.
103. Ibid., p. 155.
104. Ibid., p. 153.

105. Ibid., p. 154.

106. Mary Carmel Bourke, *A Woman Sings of Mercy: Reflections on the Life and Spirit of Mother Catherine McAuley, Foundress of the Sisters of Mercy* (Sydney, Australia: E. J. Dwyer, 1897), p. 22.

107. Lou Baldwin, *A Call to Sanctity: The Formation and Life of Mother Katharine Drexel* (Philadelphia: The Catholic Standard and Times, 1987), p. 24.

108. Ibid., pp. 20-21.

109. Ibid., pp. 13-14.

110. Ibid., p. 33.

111. Ibid., pp. 33-34.

112. Ibid., p. 37.

113. Ibid., p. 38.

114. Ibid., pp. 38-39.

115. Joseph Friske, "Bellarmine, Robert, St.," in *New Catholic Encyclopedia*, vol. 2, p. 251.

116. Ibid.

117. A Benedictine monk, p. 172.

118. The two "evil stewards," Popes Innocent VIII (1484-1492) and Alexander VI (1492-1503), failed egregiously their individual and institutional responsibilities by committing unconscionably the worst cardinal sins and crimes imaginable.

119. Popes Paul III (1534-1549), Julius III (1550-1555), and Paul IV (1555-1559) were all guilty of nepotism. Pope Pius IV (1559-1565) appointed as cardinal of Milan his nephew Charles Borromeo. Although Pope Marcellus II (1555) was uncle to Robert Bellarmine, Marcellus forbade job-seeking relatives to come near Rome; and Robert was only thirteen years old when his uncle died after serving only twenty-two days as pope.

120. Walter Jackson Ong, "Humanism," in *New Catholic Encyclopedia*, vol. 7, p. 221.

121. John Cumming, ed., *Letters from Saints to Sinners* (New York: The Crossroad Publishing Co., 1996), p. 191.

122. Ibid.

123. Ibid., p. 192.

124. Ibid.

125. Francis Trochu, *The Curé D'Ars. St. Jean Marie Baptiste (1786-1859) According to the Acts of the Process of Canonization and Numerous Hitherto Unpublished Documents*, tr. by Ernest Graf (London: Burns, Oates and Washbourne, Ltd., 1927), p. 76.

126. Ibid., p. 85.

127. Ibid.

128. Ibid., p. 91.

129. Mauer Ralph Burbach, "Vianney, Jean Baptiste Marie, St.," in *New Catholic Encyclopedia*, vol. 14, p. 637.

130. John Neumann, *The Autobiography of St. John Neumann* (Boston: Daughters of St. Paul, 1977), p. 23.

131. Ibid.

132. Ibid., pp. 24-25.

133. Ibid., p. 25.

134. Ibid.

135. Ibid.

136. Ibid., p. 27.

137. Ibid.

138. Ibid., p. 28.

139. Newman's diocese of Philadelphia was later divided and subdivided into the present dioceses of Trenton, Camden, Wilmington, Harrisburg, Allentown, and part of Altoona-Johnstown.

140. Neumann, pp. 49-50.

141. Joseph I. Dirvin, *Saint Catherine Labouré of the Miraculous Medal* (New York: Farrar, Straus and Cudahy, 1958), p. 67.

142. Ibid., p. 74.

143. Ibid., p. 86.

144. Ibid., p. 89.

145. Ibid., p. 94.

146. Butler, vol. IV, p. 444.

147. Michel Lloret, *A light shining on the earth: The Message of the Miraculous Medal* (Rome: Editions du Signe, 1997), p. 18.

148. Ibid.

149. Dirvin, p. 145.

150. Ibid., pp. 144-145.

151. Ibid., p. 19.

152. Ibid., p. 105.

153. The countries in which her sisters ministered included her native Italy, the United States of America, Nicaragua, Costa Rica, Panama, Chile, Brazil, England, and Spain.

154. Butler, vol. IV, p. 594.

155. Mary Louise Sullivan, *Mother Cabrini: "Italian Immigrant of the Century"* (Staten Island, N.Y.: The Center for Migration Studies of New York, Inc., 1992), p. 339.

156. Ibid., p. 156.

157. Ibid., p. 170.

158. Ibid., p. 91.
159. Ibid., pp. 365-366.
160. 1 Corinthians 4:13.
161. 2 Corinthians 4:8.
162. Ibid., 6:8, 10.
163. Ibid., 12:8.
164. Philippians 4:12.
165. Romans 8:35.
166. 2 Corinthians 11:23-28.
167. Acts of the Apostles 9:4, 5.
168. Ibid., 9:15, 16.
169. Philippians 3:8.
170. "The use of a Greek or Latin name in addition to or in place of a Jewish name was common among Jews of the Diaspora" (John McKenzie, *Dictionary of the Bible* [Milwaukee: The Bruce Publishing Co., 1965], p. 648).
171. Colossians 1:22, 23.

PART 4

Life in the World

Pope St. Leo the Great

Leo (d. 461) is the first of only three popes to be heralded as "the great."[1] He defended the Church theologically against the heresies of Manichaeanism, Pelagianism, Priscillianism, and Nestorianism; and politically against the most feared military leaders of his day.

As papal legate in Gaul, Leo entreated rival Roman generals to stop fighting against one another so that they could join forces against the encroaching barbarians. Otherwise, Leo noted, the Romans would exhaust themselves in internecine battles and the barbarians would invade unopposed into the western province of the empire.

As pope, Leo castigated the emperor who had convened the infamous Robber Synod, whose members physically attacked and removed from office the patriarch of Constantinople. Leo convened the famous General Council of Chalcedon, which in 451 excommunicated the pretending patriarch and promulgated the creed that the Church to this day prays each Sunday. The next year, Leo rode on horseback to the city gates of Rome at Pischiera to confront Attila the Hun, who had devastated everything and everyone from the central Asian steppes up to the walls of Rome. This crafty general responded favorably to the God-fearing but otherwise fearless pope. Leo persuaded Attila to accept an annual tribute in exchange for sparing Rome.

On the first anniversary of his confrontation with Attila, known as "the scourge of God," Leo pleads that the Romans not forget their recent deliverance by God.

> The fewness of those who were present has of itself shown, dearly-beloved, that the religious devotion wherewith, in commemoration of the day of our chastisement and release, the whole body of the faithful used to flock together in order to give God thanks, has on this last occasion been almost entirely neglected: and this has caused me much sadness of heart and great fear. For there is much danger of men becoming ungrateful to God, and through forgetfulness of His benefits not feeling sorrow for the chastisement, nor joy for the liberation. Accordingly I fear, dearly-beloved, lest that utterance of the Prophet be addressed in rebuke to such men, which says, "Thou hast scourged them and they have not grieved: thou hast chastised them, and they have refused to receive correction." For what amendment is

shown by them in whom such aversion to God's service is found? One is ashamed to say it, but one must not keep silence: more is spent upon demons than upon Apostles, and mad spectacles draw greater crowds than blessed martyrdoms. Who was it that restored this city to safety? that rescued it from captivity? the games of the circus-goers or the care of the saints? Surely it was by the saints' prayers that the sentence of Divine displeasure was diverted, so that we who deserved wrath, were reserved for pardon.

Let them avail themselves betimes of God's long-suffering and return to Him. I entreat you, beloved, let those words of the Saviour touch your hearts, Who, when by the power of His mercy He had cleansed ten lepers, said that only one of them all had returned to give thanks: meaning without doubt that, though the ungrateful ones had gained soundness of body, yet their failure in this godly duty arose from ungodliness of heart. And therefore, dearly-beloved, that this brand of ingratitude may not be applied to you, return to the Lord, remembering the marvels which He has deigned to perform among us: and ascribing our release not, as the ungodly suppose, to the influences of the stars, but to the unspeakable mercy of Almighty God, Who has deigned to soften the hearts of raging barbarians, betake yourselves to the commemoration of so great a benefit with all the vigour of faith.[2]

In 455, Leo confronted another invader, Gaiseric the Vandal, whose troops had swept from eastern Spain to North Africa through the "toe" of Italy up to Rome itself. Leo's strategy was not as successful this time. Gaiseric agreed to forgo a mass slaughter and conflagration of the city, but he insisted on taking property and captives back to North Africa. The political authorities had once again fled for their safety, leaving the pope to perform both the pastoral and political roles for the sake of the Roman people.

CONFRONTATION — WITH POLITICAL AUTHORITIES

Pope St. Gregory VII

Hildebrand (c. 1021-1085), later known as Pope Gregory VII, assisted six popes beginning in 1045 before being elected pope in 1073.[3] During the first year of his pontificate, he convened a synod to deal with the abuses of concubinage, whereby clergy lived with women as if married; and simony, whereby clergy purchased positions of bishop or pastor. The synod decreed that "not only were they (corrupt priests) disqualified from exercising ecclesiastical jurisdiction or holding any benefice, but the faithful were warned not to avail themselves of their ministrations."[4]

During his second year, he convened a synod to deal with lay abuses, especially lay investiture, whereby kings appointed bishops. This synod excommunicated "any person, even if he were emperor or king, who should confer an investiture in connection with any ecclesiastical office."[5] The times and protagonists with whom Gregory VII dealt were difficult.

> To aid him in the reforms he was about to undertake, Gregory could expect little help from those in authority. Of the great rulers, the best was William the Conqueror, ruthless and cruel though he showed himself at times. Germany was governed by Henry IV, a young man of twenty-three, dissolute, greedy of gold, tyrannical; whilst of Philip I, king of France, it has been said, "His reign was the longest and most discreditable which the annals of France have known." The leaders of the Church were as corrupt as the rulers of the state, to whom indeed they had become subservient, bishoprics and abbeys being sold by kings and nobles to the highest bidder or bestowed on favourites. Simony was general, while clerical celibacy was so little regarded that in many districts priests openly lived as married men, squandered the tithes and offerings of the faithful on their families, and even in some cases bequeathed their livings to their children.[6]

Gregory did not back down from these challenges. William the Conqueror agreed to enforce all reforms except lay investiture. Philip I accepted the reforms in principle, but did little in practice. The recalcitrant emperor Henry IV kidnapped Gregory while he was celebrating Mass on Christmas Eve in 1075. A few days later the bishops living within the empire publicly denounced the pope, and Henry deposed Gregory. The next day, Gregory excommunicated Henry, thus freeing nobles and subjects from moral obligation to obey the emperor. This move pleased the nobles, whose self-interests coincided momentarily with the Church's interests. The empire teetered on the brink of civil war.

Henry capitulated. In the dead of winter, he, his wife, and one child trekked across the Alps to Canossa, where Gregory was residing. Kneeling in knee-deep snow outside the pope's residence, Henry begged forgiveness. Although suspicious of Henry's sincerity, Gregory absolved the emperor. In the midst of this crisis, Gregory reveals his suffering to his friend Hugh of Cluny:

Were it possible, I wish you could know all the trouble that be-
sets me, all the labour that mounts up day by day to weary me out
and deeply distress me. Then your brotherly sympathy would incline
you towards me in proportion to the tribulations of my heart, and
your own heart would pour forth a flood of tears before our Lord to
beg Him, by whom all things are made and who rules all things, to
stretch forth His hand to me in my misery, and with His wonted loving kindness set this wretched being free. Often indeed have I implored Him that even as He Himself has imposed the burden, so He
rescued me from great afflictions, nor has my life proved useful, as I
hoped it would, for the service of the Church with whose chains He
has bound me.[7]

The seeds of revolution had been sown. When Henry and his brother-
in-law warred against each other, the pope backed the brother-in-law.
After the brother-in-law was slain by Henry, he besieged Rome for three
years. Trade and tranquillity were lost. Gregory then implored the Norman
duke of Calabria to rescue Rome. Although the Normans forced Henry to
flee, they stayed and abused the citizenry. War-weary Romans blamed
Gregory for these military conflicts.

Gregory fled from Rome to Salerno on the Adriatic coast. Thirteen
of his cardinals publicly blamed him for the Roman unrest. One year later,
he begged forgiveness, forgave all his detractors, and lifted all excommu-
nications except those of Henry and his antipope. Gregory died in exile.
"Although his efforts seemed to end in failure, the ideas for which he
struggled were to prevail through his successors and helped to shape
western Christendom."[8]

CONFRONTATION — WITH MILITARY AUTHORITIES

Bl. Junípero Serra

In 1931, the United States government inducted Junípero Serra (1713-
1784) into the national hall of fame and placed a statue of him in the U.S.
Capitol. He had founded nine missions that served Native Americans from
San Diego to San Francisco.[9]

Serra was a man with a mission. After many years of teaching in
Mallorca and evangelizing in Mexico, he was named in 1767 president of
the missions in Upper California. Working indefatigably, he founded
farms, rancherias, and schools to feed, shelter, and educate the native

peoples. He learned six languages to communicate with different tribes. He endured hunger and famine, stormy seas and a near shipwreck, violent attacks and threats of attack from enemy Indians. He baptized six thousand Native Americans and confirmed five thousand. In the fifteen years that he served in California, he traveled by horseback, muleback, and on foot approximately 4,285 miles.[10]

The visionary missionary experienced his greatest challenge, however, in the constant obstruction from two military leaders: Don Pedro Fages and Don Fernando de Rivera. Because the Spanish government had feared that the Russian empire might occupy the west coast of the new continent, the crown suggested that the Church and State should work together to achieve a bloodless conquest of the region. The Church was to provide the civilizing influence and the military was to provide protection.

Fages (1770-1774) worked to ensure his own comfort, but ignored the basic needs of the soldiers, missionaries, and Native Americans. He harangued the soldiers, spoke disparagingly of the friars, and described the American Indians as "well proportioned in body, but they do not have the greatest faculties of mind."[11] He allowed the soldiers to ride into Indian territory to chase down, lasso, and rape women, while shooting dead the Native American men who rushed to defend their women. Serra's former student and closest friend, Francisco Palou, writes:

> Fages considers himself as absolute and that the missionaries count for less than the least of his soldiers, so that the missionaries cannot speak to him on the slightest matter concerning the missions. He states that he is in charge of all; that the missionaries have nothing more to do than to obey, say Mass, administer the sacraments; that all the rest devolved upon him as commander. . . . If he were a person who understood something about the missions, and Indians, one could close an eye [to his actions], but the fact is he understands nothing about such things and is an unbearable character.[12]

For the sake of the mission, Serra decided to meet face-to-face with the viceroy and to request that the incorrigible Fages be removed. The sixty-year-old Serra, already suffering from asthma and an ulcerated leg, traveled five hundred miles overland and another fifteen hundred miles by sea. Departing from San Diego in October 1772, Serra met with the viceroy in Mexico City over a period of seven months, and returned in March 1774. Of the thirty-two recommendations that Serra submitted, the viceroy accepted twenty-nine, including the removal of Fages.

Fages's replacement was the timid Rivera (1774-1777). He repeatedly refused to send soldiers to assist the friars in settling new missions because he feared diminishing the protection of the presidio. One time, he and his men even watched from the presidio as the Indians burned to the ground the San Diego mission and murdered one of the friars. Rivera claimed that he and his men slept through the entire incident. Rivera's repeated inaction angered not only Serra and his missionaries but also the political and military authorities in the capital. Eventually he was recalled from duty in California because he had brought "shame to Spanish arms."[13] Serra writes:

> When I hear that there is no possibility of sparing seven or eight men and a few animals to found a mission . . . Your Excellency may well imagine how it disturbs me. That military men should move forward with caution is well and good; but for the sake of the kingdom of God some boldness is more in keeping than all these cautions they are forever urging on me.[14]

Simply, Serra wanted to increase the number of mission sites and Native American converts, who then might reside in the missions and grow in Christian culture by example and education.

CONSCIENTIOUS OBJECTOR

St. Maximilian of Numidia

When young Maximilian (274-295) refused on religious grounds to be inducted into the Roman army, a soldier immediately beheaded him. This story "is one of that small collection of precious documents that is an authentic, contemporary, and practically unembroidered account of the trial and death of an early martyr."[15] The dialogue takes place in Numidia among Maximilian, Fabius Victor (Maximilian's father), and the proconsul Dion.

The proconsul Dion asked the young man his name, and he answered, "What is the good of replying? I cannot enlist, for I am a Christian"; and added when the proconsul told the usher to take his height, "I cannot serve, I cannot do evil. I am a Christian." The proconsul repeated his order, and the usher reported that Maximilian measured five feet ten inches. Then the proconsul said he was to be given the military badge, but Maximilian persisted, "Never! I cannot be a soldier."

Dion: You must serve or die.

Maximilian: I will never serve. You can cut off my head, but I will not be a soldier of this world, for I am a soldier of Christ.

Dion: What has put these ideas into your head?

Maximilian: My conscience and He who has called me.

Dion (to Fabius Victor): Put your son right.

Victor: He knows what he believes, and he will not change.

Dion (to Maximilian): Be a soldier and accept the emperor's badge.

Maximilian: Not at all. I carry the mark of Christ my God already.

Dion: I shall send you to your Christ at once.

Maximilian: I ask nothing better. Do it quickly, for there is my glory.

Dion (to the recruiting officer): Give him his badge.

Maximilian: I will not take the badge. If you insist, I will deface it. I am a Christian, and I am not allowed to wear that leaden seal round my neck. For I already carry the sacred sign of the Christ, the Son of the living God, whom you know not, the Christ who suffered for our salvation, whom God gave to die for our sins. It is He whom all we Christians serve, it is He whom we follow, for He is the lord of life, the author of our salvation.

Dion: Join the service and accept the seal, or else you will perish miserably.

Maximilian: I shall not perish: my name is even now before God. I refuse to serve.

Dion: You are a young man and the profession of arms befits your years. Be a soldier.

Maximilian: My army is the army of God, and I cannot fight for this world. I tell you, I am a Christian.

Dion: There are Christian soldiers serving our rulers Diocletian and Maximian, Constantius and Galerius.

Maximilian: That is their business. I also am a Christian, and I cannot serve.

Dion: But what harm do soldiers do?

Maximilian: You know well enough.

Dion: If you will not do your service, I shall condemn you to death for contempt of the army.

Maximilian: I shall not die. If I go from this earth, my soul will live with Christ my Lord.

Dion: Write his name down. Your impiety makes you refuse mili-

tary service, and you shall be punished accordingly as a warning to others. *(He then read the sentence:)* Maximilian has refused the military oath through impiety. He is to be beheaded.
Maximilian: God liveth![16]

A Christian woman retrieved Maximilian's body and transported it
to Carthage, where Maximilian was laid to rest next to the plot of the great
Cyprian, who had died a martyr in 258.

The reigning emperor was Diocletian, who ruled the Western Empire from 284 until his apparent suicide in 311. After Maximilian died,
Diocletian ordered all soldiers and governmental administrators to sacrifice to the gods or lose their jobs. Six years later, he commanded that all
bishops and clergy be killed. In 304, he ordered the same penalty for the
laity. Immediately after Diocletian died, his successor Constantine decreed, in 312, that Christianity be tolerated. Ironically, Diocletian's intol-
erance and persecution led to Constantine's tolerance and promotion of
Christianity. These events confirm the dictum of Tertullian that "the blood
of martyrs is the seed of Christians."

DEFENSE — OF ECCLESIASTICAL RIGHTS

St. Thomas Becket

King Henry II and his chancellor Thomas Becket (1118-1170) were constant companions and best friends. They rivaled each other in enjoying
luxury, power, and prestige. When the archbishop of Canterbury died,
Henry nominated Thomas as archbishop. Although he protested vigor-
ously, Thomas was elected and took his position in 1162. Thomas took
seriously his new position. "Once elected, he changed dramatically his
style of life into one of regularity, piety, and austerity, while retaining his
magnificence, his generosity, and his commanding personality."[17] He resigned his chancellorship. He was ordained priest one day and bishop
and archbishop the next day.

Henry and Thomas soon clashed over the king's attempts to wield
secular authority in ecclesiastical matters. In 1164, Thomas resisted the
king even though all the other bishops of England signed the infamous
Sixteen Constitutions of Clarendon. The king convened at Northampton
a council consisting of laymen and bishops. The laymen condemned Thomas for feudal insubordination. The bishops, who had been forbidden by
Thomas from judging him, sought the assistance of the pope against their

archbishop. Thomas fled to France for safety. "Thomas appealed to Pope Alexander III, then at Sens, but the Pope, not wishing to offend Henry, would not support Thomas."[18] Thomas took refuge in one monastery and then another. He addressed the following letter in 1166 to all the clergy of England.

> I have long kept silence, waiting if perchance the Lord should so inspire you, that you should again take courage, after you had once turned your backs in the day of battle; that even one only of you would go up against the enemy and present himself as a wall of defense for the house of Israel, even if he only made a show of contending against those who do not cease daily to reproach the army of the Lord. I waited, but there was no one to go up: I was patient, but no one stood forward: I was silent, but no one spoke. . . .
>
> May God remove the veil from your hearts, that you may perceive your duty. If there be any one among you who can say that since my promotion I have taken from him an ox or an ass, or his money: if I have judged unjustly the cause of any one, or to the injury of any one among you have procured advantage to myself, let him now speak and I will restore fourfold. But if I have offended no one, why do you leave me to fight alone in the cause of God? . . .
>
> You name to us the danger which will accrue to the Roman Church, the loss of her temporalities. This danger falls on us and on ours, but nothing is said of the danger to the soul. . . . The Church hath ever increased and multiplied under tribulation and blood-shedding. It is her peculiarity to conquer while she is injured, to possess understanding when she is refuted, to succeed when she is deserted. Do not mourn for her, my brethren, but for yourselves, who are earning for yourselves a name, but not a great one.[19]

Four years later, the king of France devised a peace plan to be signed by Henry and Thomas. Thomas returned to England, but the king broke his word and required Thomas to lift his excommunication of bishops who had infringed on the archbishop's rights. Thomas refused. He reasserted the excommunication. The king swore at his barons, "What a set of idle cowards I keep in my kingdom who allow me to be mocked so shamefully by a low-born clerk."[20] Sycophant functionaries overheard what the king voiced to everyone in general and to no one in particular. Historians wonder if the king truly wished harm to come to Thomas. Nonetheless, four henchmen murdered Thomas Becket in the cathedral at Canterbury. Thomas was popularly and immediately proclaimed a martyr. Three years later, the pope declared him a saint. Principled and courageous, Thomas died to preserve the rights of the Church.

Bishop Oscar Romero

Just weeks before the installation of Oscar Romero (1917-1980) as archbishop of El Salvador, the military tortured four priests and expelled three of them as foreigners. Six thousand protestors demonstrated against the government. Further beatings followed. Then ten thousand protestors marched. Priests received death threats. Rectories were bombed. Church walls were painted with accusations. Within two months, hundreds of poor persons and two more priests were assassinated.

With the country writhing in crisis, Romero and his predecessor decided to forgo the public ceremony of the transfer of the see, and performed the rite privately. Immediately the new archbishop insisted in the national and international media that the priests had "grasped reality with great clarity and saw that the common enemy of our people is the oligarchy."[21] Romero preached that the country's main problem was that too few people had too much wealth.

Romero's defense of the poor aroused the opposition of all but one of the Salvadoran bishops. Even the auxiliary bishop whom Romero had handselected reported to Rome that Romero was supporting Marxist priests and catechists. At a conference of Latin American bishops in Puebla, Mexico, Romero was the only archbishop not elected by his national bishops. The Vatican responded by appointing Romero as its representative.

On February 17, 1980, the archbishop wrote to Jimmy Carter, thirty-ninth president of the United States. An excerpt follows.

> According to the newspapers, your government is studying the possibility of supporting, by economic and military aid, the junta that is presently governing El Salvador. Because you are Christian and have spoken of your desire to defend human rights, I should like to express my pastoral point of view regarding what I have read and make a concrete request. . . . Prohibit all military assistance to the Salvadoran government, [and] guarantee that your government will not intervene, directly or indirectly, by means of military, economic, diplomatic, or other pressures, to influence the direction of the destiny of the Salvadoran people.[22]

The next day, the oligarchy bombed the archdiocesan radio station. Ten days later, Romero reported in an interview: "My life has been threatened many times. I have to confess that, as a Christian, I don't believe in death without resurrection. If they kill me, I will rise in the Salvadoran people. I'm not boasting, or saying this out of pride, but rather as humbly as I can. As a shepherd, I am obliged by divine law to give my life for those I love, for the entire Salvadoran people, including those Salvadorans who threaten to assassinate me. If they should go as far as to carry out their threats, I want you to know that I now offer my blood to God for justice and the resurrection of El Salvador."[23]

On March 9, aides discovered dynamite inside a church where Romero was scheduled to celebrate Mass for another assassination victim. Governmental leaders offered to meet with the archbishop to discuss the heightening tensions between Church and State, between rich and poor. Romero refused. He explained that the politico-military leaders would manipulate any meeting as a public relations ruse to cover up the oligarchy's murderous conduct.

On March 24, 1980, while Romero was celebrating Mass in a hospital chapel, masked men burst inside, raised their rifles, and shot the archbishop dead. He slumped to the ground, another martyr for human rights, especially for the poor.

DEFENSE — OF PERSECUTED PEOPLE

St. Hugh of Lincoln

Hugh of Lincoln (1140-1200) was born to a noble family in Burgundy. The lad left home at eight after his mother died. He attended a convent school where he excelled. As soon as his age permitted, he became a monk and, later, a prior. While visiting the Grande Chartreuse monastery, he decided to become a Carthusian. After his superiors noted his manner of living, they asked him to serve as prior for the first Carthusian monastery in England. King Henry II, in repentance for his part in the murder of Thomas Becket, had promised to build a monastery.

In England, Hugh challenged Henry to build the monastery as promised, to fill vacant sees, and to cease channeling the Church's income into the king's treasury. Hugh refused to contribute to the king's war chest and to tolerate the king's men who, in defense of royal forest laws, "hunt the poor as if they were wild animals and devour them as their prey."[24]

"He was one of the leaders in denouncing the persecution of the

Jews that swept England in 1190-1191, repeatedly facing down armed mobs and making them release their victims."[25] At his death he was mourned by all, "especially by the Jews, whom he had always defended and befriended."[26] His funeral bier was carried by the kings of England and Scotland.

St. Maximilian Kolbe

At the Nazi concentration camp in Auschwitz, a career soldier in the Polish army, Francis Gajowniczek, found his life preserved when the Franciscan priest Maximilian Kolbe (1894-1941) volunteered to die in his place. Francis writes of Kolbe:

> I observed him evenings in the [cell] Block praying fervently and inviting others to join him — a very dangerous activity. I participated in prayer sessions he organized, and once was among his listeners at a conference he gave right outside the Block.
>
> Another day a bunch of us were shoveling manure out of a pit. Father Kolbe was beaten very cruelly by an SS guard who hit him many times in the face while his attack dog also assaulted Father, biting him seriously. Father Kolbe bore all this not just with patience but with dignity. When he returned to the pit where we were throwing out manure, he continued to work without a word.[27]

Kolbe prayed privately and publicly, and ministered to others at risk to his own life. He heard confessions at night as prisoners crept to his bedside. The sick and dying he carried on pallets, prayed with them, and administered to them the last rites. While all prisoners craved crumbs, and some even drank urine, Kolbe gave away even his meager morsels of food and drink.

One afternoon a prisoner escaped. A siren pierced the silence. Prisoners froze in their tracks. Work ceased. "The whole camp stood at attention until we were dismissed to go to bed. No one got even a bite to eat."[28] Overnight it was discovered that the escapee had come from Kolbe's block. If the runaway were not found, the rule stated that ten men from that same block would be executed in his place.

The next day, Kolbe's block was marched to the parade grounds. The prisoners were lined up: ten rows deep, sixty men in each row. The

Kommandant's deputy-commander would choose ten men to die. He walked sometimes crisply and sometimes hesitatingly past each man. The anxiety was excruciating. One prisoner writes:

> I was in about the fifth or sixth row back and the fifth or sixth man from the end when [deputy-commander] Fritsch started. As he came closer and closer my heart was pounding. "Let him pass me, let him pass me, oh, pass, pass," I was praying. But no. He stopped directly before me. With his eyes he examined me from my head to my feet, then back again. A second complete [look] up and down. I saw the [secretary] poise his pencil to write my number. Then, in Polish, Fritsch orders, "Open your mouth." I open. He looks. He walks on. I breathe again.[29]

Ten men were selected to die. One of the men, Francis Gajowniczek, cried out: "My wife and my children." The SS officer ignored him.

> Suddenly, there is a movement in the still ranks. A prisoner several rows back has broken out and is pushing his way towards the front. The SS guards watching this Block raise their automatic rifles, while dogs at their heels tense for the order to spring. Fritsch and Palitsch too reach toward their holsters. The prisoner steps past the first row.
>
> It is Kolbe. His step is firm, his face peaceful. Angrily, the Block capo shouts at him to stop or he will be shot. Kolbe answers calmly, "I want to talk to the commander," and keeps on walking while the capo, oddly enough, neither shoots nor clubs him. Then, still at a respectful distance, Kolbe stops, his cap in his hands. Standing at attention like an officer of some sort himself, he looks at Fritsch straight in the eye.
>
> "Herr Kommandant, I wish to make a request, please," he says politely in flawless German. Survivors will later say that it is a miracle that no one shoots him. Instead, Fritsch asks, "What do you want?" "I want to die in place of this prisoner," and Kolbe points toward the sobbing Gajowniczek. He presents this audacious request without a stammer. Fritsch looks stupefied, irritated. Everyone notes how the German lord of life and death, suddenly nervous, actually steps back a pace.
>
> The prisoner explains coolly, as if they were discussing some everyday matter, that the man over there has a family. "I have no wife or children. Besides, I'm an old man, not good for anything. He's in better condition," he adds, adroitly playing on the Nazi line that only

the fit should live. "Who are you?" Fritsch croaks. [Kolbe replies:] "A Catholic priest."

Fritsch is silent. The stunned Block, audience to this drama, expect him in usual Auschwitz fashion to show no mercy but sneer, "Well, since you're so eager, we'll just let you come along too," and take both men. Instead, after a moment, the deputy-commander snaps, "Request granted." As if he needs to expel some fury, he kicks Gajowniczek, snarling, "Back to ranks, you!"[30]

St. Francis Xavier

Francis, with the possible exception of St. Paul, was the greatest of all Christian missionaries. He traveled thousands of miles to the most inaccessible places under the most harrowing conditions. His converts are estimated to have been in the hundreds of thousands; and his missionary impact on the East endured for centuries. Working with inadequate funds, little cooperation, and often actively opposed, he lived as the natives did and won them to Christianity by the fervor of his preaching, the example of his life, and his concern for them.[31]

Francis Xavier (1506-1552) left his native Basque country to study at Paris, where he met Ignatius Loyola. Overcoming initial hesitation about Ignatius and his ideas, Francis joined Ignatius' emerging band. These two and five more men vowed in 1534 to spend the rest of their lives in the service of Jesus and the Church. Ordained at Venice in 1537, Francis met with the pope at Rome in 1538, then traveled to Lisbon in 1540 for embarkation to the Far East as papal nuncio to the Indies.

The rough sailing from Lisbon to the Portuguese outpost of Goa, located on the western coast of the subcontinent of India, required thirteen months, twice as long as usual. At Goa, Francis ministered for five months. He then headed for Cape Comorin, located on the southern tip of India. There he remained for three years, baptizing so many thousands among the low-caste Indians that it is said he could barely lift his arms at the end of the day. He continued evangelizing at Malacca and Japan, where he was the first known European to enter that country. Intending to preach the Gospel on mainland China, he sailed in April 1552 for that place. Ill and exhausted, Francis died in the harbor six miles short of his destination.

When he had been at Cape Comorin, Francis witnessed attacks by non-Christians against Christians. Five years before Francis' arrival, some natives had accepted baptism, but these neophytes "just knew that they were Christians and nothing more."[32] When Francis arrived, the non-Christians took umbrage at the success of Francis' evangelization. One ruler in northern Ceylon slew six hundred newly baptized. Also the natives fought among themselves as the Badagas from the north swept down upon the Paravas in the south and "robbed, butchered, and carried off captives into slavery."[33] Francis came to the aid of the Paravas, whose bodies and souls he wished to save. He writes in June 1544 to a fellow Jesuit:

> I arrived back on Sunday evening, having heard very bad news about the Cape Comorin Christians. The Badagas, I learned, were carrying them off as slaves, and the Christians, to save themselves, had taken refuge on some rocks out in the sea, where they are now dying of hunger and thirst. . . . I shall do all in my power to help the poor souls whom it is the most pitiful thing in the world to see in such dire straits. Many of them arrive daily in Manapad, despoiled of everything and without food or clothing.
>
> I have been along the land route to the Cape to meet the stricken Christians. They made the most lamentable sight you could imagine, here a group perishing for lack of food, there some old men vainly endeavoring to keep pace with the others. And the dead were all about, and the husbands in mourning, and wives bringing babes into the world by the roadside, and many other sights to move one to tears. If you had seen what I have seen you would be as much heartbroken. . . .
>
> I have sent instructions to Father Coelho to get the boats launched and in readiness to embark all the villagers of your area, in case of emergency, for I am sure the Badagas will attempt to surprise you and capture the Christians. Make the people keep a vigilant watch on the mainland, as those Badagas who are mounted, pounce at night and capture the folk before they have time to get into their boats. Keep a close eye on your Christians, for they have so little sense that to save two fanams they would abandon their sentry duties. Make them launch all their boats at once and put their belongings into them, and get the women and children to pray, now as never before, for we have none to help us but God. Above all, see to it that a most vigilant watch is maintained at night and that spies are posted on the mainland. I greatly fear that with the moon now at the full they may come to the coast by night on a foray, so mind that your people are on the alert during the night hours. May our Lord be your protector.[34]

Ven. Pierre Toussaint

The Vatican declared in 1996 that Pierre Toussaint (c. 1778-1853) had lived a life of "heroic virtues" worthy of imitation.[35] The Haitian-born New Yorker may be declared the first black saint from the United States. In New York City, however, he was prohibited because of his color from boarding a public horse-drawn carriage and from entering a Catholic Church outside of his neighborhood.

Pierre was raised in the home of French colonists named Berard. As their domestic slave, he was taught "to read and write and to play the violin."[36] He learned fine manners and became familiar with the ways of the wealthy. Because Haiti was experiencing slave revolts and suffered "numerous massacres and atrocities on both sides," the Berards and their servants fled in 1797 to New York City.[37]

Having lost all his money in a new business that failed and having already lost all his property in Haiti, Berard became ill and died in 1801. His wife was hounded by creditors. At this time, Pierre sustained the household through the lucrative trade of hairdresser, which Mr. Berard had insisted Pierre learn. Just days before Mrs. Berard died in 1807, she signed at the French consulate the papers granting Pierre his freedom. She and he exchanged the following conversation:

> *Madame:* My dear Toussaint, I thank you for all you have done
>   for me; I cannot reward you but God will.
> *Pierre:* O Madame, I have only done my duty.
> *Madame:* You have done much more. You have been everything
>   for me. There is no earthly remuneration for such services.[38]

Pierre married Juliette Gaston in 1811. After years of being childless, they adopted Pierre's niece when she was six months old and cared for her until she died from tuberculosis at fourteen. Pierre had taken her almost daily to Battery Park to enjoy the sea air.

In and around the parish of St. Peter's on Barclay Street, Pierre became well known for his generosity and prayerfulness. He visited the sick during yellow fever epidemics, and at times nursed white and black persons in his home. He attended daily Mass at his parish church and inspired his hairdressing clients with his sage advice from the Scriptures, the *Imitation of Christ,* and Bossuet.

On at least two occasions Pierre suffered racial discrimination. Once, he was refused entrance to the original St. Patrick's on Mott Street, where today "Little Italy" and "Chinatown" meet.

> One day in 1842, Pierre took Juliette and another black lady to a special event in the Cathedral; by then he was known as an outstanding member of the Catholic community of New York, admired for his piety and charity. As they entered the Cathedral, they were stopped by a young white usher who told them that there were no pews for blacks and ordered them to leave. They left with as much dignity as they could muster in the circumstances. It was a humiliating public insult, such as blacks suffered daily. It must be said to the credit of the Cathedral authorities that the President of the Board of Trustees subsequently wrote a letter of apology to Mr. Toussaint.[39]

On another occasion a nonblack friend advised the arthritic septuagenarian to take an omnibus. Pierre responded: "I cannot; they will not let me."[40] This incident occurred when he was recently heartbroken from his wife's death and shortly before his death.

DISCRIMINATION — BECAUSE OF A DISABILITY

St. Joan of Valois

Joan (1464-1505) was blessed with wealth but not health. She was born a princess with a deformed spine. As was the custom, she was betrothed at age two by her father. Her betrothed's family never met her until her future mother-in-law visited when Joan was nine. Immediately, the woman wished to break off the engagement. Joan's father threatened to put the woman's son in a bag and hurl him into the sea if he dared to renege on his promise.

When Joan was twelve, the young couple wed and separated immediately, as was usual. Returning to her father's castle, Joan dreamt of her husband. Returning to his family estates, her husband continued his life of leisure and pleasure-seeking with other women, bewailing his misfortune in having married Joan. The king insisted on a few annual visits between husband and wife. Even on these occasions, the husband paid little or no attention to his wife. He "treated her with utmost contempt."[41] The king's guards forcibly escorted them to the bedchambers.

Joan's father died and her brother ascended the throne when she was nineteen. The new king suspected Joan's husband and others of political conspiracy. Joan interceded for her imprisoned husband. She had him removed from a dreary cell to two comfortable rooms. She effected the delay of his execution and his release three years later. Her husband finally agreed to travel in her company.

When Joan's brother died in 1498, her husband ascended the throne. His first royal act was to send an envoy to the pope to seek an annulment after twenty-two years of marriage. He explained that he had been forced into marriage and that Joan was incapable of performing sexual intercourse and bearing children. Joan was crushed. She had the highest hopes for her husband and their future. After four months of hearings and forty-four witnesses, the pope decreed the marriage invalid.

Joan moved to an estate provided by her former husband. She spent her days praying and caring for the poor. Women of like spirit gathered around her and formed the contemplative order of nuns called the Franciscan Annunciades of Bourges. In 1501, the religious community was approved. Three years later, Joan professed her vows and the next year she died.

DISCRIMINATION — BECAUSE OF THE ROMAN CATHOLIC FAITH

St. Justin de Jacobis

In seventeenth-century Ethiopia, Portuguese colonists regularly abused the local populace. Because the Roman Catholic clergy did not condemn this behavior, the natives concluded that the Roman Church condoned it. When the indigenous population revolted in 1632 against the colonizers, the Coptic Ethiopians joined in the persecution against the Roman Catholic Europeans. Persecutions continued intermittently for two hundred years.

The original hostility was latent in 1839, when Western diplomats and native officials agreed to open a Roman Catholic mission in Ethiopia. Justin de Jacobis (1800-1860) was one of three priests sent there by the Vatican. He was named the vicar apostolic. He respected the Ethiopians, and they in turn respected him. His homily describes his affection for the Ethiopians.

> The door of the heart is the mouth, and the key to the heart is
> the word. As soon as I open my mouth and speak, I open the door of
> my heart. And when I speak, I offer you the key to my heart. Come

and see: in my heart the Holy Spirit has kindled a great love for the Christians of Ethiopia. I was living in my own country. There I received the message that there were Christians in Ethiopia. Then I said to my father and mother: "Father, give me your blessing; mother, give me your blessing, for I want to go and visit my very dear brothers in Ethiopia. I want to tell those Christians how much I love them."

God has answered my prayers. God has granted me the grace of seeing those beloved Christians of Ethiopia. I have seen you, I have come to know you, and now I am happy; and I praise you, my God, and am now praying you even to let me die, if that should be your pleasure, for now I am content. If God leaves me one more day, or two, or more, or however many days of life he may wish, I shall devote them all to you, since God has reserved them for you. You are the owners of my life because God has given me this life for you. If you desire my blood, come and open my veins and take it all: it is yours, you are its owners; I shall be happy to die at your hands. Unless it might please you to inflict on me this kind of death which I greatly desire, I shall spend all my life for you. If you are afflicted, I shall come to comfort you in the name of Jesus Christ. If you are naked, I shall give my clothing to cover you; if you are hungry, I shall give my bread to feed you; if you are ill, I shall visit you. If you want me to teach you what I know, I shall be happy to do that. I no longer possess anything in this world: no father, no mother, no native land. Only one thing is left to me: God and the Christian people of Ethiopia. Who possess my heart? God and the Christian people of Ethiopia.[42]

In 1841, civil and religious leaders invited Justin to join a quartet of ambassadors to implore the patriarch of Alexandria to appoint an Ethiopian as primate of Ethiopia, a see that had been vacant for twelve years. The Ethiopian leaders believed that an educated European priest would enhance the dignity of their mission. As a Roman representative, Justin added two requests: that the patriarch consider reunion with the see at Rome and that the delegation continue to Rome to signify its interest in reunion.

The journey was pleasant, but the visit with the patriarch was not. While Justin impressed his companions by his humble and holy manner, the patriarch repulsed them by his arrogant and abusive bearing. The patriarch, having rejected the suggestion that a local candidate be appointed, selected instead an alien candidate who had not even attained the canonical age. Furthermore, the patriarch threatened the group with excommunication if they dared to go to Rome. The disheartened envoys nonetheless traveled on to Rome, where the pope honored them with a private audience and celebrated Mass with them.

Anti-Roman Catholic persecution began anew with the rising popularity of Justin, known affectionately as "Abuna Jacob." The primate of the national church, Abuna Salama, despised Abuna Jacob. He decreed that Copts who gave food or drink to Justin would be excommunicated. That proclamation had little or no effect. In 1846, "Salama's patron Subagadis wrote to his chiefs: 'Kill Abba Jacob and all his people. To kill only one who follows his religion is to earn seven heavenly crowns hereafter.' "[43] Catholics, however, continued to grow in number. In 1848, Justin was ordained a bishop with authority in both the Roman and Ethiopian rites.

In 1855, Justin was arrested. After several months' imprisonment, his captors allowed him to escape. Five years later, Justin was rearrested. The deprivations of prison life and forced marches exhausted the sixty-year-old missioner. With his health fading, he was released to the care of his fellow priests. He died on the way home.

DISCRIMINATION — BECAUSE OF GENDER

Bl. Julian of Norwich

Julian of Norwich (c. 1342-1423) appears to have been a victim of fourteenth-century sexism.[44] This "first woman of letters in the English language" produced spiritual writing and doctrinal theology that far outshone in profundity the works of her male counterparts, including the author of *The Cloud of Unknowing*.[45] Nonetheless, her work enjoyed little publicity and she felt called to defend her orthodoxy.

Did suspicions arise because she was a woman teaching spiritual truths? She asks: "Because I am a woman, ought I therefore to believe that I should not tell you of the goodness of God, when I saw at that same time that it is his will that it be known?"[46] Citizens of the Middle Ages, however, already knew many outstanding women teachers.[47] Although these women were not lecturers in the burgeoning universities of Western civilization, they taught through their writing and advising.

Did suspicions arise because Julian used the feminine analogy in describing God or Jesus as mother? The feminine image to describe God long predated Julian. Both the Old and New Testaments are replete with feminine references to the divine. Also, numerous Fathers of the Church used feminine images for the divine. Julian's work is original, however, for "the theological precision with which she applies this symbolism (the feminine analogy) to the Trinitarian interrelationships."[48]

Suspicions arose in fact about Julian's orthodoxy because her teachings attempted to reconcile God's mercy and judgment in a way that seemed similar to the heretical teachings of the Free Spirit movement. Julian questioned if a loving God could in fact condemn anyone, since God's limitless love forgives all sinners. She reasoned that although all people sin, and no one "is continually protected from falling," she asked whether sin, however, can be an occasion for the sinner's return to God.[49] Sin does not possess the horror that some attach to it, since "sin can become cause for glory rather than damnation."[50] She advised sinners not to dwell upon their sins and be anxious, but to dwell upon God's love and be consoled. She writes: "He loves us endlessly, and we sin customarily, and he reveals it to us most gently."[51] Julian's orthodox views were supported by the Free Spirit adherents, who taught additionally that some people attain a spiritual height where sin is no longer possible. Julian never subscribed to this heretical view.

> She may have known about the decree *Cum de quibusdam mulieribus* of the Council of Vienne, cited throughout the fourteenth century as the authoritative document legitimizing the investigation of women "commonly known as beguines" who dared to "discourse on the Trinity and the divine essence," and in doing so, spread opinions contrary to the faith, leading simple folk into error under their pretense of sanctity. The fact that Julian was not a beguine would not have exempted her from suspicion; women who were not beguines were prosecuted under *Cum de quibusdam mulieribus*.[52]

Accepting the dictum that "something will be misunderstood if it can be misunderstood," it is understandable that some contemporaries failed to appreciate her distinctions. Julian repeatedly defends her orthodoxy.

> But in everything, I believe as Holy Church preaches and teaches. For the faith of Holy Church, which I had before I had understanding, and which, as I hope by the grace of God, I intend to preserve whole and to practice, was always in my sight, and I wished and intended never to accept anything which might be contrary to it. And to this end and with this intention I contemplated the revelation with all diligence, for throughout this blessed revelation I contemplated it as God intended.[53]

Julian's fourteenth century has been described as history's "most calamitous century."[54] Interestingly, Julian never alluded to any of the calamitous events.[55] She was aware of people's sufferings and consoled many by sharing with them God's message: "I can make all things well. I will make all things well. I shall make all things well. And thou shalt see for thyself that all manner of things shall be well."[56] She responded compassionately to people torn by the confusion of radically changing times.

Her revelations occurred when Julian was deathly ill. On the night of May 13, 1373, she was blessed with a series of fifteen visions and a sixteenth on the next day. She recovered from her illness and spent the next twenty years contemplating and writing about these visions.[57] Her *Revelations of Divine Love* has been described as "perhaps the most beautiful and certainly the tenderest exposition of divine love that has ever been written in the English language."[58]

St. Dunstan

The "most famous of all the Anglo-Saxon saints" was banished from England for criticizing the immorality of the king and his chief defenders.[59] King Edwy was not impressed that Dunstan (c. 910-988) had served and advised the three previous kings of his lineage, Athelston, Edmund, and Edred; and that three more kings, Edgar, Edmund the Martyr, and Ethelred, would later employ his services. What mattered to Edwy was that Dunstan had criticized Edwy.

One incident that particularly riled Edwy took place when the sixteen-year-old lad absented himself from his post-coronation banquet to enjoy dalliances with his girl friend Elgiva and her mother. Dunstan and another man known to be "*constantissimo animo*" were selected to search for and bring back Edwy. Dunstan himself described "how they found the royal crown upon the floor, and how the king had to be almost forced from his place between the two ladies, and once more crowned and brought back to the feast."[60] Dunstan sharply rebuked Edwy and his two companions.[61] This reprimand "gave to Edwy a lasting personal dislike of Dunstan."[62] As other controversies arose, Dunstan continued to criticize the king and his West Saxon political defenders. Edwy, resolving to rid himself of further reproaches, confiscated Dunstan's property and exiled him. Dunstan fled to Ghent in Flanders.

In 957, two years after Dunstan's exile began, Edwy's younger brother

Edgar challenged the king and recalled Dunstan to serve as an adviser. Edgar won the politico-military war, during which Edwy lost his life in 959.

Appointed as bishop to the vacant sees of Worcester and London, and eventually as archbishop of Canterbury, Dunstan sought the assistance of two former Benedictine monks — namely Ethelwold, bishop of Abingdon, and Oswald, bishop of Westbury — to reform England. Because Dunstan's exile fortuitously had exposed him to the Benedictine model of monasticism, he was more convinced than ever of the need to enforce clerical celibacy, remove incompetent and/or immoral clergy, replace them with monks, build or rebuild monasteries, and reestablish the social order by reconciling to the English the Danes who had invaded the country the century before. The restoration of monasteries as centers of scholarship and sanctity is regarded as "the turning point in our (English) religious history."[63] Monastic life had deteriorated so badly, with rules being ignored and buildings abandoned, that one scholar opines, "(Dunstan's) renewal of discipline was really a foundation rather than a revival."[64]

After sixteen years of advising Edgar, plus brief stints with his two successors, Dunstan retired to Canterbury. There he spent his final years as a teacher of young people.

EXILE IMPOSED — BY THE EMPEROR

St. John Chrysostom

In twentieth-century parlance, John Chrysostom (c. 347-407) had the unique ability to "say it like it is." He possessed strong convictions and the courage to express them. Baptized at twenty, as was then customary, John spent the next six years as a hermit under Basil the Great. After excessive asceticism broke his health, he returned to Antioch of Syria, where he was ordained a priest and gained a reputation as an excellent preacher.[65] In 398, he was named patriarch of Constantinople.

He imposed much-needed discipline. He forbade priests from continuing the suspicious practice of having young deaconesses serve as housekeepers. Wandering monks were told to find monasteries and to stay in them. Worldly widows were advised either to marry or to live according to their state of mourning. Wealthy courtiers were warned to moderate their celebrations and to make donations to the sick and the poor.

John made many enemies. He had alienated many clergy and courtiers because he criticized their laxity and luxury. He aroused the envy and enmity of religious rivals who thought that they and not he should occupy the prestigious see of Constantinople. Opposition to John coalesced in 403 and reached its denouement four years later. The patriarch of Alexandria convened in Constantinople the illegal Synod of the Oak, in which thirty-six bishops deposed John from the office of patriarch. The secular authority then implemented the ecclesiastical decree. Although the common people threatened to riot to defend him, John was whisked out of town into exile.

The emperor's troops marched John initially to Cucusus on the Armenian border, a journey of about seventy days. This distance did not discourage John's followers from visiting him. For three years, he continued to act as patriarch. From Cucusus, he wrote two hundred eighty-three letters, of which he sent seventeen to his dear friend Olympias, a philanthropic and religious widow. He writes to her:

> Please listen to what I have to say. I am going to try to make you a little less depressed and to get rid of the dark clouds in your mind. Why are you so worried, sad, agitated? Because the storm that has attacked the churches is harsh and menacing, and because it has wrapped everything in unrelieved darkness? Because it is approaching crisis-point? Because it brings dreadful shipwrecks every day, while the whole world collapses about us?
>
> We see the ocean whirling up from its uttermost depths and sailors' bodies floating on it. We see others overcome by the force of the waves, broken decks, torn sails, shattered masts, oars ripped from the oarsmen's grasp, and the helmsmen idle on the deck opposite the tillers, with their hands resting on their knees. It is all so hopeless that they can only scream, groan, cry and weep. Neither sky nor sea can be seen. Profound, unmitigated and desolate darkness covers everything. No one can see anyone else. The waves rise up and thunder all about. Everywhere monsters of the deep rear up and threaten travellers. But no mere words can express the unutterable. No terminology I can think of can adequately convey the terrors of these times. Though I am well aware of all these miseries, I never cease to lose hope. I always remember the universal Pilot. He does not rely on a steersman's ship to suffer the storm.[66]

Even in exile, John remained popular and influential. The emperor grew frustrated at his failed plan to neutralize the popular prelate. The emperor ordered in 407 that the sixty-year-old ecclesiastic be transferred to Pityus, at the remote eastern end of the Black Sea. The trip was to cover more than six hundred miles across six mountain ranges. "His guard forced him to march bareheaded in sun and rain. Worn out with hardship and fever, he died along the way to Comana in Pontus."[67]

Bl. Margaret Pole

Margaret Pole (1471-1541) was found guilty of treason and was beheaded without the benefit of a trial. Evidence was planted to show that "bulls from the Pope were found in the Countess's house, that she kept correspondence with her son (the Cardinal), and that she forbade her tenants to have the New Testament in English or any other of the books that had been published by the King's authority."[68] The real reason for murdering Margaret was to hurt her son, John Cardinal Pole, who had refused to concur with King Henry VIII's decree of divorce.[69] Since John had fled to France beyond the clutches of the king, the king killed John's mother.

Margaret was an unusual victim. She was the king's aunt. He had described her publicly as the "saintliest woman in England."[70] He personally had chosen Margaret to be the governess of his children. Since Henry's advisers knew that they could never defeat her in a legitimate court, Cromwell suggested the charge of treason, which did not require a court trial. He reasoned, "Since the Court of Parliament was supreme, a writ of Parliament to arrest Margaret on any grounds, even without any evidence, would be good law!"[71] The king wrote a baseless writ to give the appearance of legality. The son writes of his mother:

> You have heard, I believe, of my mother being condemned by the public council to death, or rather to eternal life. Not only has he who condemned her condemned to death a woman of seventy, than whom he has no nearer relation except his daughter, and of whom he used to say there was no holier woman in his kingdom, but at the same time, her grandson, son of my brother, a child, the remaining hope of our race. See how far this tyranny has gone, which began with priests, in whose order it only consumed the best, then [went on] to nobles, and there too destroyed the best. At length it has come to women and innocent children; for not only my mother is condemned, but the wife of that marquis who was slain with my brother, whose goodness was famous, and whose little son is to follow her. Compar-

ing these things with what the Turk has done in the East, there is no doubt but that Christians can suffer worse under this Western Turk.[72]

The investigators found Margaret unshakable in her position. No tricks, insults, or cajolery could make her waver. They write of their simultaneous frustration with and admiration for her.

> Please it your good Lordship to be advertised that as by our other letters we signified to the same we would, so yesterday, the 13th of this November, we travailed with the Lady of Salisbury all day both before and after noon, till almost night. Albeit for all that we could do, though we used her diversely, she should utter and confess little or nothing more than the first day she did, but still stood and persisted in the denial of all together. . . .
> Surely if it like your Lordship we suppose that there hath not been seen or [heard of] a woman so earnest, . . . so manlike in continuance, . . . and so precise as well in gesture as in words, that wonder is to behold. For in her answer and declaration she behaveth herself so, . . . sincere, pure and upright.[73]

The jailers confiscated her personal effects. They detained her in prison for nine months before transferring her to the Tower of London, where she remained for two years. She was provided neither proper clothing nor firewood to protect her against the winter weather. Even her jailer begged unsuccessfully to his superiors that this revered woman be given the basic necessities of food, clothing, and shelter. On May 28, 1541, she was beheaded.

FALSE CHARGES — SEXUAL

St. Mary Magdalene

Mary Magdalene (first century), whom Jesus befriended, has suffered a tarnished reputation for nearly two thousand years. Christians have identified Mary traditionally as a public sinner and have inferred that her sin was sexual.

She has been judged guilty by association. The seventh chapter of Luke's Gospel concludes with the story of an anonymous repentant woman, "a woman of the city, who was a sinner," a woman who washed Jesus' feet in Simon's home.[74] The eighth chapter begins with Jesus journeying through various towns and villages, accompanied by "some women who had been healed of evil spirits and infirmities: Mary, called Magdalene, from whom seven demons had gone out, and Joanna, . . . and Susanna, and many others."[75] To this day, Mary Magdalene has been identified with the public sinner who is imagined to be a prostitute, although "there is no reason to identify Mary Magdalene with the sinful woman of 7:36ff.; Luke introduces Mary as someone new."[76]

What do we know about Mary Magdalene? The Scriptures state clearly that she had seven demons cast from her (Luke 8:2), ministered to Jesus in Galilee (Luke 7:37-50), remained with Jesus at the foot of the cross on Cavalry (Mark 15:40; John 19:25), witnessed where Jesus was entombed (Mark 15:47), discovered the empty tomb (John 20:1) and heard the angel announce Jesus' resurrection (Mark 16:1-8), and was the first person to whom the resurrected Jesus appeared (Mark 16:9; John 20:14-17)). Although Mary Magdalene is thought by some to be the sister of Martha and Lazarus, no scriptural evidence exists to support this conclusion.

LUST

Ven. Charles de Foucauld

Charles de Foucauld (1858-1916) told his women of the night: "I rent by the hour; I don't sign a lease."[77] Most of his sexual liaisons were one-night stands.

Charles was born into an aristocratic family whose Foucauld lineage included numerous ecclesiastical and political leaders, as well as military heroes. Born into wealth, he never wanted for money. When Charles was five, his mother died of a miscarriage and his father of consumption. A rich uncle accepted responsibility for raising the nephew, but the uncle failed to perform his duty.

Charles led a rather purposeless life from ages fifteen to twenty-seven, when he was expelled from the French Foreign Legion. That the Legion, which had a reputation for attracting and tolerating innumerable social misfits and rogues, could not tolerate Charles indicates how extreme was his misbehavior. He tested in the top fifth of his class, but finished preparatory school 333rd out of 386 students. Immediately after graduation, he entered Cavalry School, where he finished last out of eighty-seven students. During the ninety days of summer in military school, he spent twenty-one days under simple house arrest and forty-five days in strict confinement.

Nothing shamed him. He and a cousin, also rich and undisciplined, ordered into their private quarters the choicest meats, wines, and paid women. At the end of the one-year Cavalry School, one month after his twenty-first birthday, the inspector general of the school writes of Charles: "Has a certain distinction and has been well brought up. But is empty-headed and thinks of nothing but amusing himself."[78]

Because Charles was commissioned in October 1879 to a remote region, which proved boring for him, he rented a bachelor's apartment in Paris. There he met Mimi Cardinale, "who was as witty as she was unvirtuous."[79] He lived with her for six months. Other courtesans came and went as he needed them. In December 1880, when his regiment was transferred to Algeria, he took Mimi with him.

> When the colonel and the officers arrived later with their wives and the whole regiment, the scandal was without precedent. The colonel remonstrated with his sublieutenant. However, the latter had no intention of giving in. He showed himself the more publicly with Mimi while the hue and cry increased. The colonel was beset by protests and asked the sublieutenant to make his choice between Mimi and the regiment. Foucauld did not hesitate; he would not send his mistress away.[80]

In March 1881, he had been forcibly retired from the military for "disobedience and notorious misconduct."[81] In June of that year, however, when war broke out in Algeria, he begged to be readmitted to his regiment. The same option was repeated: Mimi or the military. Charles, now tired of Mimi, opted for war.

Charles traveled to North Africa and fought admirably in the desert warfare. A companion from his preparatory school was surprised by the change in him. The companion writes, "In the midst of the dangers and the deprivations of the expeditionary columns this well-read playboy revealed himself to be a soldier and a leader, bearing the worst trials gaily, giving of himself constantly, taking devoted care of his men."[82] The war lasted half a year. Because Charles could not accept the quiet of a peacetime military life, he resigned again from the military.

He traveled to Morocco, where he studied its geography. Charles "wrote two books that won gold prizes from the French Geographical Society in 1885."[83] The next year he moved back to Paris, where he found lodging close to the home of his dear cousin Marie and her husband. Marie never said a single word about his misconduct. By her silent example of daily Mass and Communion, she occasioned his conversion. Before the year was over, he wrote to his cousin, "You have brought me back to Jesus."[84]

This previously profligate playboy completely changed his life. In 1901, he returned to the Moroccan desert in order to establish a Christian presence in the midst of the Muslim world. His ministry was to be like that of his cousin Marie: silent example that encourages conversion.

St. John Gabriel Perboyre

China's first saint, the Vincentian priest John Gabriel Perboyre (1802-1840), was born during the French Revolution's anti-Catholic persecution, and he died during a xenophobic Chinese anti-Christian persecution. John had always longed to be a missionary in China, but his weak health repeatedly prevented his superiors from granting permission.

Finally, after nine years of teaching and serving as director of novices, John and two Vincentian confreres sailed in March 1835 from LaHavre, France, for China. Six months later, they arrived at Macao and prepared to enter China under the cover of darkness because priests were forbidden by imperial decree from ministering on the mainland. John's destination was Honan Province, a journey of six hundred miles up the Yangtze River and another six hundred miles inland.

Persecution awaited him. "Eighteenth-century edicts which outlawed Christianity and condemned to death all Europeans who spread the faith remained on the books. They were enforced intermittently, subject to the mood and venality of the local authorities."[85] In 1839, a well-planned persecution erupted: "It broke out simultaneously throughout the province and the mandarins knew the names of the priests and catechists and the location of all the chapels."[86] Soldiers arrested John and three Christian laymen. The prisoners were handed over successively to the local mandarin, the provincial mandarin, and the viceroy.

The viceroy mistreated John cruelly with a variety of beatings: a hundred strokes with a bamboo rod or a leather strap across the lower back and kidneys, seventy strokes across the mouth, and forty strokes across the face. He remained chained at all times: in prison, in transit, and during tortures. Repeatedly he was forced to kneel on broken glass and shards of pottery. Guards forced down his throat the boiling blood of a dog. He was ordered to trample the crucifix, worship pagan idols, and deliver the names of other Christians. These betrayals John always refused to perform. The viceroy himself then beat John and ordered his face to be branded by a hot iron rod with characters that read: "Preacher of a false religion."[87]

The torturers regularly brought John to the brink of death, and then relented. As soon as he began recovering, the soldiers then renewed their tortures. John's last letter from prison describes the experience.

> When I came to Gucheng, I was treated with great humanity during the time I was there, although I had to undergo two interrogations by the sub-prefect. At Xiangyang, I underwent four interrogations. During one of these, I had to stay for half a day with my bare knees on iron chains and hung from the *hangtse*. At Wuchang, I underwent more than twenty interrogations, and during almost all of them I experienced various tortures, because I was unwilling to say what the mandarins wanted to know. Had I said anything, it would certainly have unleashed a general persecution quickly throughout the empire. Nevertheless, what I suffered at Xiangyang was only because of my religion. At Wuchang I received 110 blows with the *bienze* since I was unwilling to trample the Cross under foot.[88]

In May 1840, the viceroy imposed the death sentence on John. The emperor's confirmation was sought and received. Implementation followed immediately. In the company of other prisoners, John was force-marched. One soldier lined up on each side of each convict. The military clashed their cymbals sporadically to terrorize the crowd. The group then ran to the place of execution, near a lake.

> First, the executioners dispatched the criminals. They were decapitated and their heads were collected and exposed. During this time, John Gabriel knelt down and prayed. Some of the spectators said: "Look at the European on his knees, praying." Many took offense that a man who had given example of all the virtues should be condemned to death. John Gabriel had his red tunic removed, leaving him only some wretched shorts. Then they tied him to a gallows shaped like a low cross. His arms were attached to the back of this cross. They bent his legs as if he were kneeling, and tied his ankles to the post a few inches from the ground. To kill him, the executioner then placed a cord around his neck, and slipped a piece of bamboo into the knot. With a strong twist, he tightened the cord around the convict's neck, and then he loosened the cord to give the poor sufferer a moment to catch his breath. Then he tightened the cord a sec-

ond time, and relaxed it again. Only after the third twist did he keep the cord tightened until death followed. To hasten his death in accordance with the normal procedure, an assistant to the executioner then gave John Gabriel a violent kick in the abdomen. The martyr's head fell forward.[89]

During the execution of Perboyre, a sign of the cross appeared in the sky. This sign of the cross appears in most depictions of the death of John Gabriel Perboyre.

> When the bishop learned of the events that I have just recounted (the phenomenon of the sign of the cross), he did not put much faith in them at the beginning. But later, struck by the great number and importance of the witnesses, he launched a formal inquiry. As a result, he stated that a large, luminous and well formed cross had appeared in the sky, and that a large number of witnesses, both Christian and pagan, had seen it at the same time, in the same shape and size, and in the same place in the sky. These witnesses lived in districts quite far from one another, and had no way of communicating with one another. The bishop also questioned the Christians who had known Father Perboyre, and they all regarded him as a great saint.[90]

Observers noted that John had conducted himself in a saintly manner long before he was martyred. Martyrdom confirmed his sanctity.

MARTYRED — IN CONSTANTINOPLE

St. Andrew of Crete

The Church lists two saints named Andrew of Crete. They died twenty-five years apart. The Andrew (d. 766) in this story is the younger, known also as Andrew of Krisis, indicating where he was buried.

Eighth- and ninth-century Constantinople became embroiled over the veneration of images. Even though this veneration had been practiced since the first century, opposition to images arose from the heretical sect of Christian Monophysitism and image-forbidding Islam. Two emperors from Asia Minor, Leo III and his son Constantine V, decided to impose their iconoclastic views. The penalties for venerating images ranged from confiscation of property to exile and, at times, even mutilation. Constantine V convened at Hiereia, in 752, a council of three hundred thirty-eight bishops and appointed archbishops from Asia Minor as leaders of the council.

> After denouncing all pictorial representations as idols, they [the council Fathers] declared further that any such representation of Christ was false because it must necessarily either separate his two natures or circumscribe the person of the Word who has no limits. Only one image in Christianity has the divine guarantee and presents Christ in His totality: the Eucharist. And representation of a saint was rejected for moral reasons, i.e., as an affront to his present glorious state of being freed of matter.[91]

Andrew left home and protested publicly in Constantinople against the emperor's persecution and heretical position. The imperial entourage pounced upon him. They imprisoned and tortured him for two days. Then, as the soldiers dragged Andrew through the city's streets, an iconoclast in the crowd thrust a fish spear at Andrew and stabbed him to death.[92] Andrew is the first of four monks memorialized as martyrs of the iconoclastic controversy.[93]

This first wave of iconoclasm was followed by a respite of forty years. It culminated in 787 with the condemnation of the Council of Hiereia by the Eastern Church's patriarchs who lived outside of Constantinople. In 813, however, the army backed a new father-son pair of emperors, who led a second wave of iconoclastic persecution. The father convened a council of bishops, which annulled the previous annulment of Hiereia, and the son waged a violent persecution. As soon as they died, their successors restored the practice of the veneration of images, which was confirmed by a new council. Unfortunately, this entire controversy failed to develop a sophisticated theology of icons.

MARTYRED — IN LONDON

St. Edmund Campion

Born and raised Catholic, Edmund Campion (c. 1540-1581) converted to Anglicanism when Protestant Queen Elizabeth ascended the throne in 1558. As a deacon studying the Church Fathers, however, he increasingly questioned the doctrinal and moral positions of the Protestant churches. Peers and patrons began to accuse him of "papistical tendencies."[94] He traveled to Dublin, where he wrote a history of Ireland and studied further the division of the churches. When the pope excommunicated Queen Elizabeth, Edmund moved closer to the Catholic position. Returning to England in 1571, he happened upon the trial of a priest, who was judged guilty and martyred for being Catholic. Edmund prayed for right faith and discernment, and converted back to Catholicism. He traveled to Douay, France, where he continued his studies for the priesthood, and went on to Rome, where he joined the Society of Jesus in 1573. After teaching in Prague and there being ordained a priest, he and a fellow Jesuit were chosen to minister in their native England.

Edmund and his companion entered England in 1580. Edmund himself donned a variety of disguises — for example, at one time, that of an illiterate servant; and at another time, that of a jewel merchant. When the government learned of the priests' whereabouts, the priests fled from London to Berkshire, Oxfordshire, Northamptonshire, and Lancashire, staying one step ahead of the authorities. Edmund's teaching, preaching, and celebrating Mass resulted in many converts, but he knew his safety was at risk. He writes to his Jesuit superior: "I ride about some piece of the country every day. The harvest is wonderful great. . . . I cannot long escape the hands of the heretics . . . I am in apparel very ridiculous; I often change it and my name also."[95]

While on the run, he composed his *Decem Rationes*, that is, ten points on which he challenged Protestant theologians to debate their religion. In June 1581, four hundred copies of this text were distributed surreptitiously in the pews of the university church at Oxford. This audacious action embarrassed the Protestants. They responded with a flurry of efforts to capture Edmund. Three weeks later, he was behind bars, having been betrayed by one of those attending Mass in a private home.

Noblemen and even the queen tried to persuade him, going so far as to torture him and bribe him to change his theological position. These officials intervened four times, all to no avail. He was racked each time. Edmund had studied too hard and had prayed too long to be swayed by superficial arguments and temporary discomfort. He was indicted and eventually convicted "on the fabricated charge of having plotted at Rome and Rheims to raise a rebellion in England."[96] Campion responded to the guilty verdict:

> It was not our death that ever we feared. But we knew that we were not lords of our lives, and therefore for want of answer would not be guilty of our own deaths. The only thing we have now to say is that if our religion does make us traitors, we are worthy to be condemned; but otherwise are and have been as true subjects as ever the

Queen had. In condemning us you condemn all your own ancestors — all the ancient bishops, priests, and kings, — all that was once the glory of England, the island of saints, and the most devoted child of the See of Peter. For what have we taught, however you may qualify it with the odious name of treason, that they did not uniformly teach? To be condemned with these old lights — not of England only, but of the world — by their degenerate descendants is both gladness and glory to us. God lives; posterity will live; their judgment is not so liable to corruption as that of those who now sentence us to death.[97]

MARTYRED — IN NORTH AMERICA

St. Isaac Jogues

Isaac Jogues (1607-1646) attended Jesuit schools from ages ten to seventeen in his native Orléans before joining the Society of Jesus. Upon ordination in 1636, he volunteered for the North American mission. Sailing from Dieppe, he arrived at Quebec three months later. He was missioned to the Hurons in the north country at Sault St. Marie, six hundred miles from the Jesuit headquarters at Three Rivers.

In 1642, while Isaac and about forty other men were returning from a supply trip to Quebec, an Iroquois raiding party ambushed the heavily laden canoes. Some men escaped, some were killed, and twenty-two were captured and brought to Ossernenon, near Albany, New York. Upon arrival in the village, three Hurons were burned alive. "The nightmare of torture began. The enemy fell upon their captives in a great rage, ripping out their finger nails, chewing their fingers and beating them with clubs."[98]

On September 29, Isaac Jogues and René Goupil were walking along the perimeter of the village to which they were confined. Two braves accosted them. One youth suddenly swung a tomahawk over René's head, splitting the lay missionary's head in two. Isaac knelt down, expecting the same treatment. Instead, the braves left him kneeling over his dead companion. Back in the village, Isaac continued his ministry of comforting, praying with, and baptizing Hurons and Iroquois.

Almost a year later, Isaac escaped with the help of Dutch traders who had distracted the Iroquois during trading negotiations. Sailing down the Hudson River to New Amsterdam, which is present-day New York City, Isaac wrote to his superior in France. The missionary described the tortures that he and others suffered for the Gospel.

The natives attacked first Guillaume Cousture, one of the lay members of the group. "They stripped him naked, and like mad dogs ripped away his nails with their teeth, bit his fingers off, and pierced his right hand with a spear." Next, the attackers tortured Isaac, who writes, "They turned on me with their fists and knotted sticks, left me half-dead on the ground, and a little later tore away my nails in the same way, and bit off my two forefingers which caused me incredible agony." He continues the description of the torture.

We suffered many hardships during this journey of thirty-eight days — hunger, intense heat, threats, blows, as well as the cruel pain of our unhealed wounds, which so putrefied that worms dropped off them. The enemy went even further. In cold blood, they inhumanly tore out our hair and beards, and with their nails, which are extremely sharp, they wounded us in the most tender and sensitive parts of the body. On the eighth day of our travel, we fell in with two hundred savages on their way to attack the French. These gave thanks to the sun, who directs the fortunes of war, so they believe, fired their guns to signal their joy, and forced us to disembark, whereupon they welcomed us with a rain of sticks. I being the last, and therefore more exposed to their beating, fell halfway along the road and thought I must die there, unable and unwilling as I was to rise. What I suffered is known only to One for whose love and in whose cause it is pleasing and glorious to suffer. They wanted, however, to take me into their country alive. So moved by cruel mercy, they carried me covered in blood from wounds — especially in the face — to a hill on which they had erected a stage. They now loaded me with a thousand insults and dealt me fresh blows on neck and body. They burned one of my fingers, crushed another under their teeth, and so twisted the bruised and torn sinews of the remainder, that although at present partially healed, they are crippled and deformed.

In the afternoon of the tenth day, we left the canoes to make the rest of the four days' journey on foot. Hunger was our constant companion. We went for three days without food, but on the fourth found some wild fruits. At last, on the eve of the Assumption of the Most Blessed Virgin, we arrived at the first village of the Iroquois. They and the Huron slaves awaited us on either bank of the river, the Hurons to warn us to get away for otherwise we should be burned to death, the Iroquois to belabour us with sticks, fists, and stones aimed especially at my head, for they hate a head shaven and shorn. Two nails had been left me; these they now tore out with their teeth, and with their razor-sharp nails they ripped away the underlying flesh to the very bone. They then led us to a village situated on another hill.[99]

Again, the visitors were welcomed by having to run the gauntlet manned by young braves who beat their victims with sticks and iron rods the Dutch had delivered to the Native Americans.

Virtually all of France had been reading the missionaries' spellbinding accounts in *The Jesuit Relations.* When Isaac arrived at Rennes, France, on January 5, 1644, Jesuits came from near and far to visit him. "Everyone from the Queen down wished to meet and talk with him."[100]

In spring 1644, Isaac returned to his mission, not to Sault St. Marie, but instead to Montreal, where the Jesuit superiors wanted him to assist government officials in New France in preparing a peace treaty. Isaac made two peacemaking trips. The first one was helpful, but inconclusive. The second ended with Isaac's being tomahawked to death. His Huron guides abandoned Isaac and John Lalande when some Iroquois warned the group that other Iroquois were lying in wait to kill them. Despite that news, Isaac and John pushed on. News of their deaths reached Quebec nine months later.

MARTYRED — IN ROME

St. Ignatius of Antioch

In his letters Ignatius (d.c. 107) calls himself Theophorus, that is, the God-bearer. This Syrian convert served as bishop of Antioch for forty years. Scholars suggest that Ignatius was a disciple of John the apostle, and Polycarp of Smyrna was Ignatius' disciple.

The emperor Trajan decreed that governors should not initiate a persecution against Christians, but only respond after public accusations had been brought forth. "Trajan was a magnanimous and humane man, yet the very gratitude that he felt he owed his gods for his victories . . . led him subsequently to persecute Christians for refusing to acknowledge these divinities."[101] When an informer identified Ignatius as a Christian, the governor ordered Ignatius' arrest. He was transported in chains from Antioch, overland to Seleucia, where he was boarded on a ship bound for Rome. Rather than sailing directly to Rome, the ship's captain hugged the coastline of Asia Minor and Greece, stopping at Smyrna, Troas, Neapolis, and Philippi. The party portaged on foot from Macedonia to Epirus, where they continued sailing to Epidamnum, in current-day Albania. All along the route, local bishops, priests, and parishioners met with Ignatius. At Smyrna and Troas, Ignatius dictated seven letters, "which are among the most important of the earliest Christian writings."[102]

Reaching Rome on December 20, the final day of the public games, Ignatius was marched first to the emperor and then immediately to the amphitheater, where two lions devoured him as thousands of revelers cheered. Ignatius' request in his letter to the Christians at Rome was respected: that they not obstruct his becoming "the food of beasts . . . the wheat of God."[103]

You have never begrudged the martyrs their triumph but rather trained them for it. And so I am asking you to be consistent with the lessons you teach them. Just beg for me the courage and endurance not only to speak but also to will what is right, so that I may not only be called a Christian, but prove to be one. For if I prove myself to be a Christian by martyrdom, then people will call me one, and my loyalty to Christ will be apparent when the world sees me no more. Nothing you can see is truly good. For our Lord Jesus Christ, now that he has returned to his Father, has revealed himself more clearly. Our task is not one of producing persuasive propaganda; Christianity shows its greatness when it is hated by the world.

I am writing to all the churches to declare to them all that I am glad to die for God, providing you do not hinder me. I beg you not to show me a misplaced kindness. Let me be the food of beasts that I may come to God. I am his wheat, and I shall be ground by the teeth of beasts, that I may become Christ's pure bread.

I would rather that you coaxed the beasts to become my tomb and to leave no scrap of me behind; then when I have died I will be a burden to no one. I shall be a true disciple of Christ when the world no longer sees my body. Pray to Christ for me that by these means I may become a sacrifice to God. I do not give you orders like Peter and Paul. They were apostles, I am a condemned criminal; they were free, I am still a slave. But if I suffer, I shall become the freedman of Jesus Christ and I shall rise again to freedom in him.

Now as a prisoner I am learning to give up my own wishes. All the way from Syria to Rome I am fighting wild beasts, by land and by sea, by day and by night, chained as I am to ten leopards, I mean the detachment of soldiers who guard me; the better you treat them, the worse they become. I am more and more trained in discipleship by their ill-usage of me, but I am not therefore justified. . . . Bear with me, for I know what is good for me. Now I am beginning to be a disciple. May nothing visible or invisible rob me of my prize, which is Jesus Christ! The fire, the cross, packs of wild beasts, lacerations, rendings, wrenching of bones, mangling of limbs, crushing of the whole body, the horrible tortures of the devil — let all these things come upon me, if only I may gain Jesus Christ![104]

St. Hallvard

A story, apparently based as much in fiction as in fact, is told about Hallvard (d. 1043), a Norwegian sailor. While working in the Drammenfjord Islands in the Baltic Sea, Hallvard was standing at dockside preparing his boat for departure. A young woman, who in some renditions of the story is described as pregnant, came running to him. She begged him to let her seek safety on his boat. He acquiesced. Soon, three men came running in hot pursuit of the woman. The three demanded that he hand her over to them. They accused her of stealing from them. Hallvard refused. "He said he was willing to give them the value of what she was accused of stealing."[105]

The pursuers rejected his offer. They wanted the woman. Neither the three men nor Hallvard gave in. One of the three assailants then raised his bow and shot to death Hallvard and the woman. The attackers tried to hide the evidence of their crime. They tied a large rock to Hallvard's neck and threw the body overboard. The corpse sank momentarily and then surfaced. Hallvard's killers were found out. Hallvard became famous as a hero in defense of innocent life.

St. Margaret of Scotland

Margaret (1045-1093) was born to an English prince and a German princess who were residing in exile at the court of King Stephen of Hungary, whose wife was related to Margaret's family. At twelve years of age, Margaret traveled to England, where she lived at the court of King Edward the Confessor. Nine years later, Margaret and her mother fled from England during the famous Battle of Hastings in 1066. They were received in Scotland by King Malcolm III, who married Margaret four years later.

Margaret brought much Christian, Hungarian, and English culture to relatively unchristianized and uncultured Scotland. She promoted faith and religion, the arts and education. She gained fame for her prayerfulness and practical charities for the poor. She gave birth to eight children, one of whom is also recognized as a saint.

Margaret was lying sick in bed at Edinburgh Castle when she received word that her husband and son had been killed by rebels at Alwick Castle. She prayed for mercy on the souls of all the deceased and that God would take her soul. When the rebels who had murdered her husband and son barged through the castle gates to kill her, she had already expired, having died from a broken heart.

St. John Baptist de la Salle

When John Baptist de la Salle (1651-1719) established schools to teach poor boys at no cost to them, he encountered vociferous opposition from teachers who taught for pay in other schools. His charity was undermining their livelihood, they complained.

The structure of the educational system in France at that time included three types of schools: first, "small schools" operated by lay teachers who received payment from approximately ten students of diverse age, ability, and accumulated knowledge; second, "bush schools" operated by priest-schoolmasters at a small cost to students who attended sporadically; and third, "charity schools" operated by La Salle's community of Brothers of the Christian Schools, who taught large classes gratis.

La Salle revolutionized the way in which teaching had been conducted since the classical philosophers in 500 B.C. In 1720, he published his well-practiced method, which remains in vogue almost three hundred years later. We glean from his book, *The Conduct of Schools*, his innovations that we take for granted now. His followers would not teach a dozen students in different subjects in a one-on-one context, but forty or fifty students the same subject at the same time, a method he called simultaneous education. His disciples would not teach in esoteric Latin, but in the vernacular. They would not teach for a price, but for free. La Salle's students were poor boys whom other teachers would have exiled to manual labor. La Salle's group taught not only the three R's but also religion, which was viewed as the main purpose of their schools and which integrated all other learning and activity. In order to provide qualified teachers, La Salle introduced Western civilization's first teacher-training colleges by inviting these new schoolmasters into his home for instruction. A close friend of La Salle and former superior of the brothers at Rouen produced the most reliable contemporary biography of La Salle. The friend writes:

> On this occasion the world expressed every disparaging remark that it could think of against good work in general and against those who devote themselves to them. With regard to this particular project and to its author, everybody expressed all the criticism, mockery and ridicule that the world's false wisdom, its characteristic spirit and its natural malignity suggested. The canon was cited to answer for his behavior before as many tribunals as there were families in the city. Everyone investigated him and set himself up as a judge; there were as many different sentences handed down as there were judges. But however diverse these verdicts were, in one respect, they all agreed: he was guilty and should be condemned.[106]

These changes upset not only the established pedagogy but more importantly the economic order of the teaching profession. The paid teachers protested in the streets. They gained the support of political and ecclesiastical leaders. They took La Salle to court and burdened him with lawsuits. They shut down temporarily his community's schools and houses throughout Paris and its suburbs. One biographer describes the situation.

> De la Salle, who detested suits, found himself dragged at the same time before the tribunals of the Church and the State. This double suit was due to the fact that the schoolmasters were under ecclesiastical protection, while the writing masters were protected by the civil authorities. Hence the municipality of Paris took the side of the latter and their case was tried before the ordinary magistrates. Like most legal battles, the war was waged on many fronts. To save a good deal of time, we may understand that the Brothers got the worst of it, for their work was attacked, their schools were closed, their books and furniture were confiscated, and large fines were imposed upon them. They were then forbidden to live in Paris or to form any Community there until they were in a position to produce a special permission from the King himself. Furthermore, this sentence was executed with the utmost severity. It was placarded in Paris, emissaries of the police appeared before the house occupied by them in the parish of St. Paul, their title was torn down from over the door and the

premises were ransacked and pillaged and left destitute of furniture, books, and Brothers.[107]

Many relatives and friends criticized La Salle for associating with low-born teachers and students, and for abdicating his aristocratic roots to pursue the pedestrian career of becoming a teacher. They judged him guilty, at best, of misguided altruism.

We know of these tirades against La Salle through his biographers. His own letters refer rarely and briefly to his sufferings. After the incidents described above, La Salle, at the end of a long letter to one of his brothers, writes simply: "Pray hard for us, who need it badly; we also shall pray for you."[108]

La Salle suffered when the poor suffered. To allow the educational system to continue the ancient way of instruction would continue the exclusion of the poor from the classroom and from a place among the burgeoning bourgeoisie. This idea of teaching poor boys was perceived as a divine call. "Once he [La Salle] became convinced that this was a divinely appointed mission, he threw himself wholeheartedly into the work, left home and family, abandoned his canonry, gave away his fortune and reduced himself to the level of the poor to whom he henceforth consecrated his life."[109]

REJECTION — FOR EDUCATING POOR GIRLS

St. Mary Mazzarello

The men and women of Mornese in the lower Piedmont region of Italy worked for five years to construct a school for boys. The pastor provided the vision and most of the money. The townspeople provided free labor on weekends and holidays. The saintly Don Bosco visited the town frequently and blessed the building, the laborers, and all the villagers. He continuously encouraged the townsfolk in their project, which reflected his own commitment to educate boys.

Just as the building was nearing completion in 1871, Bosco, however, felt called by God to found a community of nuns to do for girls what he had been doing for boys. This call was confirmed, he felt, when the bishop, who had just built a minor seminary for boys, wanted no competition for students from nearby Mornese. Bosco shared his idea with the pope, who responded, "In my opinion the Sisters should do for girls what the Salesians are doing for boys."[110] Bosco then confided his vision, as well as the bishop's and pope's positions, to the pastor. The saintly founder then swore the pastor to secrecy regarding the persons responsible for making this change; the pastor alone would have to accept responsibility.

Bosco's idea for the community of nuns was influenced by the exemplary work of Mary Mazzarello (1837-1881). Bosco had met Mary in Mornese in 1865, when he visited the sodality of the Daughters of Mary Immaculate and observed their "teaching catechism to children, organizing games, ministering to the sick, holding workshops in dressmaking, and doing little things for those in need."[111] Bosco tried to persuade these laywomen to become nuns. He urged them to educate girls, even though most of these peasant women themselves had never spent one day in school.

How might the pastor move the fledgling community of nuns into the school? Providence intervened. The parishioners, wanting to repair the pastor's home, suggested that he move temporarily into the Daughters' house next to the church and the Daughters move into the school. The move occurred, however, under the cover of darkness because the women were transferring more than temporary supplies. The townsfolk grew suspicious.

> Since it was Father Pestarino who had initiated the [school] project, who had persuaded the village council to endorse it and had aroused the enthusiasm of the whole community for it, they concluded that he had the most say in it. It followed, in their minds, that he had also played the key role in this betrayal. On his part, Father Pestarino felt bound to observe the promise of secrecy he made to Don Bosco, in the latter's attempt to save the good name of the Church. So perilous did his situation become that several men had to be posted outside his home to protect him! Part of the ire of the angry villagers now fell on the object of Father Pestarino's attentions, that is, on the girls themselves. Where before these had been of some service to the community, now they intended to withdraw from it and from the parents who had raised them. "What sort of gratitude was this?" they wanted to know. Just to please them, Father Pestarino seemed ready to sacrifice everything and everybody, even to the extent of neglecting his responsibilities to the rest of the flock. . . . It was not a pleasant time for Father Pestarino but he bore it all with characteristic silence and fortitude. The daughters had also to share in his sufferings.[112]

Many families refused permission to their elder daughters to associate with Mary, lest they become nuns and not marry. Families withdrew their younger daughters from Mary's workshops to demonstrate their opposition to her ministry. Neighbors ceased providing food and funds, which had supported Mary and her company. Mary kept encouraging her band, saying: "We may be women but that doesn't mean we're going to let people walk all over us. We have given ourselves to the Lord. Let the world say what it likes and let us do what we have to do to become saints."[113] The company of women became known as the Daughters of Our Lady Help of Christians, or the Salesian Sisters. At the time of Mary's death, ten years after their founding, the community had grown to thirty convents.

REJECTION — FOR LEADING AN ARMY

St. Joan of Arc

Joan of Arc (1412-1431) heard saints' voices instructing her to save France. But who would listen to Joan's voice? Military leaders listened only after her specific prophecies proved true and their military plans ended in defeat. Church leaders listened, and although they detected no theological errors, recommended that she be treated with suspicion. Lay leaders listened to her and followed her for a short while, but abandoned her soon after the army won its victories.

France's spirit was sapped by too many wars and too little leadership. France was in the throes of the Hundred Years' War against England, which had begun in 1337 and continued to 1457. During this century, there occurred also civil wars between the dukes of Burgundy and Orléans, the traitorous support of England by the Burgundians against Orléans, and the peasant revolts throughout the countryside. Political leadership failed to assert itself because King Charles VI was insane and the self-indulgent Charles VII preferred pleasures and pastimes to political responsibilities. Into this military maelstrom and political vacuum entered fourteen-year-old Joan of Arc.

Joan left the town of Domremy in the Lorraine region, presented herself to Charles VII at Chinon, and persuaded him to let her lead his army. Charles had nothing to lose; his back was against the wall of the Pyrennees. Joan then led the army, and in eight days freed the city of Orléans, which had been under siege for eight months. This seemed like a miracle. During the next two months, Joan literally cleared the way for Charles to travel from Orléans to Rheims, where he was crowned king. Joan wanted to continue the campaign, but the king and others refused to support her. She writes in 1429 to the inhabitants of the town of Riom:

Dear and good friends, you know well how the town of Saint-Pierre le Moustier was taken under assault, and, with God's help, I intend to free the other places that are against the king; but because a great amount of gunpowder, many arrows and other necessities of war were used before the said town, and the lords in that town and I are poorly provided to lay siege to La Charité, where we shall soon make our way, I beg you by your great love for the well-being and honor of the king, and also of all others thereafter, without delay to assist us in the said siege by sending powder, saltpeter, sulphur, arrows, strong crossbows and other necessities of war. For, consider, if we have the said powder and other necessities of war, the matter will soon be settled and no one will accuse you of negligence or refusing to help. Dear and good friends, may our Lord take care of you.[114]

The king ordered the attack, but did not provide sufficient resources. The town of Riom promised supplies, but did not deliver them. The grateful city of Orléans provided food, clothing, munitions, and money, but not in sufficient amounts. Joan laid siege to Saint-Pierre le Moustier, but she failed in her fight. Six months later, she was captured. The duke of Burgundy sold her to the English at a great price.

The English at Rouen tried her on the charges of heresy and witchcraft. The bishop of Beauvais, who allegedly hoped the English would appoint him the archbishop of Rouen, presided over the trial.[115] After three months of fierce and unsuccessful interrogation by learned theologians who were oftentimes outwitted by the unlearned Maid of Orléans, the episcopal judge tricked Joan into admitting apparent guilt. On May 30, having been found guilty of being a relapsed heretic, Joan was excommunicated, handed over to secular authorities, whose henchmen lit the fire surrounding the stake to which she was tied. She died, declaring her innocence.

Two decades after Joan's death, her mother and two siblings requested a review of the court proceedings. Joan's innocence was attested to by one hundred fifteen witnesses. The Church pondered the new evidence. Pope Callistus overrode the local bishop's earlier decision, but it was twenty-five years after Joan had been burned at the stake. She was canonized in 1920 by Pope Benedict XV.

St. Andrew Avellino

Andrew (1521-1608) was the religious name taken when the young priest Lancelot Avellino transferred in 1557 from the diocese of Naples and joined the new Theatine community founded by Cajetan.

As a young cleric, Lancelot received doctoral degrees in civil and canon law. After he found himself in a compromising legal position, he gave up the practice of law in favor of the pastoral care of souls.

In 1556 he was assigned by the local cardinal to reform the nuns of the convent of Sant' Archangelo at Baiano. "This convent had an evil reputation, and the efforts of the young priest were ill received by some of the nuns and certain men who used to visit them. These did not stop short of physical violence."[116] Actually "he was almost killed by those opposing his reforms."[117] His efforts at reform affected the nuns very little, and eventually the convent was suppressed.

St. Louis de Montfort

What is a hospital at the end of the seventeenth century? It would be naïve to imagine it as a place of medical care in the modern sense. A place for care, yes, and a place to die, but it is also an orphanage and a mental hospital, a prison, as well as a correctional institution. "Promiscuity, misery and infection reigned there." . . . "Hospitals were given such sweet names as Charity, Mercy, Good Shepherd, House of God, but they fooled no one. The sick hid for fear of being dragged there."[118]

Newly ordained, Louis Marie Grignion (1673-1716) entered the hospital at Poitiers to bring order into the "house of disorder where there is no peace whatsoever."[119] The hospital had one hundred fifty beds for three hundred patients. The staff consisted of volunteers only, who paid for their meals rather than eat the hospital-issued black bread. The institution had no resources except the charity of the local populace. Louis accepted the challenge: "All that I had been told by a number of experienced priests of the town to dissuade me from going to this ill-regulated house only increased my determination to undertake this work."[120]

Louis reformed the organization and operation of the hospital. He arranged for guests to eat in a common place at a common time; and even he himself took to begging in the streets for their food. Performing the lowliest housekeeping chores, he maintained the building as neat and clean as possible. He replaced the chaplain who had been doing the minimum of ministry, by naming himself to that position. "The poor felt the sublime quality in his goodness to them. Fed, taught, edified, loved, they were attached heart and soul to their chaplain and director."[121] The staff and administrators, however, perceived him as odd at best, probably insane, and a troublemaker no matter what his motivation.[122] They finally forced him to leave the hospital. Louis laments:

> I did this for three months, enduring opposition and snubs, which went on increasing day after day to such an extent that ultimately, through the disapproval of a certain gentleman and the matron of the workhouse, I was obliged to give up providing food for the dining-room of the poor. In giving this up, I acted in obedience to my director although the reorganization of the dining room had been a great help to the administration of the establishment.[123]

Then a plague struck the hospital. For two weeks, it took the lives of inmates and staff alike, including Louis's two major critics: his immediate superior and the overall supervisor. Louis was invited to return. He writes: "More than eighty of the poor inmates fell ill and some of them died, and the whole town began to say that there was a plague in the poorhouse and that the place was cursed. Through all this period of sickness, and in spite of my involvement with the dying, I was the only one not to be affected with the disease."[124]

After about two years' service, Louis was forced to resign by common complaint of the staff and inmates, as well as the priests and bishop. Even his spiritual director found Louis difficult and asked to be relieved of his duty: "As your conduct is not ordinary, it might be difficult for me to stand for all that you do, whilst I do not wish to set limits to the grace which perhaps draws you to act as you do."[125] Although he left the hospital, he remained at Poitiers in order to preach missions. In that ministry too, he offended so many ordinary people that the bishop withdrew from Louis permission to preach. Louis then walked to Rome, where the pope named him missionary apostolic and sent him back to France. Louis returned to his native Brittany, where he enjoyed success, although criticism surfaced again and many parishes and even some dioceses refused him permission to preach.

He achieved a great deal in his sixteen years in the priesthood. Ordained in 1700 at age twenty-eight, he founded the women's community of the Daughters of Divine Wisdom in 1702 and the men's community of Missionaries of the Company of Mary in 1715. "He composed more than 23,400 verses of hymns."[126] He wrote numerous books. His constant theme was: "Surrender to Christ through Mary."[127]

St. Marguerite d'Youville

Marguerite d'Youville (1701-1771) suffered repeatedly at the hands of her family and relatives, civil and religious authorities, "acts of God," and laypeople. These sufferings developed in her a deep sensitivity to render practical service to people in need. Her love was affective and effective.

Death took early and often those whom she loved. Her father died when she was seven. She married at twenty, and her husband died eight years later. Four of their six children died in infancy.

Dreams of blissful marriage unfolded into a nightmare. At eighteen, she was engaged to a young man who called off the wedding when Marguerite's widowed mother married beneath her class. She then married François d'Youville, who turned out to be a contemptible husband.

When she began a hospital for the poor, her family, civil and Church authorities, her two brothers-in-law, the king's intendant, and the bishop of Quebec opposed her work. Two fires razed the hospital in which she had invested all her earnings and efforts.

Unfounded rumors circulated about her romantic involvement with a priest. Another priest reacted by publicly refusing her and her nuns Holy Communion as they knelt at the altar rail.

During the seven-year War of 1753, she nursed soldiers of both the opposing French and English sides. When the war was over, the victorious English refused to provide her with any information about her priest-son whom the English had captured and kept imprisoned for four years.

Laypeople ridiculed Marguerite and her religious sisters for caring for people below the nuns' social class. Many of these poor were Native Americans who suffered from excessive drinking, which Marguerite's husband had promoted by trading them liquor for furs. The French word "*gris*" has a double meaning: gray, which describes the color of the nuns' habit; and drunk, which describes the habit of many of the people whom the sisters assisted. Marguerite and her nuns became known as, *Les soeurs grises* — The tipsy nuns![128]

The superior of the Sulpician priests, a Father Normant, assisted the nuns in acquiring the administration of the General Hospital. Another religious community had founded the hospital, but because of fiscal mismanagement had driven the institution into bankruptcy. The city's old guard, however, resisted what they called a "takeover" by the nuns.

> On the feast of All Saints, the four women, leaving together to attend Mass at Notre Dame, were openly assailed in the street. Angry citizens, persuaded now that Father Normant intended to get these women into their General Hospital, blocked their way, hissing, mocking, reviling them. *"Les soeurs grises!"* they shouted. *"Grises! Grises!"* Madame d'Youville, imperious in her spiritual strength, made her way in silence through the crowd, followed by her companions, equally silent, equally courageous. Several men, infuriated by their unassailable peace, picked up stones and savagely hurled them, striking the gentle women as they passed on.[129]

Marguerite transcended all these hurts as she and her colleagues signed their Original Commitment, which every Grey Nun since 1745 has signed. The document reads in part:

> We, the undersigned, for the greater glory of God, the salvation of our souls, and the relief of the poor, wishing sincerely to leave the world and to renounce everything that we possess in order to consecrate ourselves to the service of the destitute, united only by the bonds of charity (without any intention on our part of forming a new community), in order to live and die together, so that this union may be firm and lasting, have unanimously agreed and of our own free will have promised the following: . . . to live together for the rest of our lives in perfect union and charity, . . . to consecrate our time, our days, our work, even our lives, to labor, the product thereof to be put in common to provide subsistence for the poor and for ourselves, . . . to receive, feed, shelter as many poor as we can take care by ourselves or by the alms of the faithful.[130]

SEXUAL HARASSMENT

St. Charles Lwanga

The Christian faith was brought to Uganda in Central Africa in 1879, when the White Fathers evangelized and baptized the natives. Seven years later, Charles Lwanga and a group of twenty-two companions died for the faith.

Chief Mtesa, who originally received the White Fathers, was succeeded by Chief Mwanga, who rejected outright the teachings of the Christian faith. "Mwanga was addicted to unnatural vice," and his fears of mutiny and a coup by ambitious soldiers were intensified "by the refusal of Christian boys in his service to minister to his wickedness."[131]

The master of the royal pages oversaw the behavior of the young men. Charles's predecessor as master of the pages, Joseph Mkasa, was a good Christian who hid the pages from the chief's sexual advances. After Joseph admonished Mwanga for his immoral behavior, the chief beheaded Joseph. This murder occurred in November 1885.

In May 1886, Mwanga invited a young page, Mwafu, to the royal quarters for immoral purposes. Mwafu resisted the advances of the chief. Mwafu excused himself, saying that the behavior was contrary to Christian teaching, which he had begun studying recently. The chief became furious at the promoters of this religion that prohibited his indulgence. The chief called to his quarters Mwafu's instructor, Denis Sebuggwawo, and thrust a spear through his throat. Immediately, soldiers surrounded the encampment of the royal pages so that none could escape.

During that night of arrest, Charles Lwanga baptized four of the boys who were already catechumens. At daylight, the soldiers ordered all the pages to gather and then to divide themselves into two groups: Christian and non-Christian. Fifteen followers of Christ, boys between the ages of fifteen and twenty-five, stepped forward immediately. Two other youths and two soldiers then joined the group. "Mwanga asked them if they intended to remain Christian. 'Till death!' came the response; 'then put them to death,' he replied!"[132]

The group was force-marched to a camp thirty-seven miles away. Three boys were killed along the route. The others, once having arrived in camp, were tortured for seven days. Finally, a huge funeral pyre was readied, the boys were stripped naked, wrapped in a garment of reed, and laid on the pyre, which was set afire. Among the boys was the son of the chief executioner, who eased his son's sufferings by killing him before placing him on the pyre. Words praising Jesus could be heard from the boys' lips as they writhed in the flames consuming their bodies.

As always, the blood of martyrs is the seed of Christians. Within a year after the death of Charles Lwanga and his companions, the number of baptized and catechumens tripled.

Endnotes

1. The two other popes are St. Gregory the Great, who reigned from 590 to 604, and St. Nicholas the Great, who reigned from 858 to 867.
2. Leo the Great, sermon LXXXIV, 9, "Concerning the Neglect of the Commemoration," in *The Letters and Sermons of Leo the Great, Bishop of Rome*, tr. by Charles Lett Feltoe. *Nicene and Post-Nicene Fathers of the Christian Church*. Second Series. Ed. by Philip Schaff and Henry Wace, 1956 (New York: The Christian Literature Co., 1889), vol. XII.
3. Gregory's former teacher, John Gratian, upon being named pope as Gregory VI in 1045, appointed Hildebrand as his archdeacon. When Gregory VI died, Hildebrand entered the monastery, probably at Cluny, where his friend Hugh was abbot. After two years in which two popes came, served, and passed quickly to eternal life, the next five popes asked Hildebrand to serve as their chief adviser.
4. *Butler's Lives of the Saints,* ed. by Herbert Thurston and Donald Attwater, four volumes (Westminster, Md.: Christian Classics, 1990), vol. II, p. 387.
5. Ibid.
6. Ibid., p. 386.
7. A Benedictine monk of Stanbrook Abbey, ed., *Letters from the Saints* (New York: Hawthorne Books, Inc., 1964), pp. 175-176.
8. J.N.D. Kelly, *The Oxford Dictionary of Popes* (New York: Oxford University Press, 1986), p. 156.
9. All nine of the churches remain active to this day: San Diego de Alcalá (1769), San Carlos de Monterrey (1770), San Antonio de Padua (1771), San Gabriel de los Temblores (1771), San Luís Obispo (1772), San Francisco (1776), San Juan Capistrano (1776), Santa Clara (1777), and San Buenaventura (1782).
10. Marion A. Habig and Francis B. Steck, *Man of Greatness: Father Junípero Serra* (Chicago: Franciscan Herald Press, 1963), p. 46.
11. Winifred E. Wise, *Fray Junípero Serra and the California Conquest* (New York: Charles Scribner's Sons, 1967), p. 85.
12. Wise, p. 95.
13. Ibid., pp. 129-130, 140.
14. Ibid., p. 113.
15. Butler, vol. I, p. 571.
16. Ibid., pp. 572-573.
17. M. David Knowles, "Becket, Thomas, St.," in *New Catholic Encyclopedia*, vol. 2, p. 213.
18. John J. Delaney, *Dictionary of Saints* (Garden City, N.Y.: Doubleday and Co., Inc., 1980), p. 553.

19. J. A. Giles, *The Life and Letters of Thomas à Becket* (London: Whittaker and Co., 1846), pp. 348-350, 361-362, 376.

20. David Knowles, *Thomas Becket* (Stanford, Calif.: Stanford University Press, 1971), p. 139.

21. Placido Erdozain, *Archbishop Romero: Martyr of Salvador*, tr. by John McFadden and Ruth Warner (Maryknoll, N.Y.: Orbis Books, 1981), p. 76.

22. Ibid., pp. 77-78.

23. Ibid., pp. 75-76.

24. Butler, vol. IV, p. 372.

25. Delaney, p. 293.

26. A Benedictine monk, p. 276.

27. Patricia Treece, *A Man for Others: Maximilian Kolbe, Saint of Auschwitz, In the Words of Those Who Knew Him* (San Francisco: Harper and Row Publishers, 1982), pp. 165-166.

28. Ibid., p. 167.

29. Ibid., p. 169.

30. Ibid., pp. 170-171.

31. Delaney, p. 237.

32. Butler, vol. IV, p. 476.

33. Josef Wicki, "Xavier, Francis, St.," in *New Catholic Encyclopedia*, vol. 14, p. 1059.

34. A Benedictine monk of Stanbrook Abbey, ed., *Letters from the Saints* (New York: Hawthorne Books, Inc., 1964), pp. 234-235.

35. *The Tablet*, vol. 89, no. 40, December 28, 1996; p. 2.

36. M.N.L. Couve de Murville, *Slave from Haiti: A Saint for New York? The Life of Pierre Toussaint* (London: Incorporated Catholic Truth Society Publications, 1995), p. 5.

37. Ibid.

38. Ibid., p. 8.

39. Ibid., p. 23.

40. Ibid., p. 26.

41. Mary Jean Dorcy, "Joan of France (Valois), St.," in *New Catholic Encyclopedia*, vol. 7, p. 993.

42. *Liturgy of the Hours: Proper of the Congregation of the Mission* (New York: Catholic Book Publishing Co., 1978), pp. 39-41.

43. Butler, vol. III, p. 233.

44. The epithet of "Blessed" was never applied to Julian by the Church officially but popularly in recognition of her widespread fame for sanctity.

45. Julian of Norwich, *Showings*, tr. by Edmund Colledge and James Walsh (New York: Paulist Press, 1978), p. 10.

46. Joan M. Nuth, *Wisdom's Daughter: The Theology of Julian of Norwich* (New York: The Crossroad Publishing Co., 1991), p. 21.

47. Among outstanding women teachers were Mechtilde of Madgeburg, Mechtilde of Hackeborn, Gertrude of Helfta, Catherine of Genoa, Catherine of Siena, Hildegard of Bingen, and Bridget of Sweden.

48. Nuth, p. 21.

49. Ibid.

50. Ibid.

51. Ibid., p. 115.

52. Ibid., pp. 20-21.

53. Ibid., p. 192.

54. Barbara Tuchman, *A Distant Mirror: The Calamitous 14th Century* (New York: Alfred A. Knopf, 1978).

55. The calamitous events include the Black Death, the Hundred Years' War, the Avignon Papacy, the Great Western Schism, the prosecution of heresy throughout western Europe, the peasants' uprising of 1381, and the troubled reign of King Richard II.

56. Butler, vol. II, p. 303.

57. Her contemplation resulted in revelations on human nature and God's divine nature, Jesus' incarnation and passion, God's grace and goodness, our lapses into sin and God's all-forgiving love. She wrote two books, a *Short Text of Showings* soon after the visions and the *Long Text of Showings* twenty years later. She was well educated; she referred to and quoted the Latin Vulgate edition of the Bible, Augustine, Gregory the Great, Thomas Aquinas, and Chaucer.

58. Butler, vol. II, pp. 302-303.

59. Ibid., p. 349.

60. Dunstan Pontifex, "St. Dunstan in His First Biography," *Downside Review*, vol. 51, 1933, p. 36.

61. Stubbs, a renowned scholar on the subject of Dunstan, writes, "The monstrous lust of such a mere child as Edwy could not have been a main feature of a story told by Dunstan himself. . . . The offense given to Dunstan may easily be accounted for the relationship of Edwy and Ethelgifu (the mother of Elgiva)" (William Stubbs, *Memorials of Saint Dunstan, Archbishop of Canterbury*, in the series *Chronicles and Memorials of Great Britain and Ireland During the Middle Ages* [Munich, Germany: Kraus Reprint Ltd., 1965]; p. lxxxix).

62. Pontifex, p. 37.

63. Ibid.

64. Stubbs, p. lxxxiv.

65. The name Chrysostom means golden-mouthed.

66. John Cumming, ed., *Letters from Saints to Sinners* (New York: The Crossroad Publishing Co., 1996), pp. 81-82.

67. Paul William Harkins, "John Chrysostom, St.," in *New Catholic Encyclopedia*, vol. 7, p. 1043.

68. Bede Camm, ed., *Lives of the English Martyrs Declared Blessed by Pope Leo XIII in 1886 and 1895*, vol. 1, *Martyrs Under Henry VIII* (London: Burnes and Oates Limited, 1904), p. 529.

69. "In 1538, two other sons [of Margaret] were arrested and executed on a charge of treason, even though Cromwell wrote that their only crime was being brothers of the cardinal" (Delaney, p. 474).

70. Butler, vol. II, p. 413.

71. Camm, p. 528.

72. Ibid., p. 530.

73. Ibid., pp. 522-523.

74. Luke 7:37.

75. Ibid., 8:2-3.

76. Carroll Stuhlmueller, "The Gospel According to Luke," in *The Jerome Biblical Commentary* (Englewood Cliffs, N.J.: Prentice-Hall, Inc., 1968), p. 138.

77. Anne Fremantle, *Desert Calling* (New York: Henry Holt and Co., 1949), p. 48.

78. Michel Carrouges, *Soldier of the Spirit: The Life of Charles de Foucauld*, tr. by Marie-Christine Hellin (New York: G. P. Putnam's Sons, 1956), p. 14.

79. Ibid., p. 16.

80. Ibid., pp. 16-17.

81. Ibid., p. 17.

82. Ibid., p. 20.

83. Vincent J. O'Malley, *Saintly Companions* (New York: Alba House, 1995), p. 110.

84. Ibid.

85. Richard J. Kehoe, "John Gabriel Perboyre, C.M.; Canonized a Saint, June 2, 1996" (published privately at St. John's University, New York City), p. 5.

86. Ibid.

87. André Sylvestre, *John Gabriel Perboyre, C.M.: China's First Saint*, tr. by John E. Rybolt (Strasbourg, France: Editions du Signe, 1996), p. 24.

88. Ibid., p. 25.

89. Ibid., p. 26.

90. Ibid., p. 27.

91. Ibid., p. 327.

92. Butler, vol. IV, p. 157.

93. The other three are named Stephen the Younger, Andrew, and Paul.

94. Butler, vol. IV, p. 466.

95. Camm, vol. II, p. 467.

96. Ibid., p. 468.

97. Ibid., pp. 348-349.

98. Angus MacDougall, *Martyrs of New France* (Midland, Ontario: Martyrs' Shrine Publication, 1972), p. 12.

99. The Benedictine monks of Ramsgate Abbey, eds., *The Book of Saints* (Wilton, Conn.: Morehouse Publishing, 1989), pp. 37-39.

100. MacDougall, p. 15.

101. Butler, vol. I, p. 219.

102. Delaney, p. 297.

103. Francis Xavier Murphy, "Ignatius of Antioch, St.," in *New Catholic Encyclopedia*, vol. 7, p. 353.

104. *Liturgy of the Hours*, vol. III (New York: Catholic Book Publishing Co., 1975), pp. 324-325.

105. Butler, vol. II, p. 322.

106. John Baptist Blain, *The Life of John Baptist de la Salle: Founder of the Brothers of the Christian Schools*, tr. by Richard Arnandez (Rouen, France: John Baptist Machuel, with the approbation and authorization of the king; 1733; and Montini High School, Lombard, Ill.), p. 65.

107. Martin Dempsey, *John Baptist de la Salle: His Life and His Institute* (Milwaukee: The Bruce Publishing Co., 1940), pp. 112-113.

108. John Baptist de la Salle, *De la Salle: Letters and Documents*, ed. by William John Battersby (London: Longmans, Green and Co., 1952), p. 59.

109. William John Battersby, "La Salle, John Baptist De, St.," in *New Catholic Encyclopedia*, vol. 8, p. 390.

110. Peter Lappin, *Halfway to Heaven* (New Rochelle, N.Y.: Don Bosco Publications, 1981), p. 84.

111. Pietro Stella, *Don Bosco: Life and Work*, tr. by John Drury (New Rochelle, N.Y.: Don Bosco Publications, 1985), p. 214.

112. Ibid.

113. Ibid., p. 93.

114. Cumming, p. 122.

115. Butler, vol. II, p. 429.

116. Ibid., vol. IV, p. 305.

117. Delaney, p. 81.

118. Benedetta Papasogli, *Wisdom of the Heart: The Story of Marie Louise Trichet* (Bayshore, N.Y.: Montfort Publications, 1993), p. 21.

119. Ibid., p. 24.

120. Louis Marie Grignion de Montfort, *The Collected Writings of St. Louis Marie de Montfort: God Alone* (Bayshore, N.Y.: Montfort Publications, 1988), p. 15.

121. George Rigault, *Saint Louis-Marie Grignion de Montfort: His Life and Work*, tr. by D.M.D.B. (Port Jefferson, N.Y.: The Montfort Fathers, 1947), p. 48.

122. "His oddities had full play here, and did not always call for imitation. He emptied slops, used the cups of those who had skin disease, and one day having cleaned an ulcer, swallowed the water with which he had done so" (Rigault, p. 48).

123. Ibid., pp. 26-27.

124. Ibid., pp. 15-16.

125. Rigault, p. 47.

126. John Patrick Gaffney, "Grignion de Montfort, Louis Marie, St.," in *New Catholic Encyclopedia*, vol. 6, p. 805.

127. Ibid.

128. Mary Pauline Fitts, *Hands to the Needy. Blessed Marguerite d'Youville: Apostle to the Poor* (Garden City, N.Y.: Doubleday and Co., Inc., 1971), p. 95.

129. Ibid., pp. 98-99.

130. Ibid., p. 115.

131. Butler, vol. II, pp. 468-469.

132. Ibid., p. 469.

Epilogue

How did the saints respond to suffering? The saints generally faced and felt their suffering, identified with Jesus in his suffering, and transcended suffering by serving other people.

The saints faced their suffering. They accepted reality; they did not deny it. For example, St. John de Brébeuf (1593-1649) explains graphically to his confreres in France the conditions Jesuit missionaries ought to expect in the New World.

> However careworn and weary you may be, we can offer you nothing but a poor mat, or at best a skin rug for a bed; added to that, you will arrive at a time of year when fleas will keep you awake almost all night. And this petty martyrdom, to say nothing of mosquitoes, sandflies, and suchlike gentry, lasts usually not less than three or four months of the summer.
>
> As for the winter, how do you imagine you will spend it? I am not exaggerating when I tell you that five to six months of winter are passed in almost continual discomforts — bitter cold, smoke, and vexations from the natives. We have a simple log cabin, but so well jointed that we have to send someone outside to see what the weather is like. The smoke is very often so thick, so stifling, and so persistent, that for five or six days at a time, unless you are completely hardened to such conditions, it is all you can do to decipher a line or two of your Breviary.
>
> So far we have looked only on the bright side. As we have Christians in almost every village, we have to reckon on making the rounds at all seasons, and on staying in any place if necessity demands for two or three whole weeks, amid indescribable annoyances. Moreover our lives hang upon a single thread. Apart from the fact that your cabin is merely, so to speak, a thing of straw, and may be burned down at any moment, the ill-will of the natives is enough to keep us in a state of almost perpetual fear. A malcontent may set you on fire, or choose some lonely spot to split your skull open. And then you are held responsible for the barrenness or fruitfulness of the earth on pain of your life: you are the cause of drought; if you cannot make rain, they go so far as threatening to do away with you. I leave you to imagine if we have any grounds for feeling secure.
>
> There is no inducement whatever here to the practice of virtue. We live among tribes who have no idea of what you mean when you

speak to them of God, and whose mouths are often filled with horrible blasphemies. You are occasionally forced to forgo offering the holy Sacrifice of the Mass; and when you are able to say it, a little corner of your cabin must serve you as chapel. . . . I need not warn you that there is not much chance of privacy with the natives all round; they scarcely ever leave you, and hardly know what it is to speak in a low tone. One point I dare not discuss: the risk of disaster from falling into their impurity, if a man's heart is not sufficiently filled with God to be steadfast in resisting this poison.[1]

The saints felt their sufferings. They were in touch with their feelings; they did not repress them. For example, St. Thérèse of Lisieux (1873-1897) describes her profound feelings at difficult moments. When she was four, Thérèse lost her mother. Thérèse writes: "The moment Mummy died, my happy disposition changed completely. I had been lively and cheerful, but I became timid and quiet and a bundle of nerves."[2] Five years later, Thérèse's heart broke further when her eldest sister, Pauline, left home to enter the monastery of Carmel. In her autobiography, Thérèse addresses her words to Pauline:

> I have to speak of that grievous separation which almost broke my heart — when Jesus took away from me that little mother [Pauline] whom I loved so dearly. . . . How can I express the agony I suffered. In a flash I understood what life was. Until then I had not seen it as too sad a business, but now I saw it as it really was — a thing of suffering and continual partings. I cried bitterly, for I knew nothing of the joy of sacrifice. I was weak, so weak that I thought it a great grace that I could endure a trial which seemed so much beyond my strength.[3]

As a teenager, Thérèse traveled to Rome with her father in order to ask the pope face-to-face for the exceptional permission to enter Carmel at the age of fifteen. At the end of Mass in the pope's private chapel, the guests were invited to receive the pope's blessing. Thérèse relates the experience.

> Not a word was uttered, but I was determined to speak. Suddenly, though, [the Vicar-General of the diocese of Bayeux] Father Reverony, who was standing on the right of His Holiness, told us in a loud voice that it was absolutely forbidden to speak to the Holy Father. With a madly beating heart I gave a questioning glance at [my sister] Céline. "Speak!" she whispered. A moment later I was kneeling

before the Pope. I kissed his slipper and he offered me his hand. Then, looking at him with my eyes wet with tears, I said: "Most Holy Father, I have a great favour to ask." He leant forward until his face almost touched mine, as if his dark, searching eyes would pierce the depths of my soul. "Most Holy Father," I said, "to mark your jubilee, allow me to enter Carmel at fifteen."[4]

The vicar-general interrupted immediately, "with a look of astonished displeasure."[5] He explained to the pope that local authorities were already investigating the matter. The pope replied, "Very well, my child, do whatever they say."[6] Thérèse blurted out, "O Most Holy Father, if you say yes, everybody will be only too willing."[7] She continues, "He gazed at me steadily and said in a clear voice, stressing every syllable, 'Come, come, . . . you will enter if God wills it.' "[8] With that, two Swiss Guards took her by the arms, lifted her up, and carried her away. Thérèse felt crushed.

> My suffering was severe. . . . That day the sun dared not shine, and from the gloomy clouds which covered the blue Italian sky the rain poured down as I wept. Everything was over: all the pleasures had gone from my journey, as the whole point of it had just been destroyed.[9]

The saints identified with Jesus. The saints believed that Jesus' "active endurance" of suffering had been redemptive.[10] Suffering was not meaningless, but meaningful. What had seemed senseless, made sense in Jesus. For example, St. Frances Xavier Cabrini (1850-1917), who emigrated from Italy to the United States and established against great odds dozens of hospitals, schools, and orphanages, provides posterity with the prayer that indicates her identification with Jesus.

> From these holy exercises, O Lord, Your mercy has urged me to wish to suffer for the love of You, Jesus, and to imitate Your life, which was a continual martyrdom. Give me the desire to humble myself for Your love. Enlighten me how to do so when humiliating occasions present themselves. When I do not feel inclined to follow Your holy inspirations, help me to do so. O Heart of Jesus, by the agonizing abandonment which You experienced in the Garden of Gethsemane, by the horror which You felt when You saw Yourself covered with sins, which made You sweat blood, help me and give me courage to overcome those obstacles which would make me less pleasing to You. Yes, yes, O most beloved Jesus, allow me to keep You company in the Gar-

den of Olives in place of Your disciples who slept. My Jesus, I long . . . to wipe from Your brow the drops of precious blood, with the hope of securing my salvation and the utmost perfection. Lord, unite me closely to You; never let me go away from You, my Love; O Heart of my heart, Life of my life! O most comforting sweetness of my soul! As You have always inspired me, O my God, behold that I offer myself to You today and for all my life as a sacrifice to share Your painful agony in the Garden of Olives.[11]

The saints transcended sufferings by serving other people. These Christian heroes and heroines reached out beyond themselves to touch the lives of other people. These saints led self-sacrificing and self-giving lives. For example, St. Louise de Marillac (1591-1660) rose above her personal hurts to reach out to the poorest of the poor. Born an illegitimate child, Louise was accepted by no family member except her father. When she attempted to enter religious life, authorities rejected her on the grounds of weak health. She married, but her husband died twelve years later. Her only child entered the seminary three times but left each time, and eventually moved in with a wayward woman by whom he fathered a child and whom he married nine years later. Because Louise constantly worried about her unsettled son, St. Vincent de Paul (1580-1660) advised her to focus attention not on her worries but on the needs of other people. Vincent, writing to Louise, gives her much the same advice he had offered to St. Jane de Chantal (1572-1641), who had a similarly restless son.

> What shall I say to you now about your son, except that, just as we were not to put too much trust in the affection he used to have for the community, we must also not be troubled about the different feeling he has now. Leave him alone then, and surrender him completely to what Our Lord wills or does not will. It rests with Him alone to direct these tender souls. He is also more interested in this than you, because he belongs more to Him than to you. When I have the pleasure of seeing you, or more time than at present to write to you, I shall tell you the thought that came to me one day and which I shared with Madame de Chantal concerning this matter. It consoled her and, by the mercy of God, freed her from a sorrow similar to that which you may be suffering. Until we next see each other then. And if your other difficulty troubles you, write to me about it and I shall answer you.
>
> Meanwhile, get ready to do an act of charity for two poor girls

whom we have decided should leave here. We shall send them to you from here in a week's time and ask you to direct them to some good woman who can find them work as servants, unless you know some upright lady who may need them.[12]

Relevancy for today. Everybody suffers. Suffering is universal and inevitable; no one escapes suffering. The reader is invited, therefore, to identify with the saints who have experienced suffering in sickness and death, with family members and friends, in the Church and in society at large. The reader is invited to respond, as did the saints, who faced and felt their suffering, identified with Jesus, and then reached out to serve others.

By their responses to suffering, the saints grew more human and more Christian. Suffering can be a blessing. When someone accepts one's limitations, that person is freed to accept Jesus' limitless love. The void in every person's life can be filled by Jesus. The Paschal Mystery, which is Jesus' experience of his suffering, death, and resurrection, models the Christian life. Although an individual cannot control much of the suffering that occurs in life, yet each individual can control much of one's response to suffering. By the grace of God, each person can become in the midst of suffering more human and more Christian. Each person can become like the saints who also suffered.

Endnotes

1. A Benedictine monk of Stanbrook Abbey, ed., *Letters from the Saints* (New York: Hawthorne Books, Inc., 1964), pp. 33-35.
2. Thérèse of Lisieux, *The Autobiography of St. Thérèse of Lisieux: The Story of a Soul,* tr. by John Beevers (Garden City, N.Y.: Image Books, 1957), p. 29.3. Ibid., p. 41.
4. Ibid., p. 83.
5. Ibid.
6. Ibid., p. 84.
7. Ibid.
8. Ibid.
9. Ibid., pp. 84-85.
10. Richard Sparks, "Suffering," in *The New Dictionary of Catholic Spirituality*, ed. by Michael Downey (Collegeville, Minn.: The Liturgical Press, 1993), p. 953.
11. Mother Frances Xavier Cabrini, *The Awakening* (New York: Missionary Sisters of the Sacred Heart, 1996), p. 45.

12. Vincent de Paul, *Correspondence, Conferences, Documents,* vol. 1, *Correspondence I (1607-1639),* newly tr. by Helen Marie Law and others, ed. by Jacqueline Kilar (Brooklyn: New City Press, 1985), pp. 34-35.

The Saints at a Glance

Saint	Century[1]	Continent[2]	Vocation[3]
Alphonsus Liguori, St.	18th	Europe	Clergy
André of Montreal, Bl.	20th	N. America	Laity, Religious
Andrew Avellino, St.	17th	Europe	Clergy
Andrew of Crete, St.	8th	Europe	Clergy
Anthony Mary Claret, St.	19th	N. America	Clergy
Augustine of Hippo, St.	5th	Africa	Clergy
Benedict Joseph Labre, St.	18th	Europe	Laity, Single
Benedict of Monte Cassino, St.	6th	Europe	Clergy
Bernadette Soubirous, St.	19th	Europe	Laity, Religious
Boniface of Canterbury, St.	8th	Europe	Clergy
Camillus de Lellis, St.	17th	Europe	Clergy
Catherine de Hueck Doherty	20th	N. America	Laity, Married
Catherine Labouré, St.	19th	Europe	Laity, Religious
Catherine McAuley, Ven.	19th	Europe	Laity, Religious
Catherine of Genoa, St.	16th	Europe	Laity, Married
Catherine of Siena, St.	14th	Europe	Laity, Single
Charles Borromeo, St.	16th	Europe	Clergy
Charles de Foucauld, Ven.	20th	Africa	Clergy
Charles Lwanga, St.	19th	Africa	Laity, Single
Clare of Assisi, St.	13th	Europe	Laity, Religious
Cyprian of Carthage, St.	3rd	Africa	Clergy
Cyril of Moravia, St.	9th	Europe	Clergy
Damien the Leper, Bl.	19th	Asia	Clergy
Dorothy Day	20th	N. America	Laity, Married
Dunstan, St.	10th	Europe	Clergy
Dymphna, St.	7th	Europe	Laity, Single
Edith Stein, St.	20th	Europe	Laity, Religious
Edmund Campion, St.	16th	Europe	Clergy
Elizabeth Ann Seton, St.	19th	N. America	Laity, Married, Religious
Fabiola, St.	4th	Europe	Laity, Married
Frances Cabrini, St.	20th	Europe, N. America	Laity, Religious
Francis Borgia, St.	16th	Europe	Laity, Married, Clergy
Francis of Assisi, St.	13th	Europe	Laity, Religious
Francis Xavier, St.	16th	Asia	Clergy
Frederic Ozanam, Bl.	19th	Europe	Laity, Married
Gregory Nazianzen, St.	4th	Asia	Clergy
Gregory the Great, St.	7th	Europe	Clergy
Gregory VII, St.	11th	Europe	Clergy
Hallvard, St.	11th	Europe	Laity, Single
Hedwig of Poland, Bl.	14th	Europe	Laity, Married
Helena of Constantinople, St.	4th	Asia	Laity, Married
Herman the Cripple, Bl.	11th	Europe	Clergy
Hildegard of Bingen, St.	12th	Europe	Laity, Religious
Hugh of Lincoln, St.	13th	Europe	Clergy
Ignatius Loyola, St.	16th	Europe	Clergy
Ignatius of Antioch, St.	2nd	Asia	Clergy
Isaac Jogues, St.	17th	N. America	Clergy
Jane Frances de Chantal, St.	17th	Europe	Laity, Married, Religious
Joan of Arc, St.	15th	Europe	Laity, Single
Joan of Valois, St.	16th	Europe	Laity, Married

1. The criterion for the century is the date of the person's death.
2. The criterion for the continent is the place where the person ministered.
3. The criterion for vocation is canon no. 207, which classifies the Christian faithful as either clergy or laity.

John Baptist de la Salle, St.	18th	Europe	Clergy
John Chrysostom, St.	5th	Asia	Clergy
John Gabriel Perboyre, St.	19th	Asia, Europe	Clergy
John Neumann, St.	19th	N. America	Clergy
John Newman, Ven.	19th	Europe	Clergy
John of God, St.	16th	Europe	Laity, Single
John of the Cross, St.	16th	Europe	Clergy
John XXIII, Pope	20th	Europe	Clergy
John Vianney, St.	19th	Europe	Clergy
Josaphat, St.	17th	Europe	Clergy
Joseph Bernardin, Cardinal	20th	N. America	Clergy
Joseph Calasanctius, St.	17th	Europe	Clergy
Julian of Norwich, Bl.	15th	Europe	Laity, Single
Junípero Serra, Bl.	18th	N. America	Clergy
Justin de Jacobis, St.	19th	Africa	Clergy
Juvenal Ancina, Bl.	17th	Europe	Clergy
Kateri Tekakwitha, Bl.	17th	N. America	Laity, Single
Katharine Drexel, Bl.	20th	N. America	Laity, Religious
Leo the Great, St.	5th	Europe	Clergy
Louis de Montfort, St.	18th	Europe	Clergy
Louis Martin	19th	Europe	Laity, Married
Louise de Marillac, St.	17th	Europe	Laity, Religious
Magdalene di Canossa, Bl.	19th	Europe	Laity, Religious
Margaret Mary Alacoque, St.	17th	Europe	Laity, Religious
Margaret of Cortona, St.	13th	Europe	Laity, Single
Margaret of Scotland, St.	11th	Europe	Laity, Married
Margaret Pole, Bl.	16th	Europe	Laity, Married
Marguerite d'Youville, St.	18th	N. America	Laity, Married, Religious
Maria Goretti, St.	20th	Europe	Laity, Single
Martin de Porres, St.	17th	S. America	Laity, Religious
Mary Magdalene, St.	1st	Asia	Laity, Single
Mary Mazzarello, St.	19th	Europe	Laity, Religious
Matt Talbot, Bl.	20th	Europe	Laity, Single
Maximilian Kolbe, St.	20th	Europe	Clergy
Maximilian of Numidia, St.	3rd	Africa	Laity, Single
Methodius, St.	9th	Europe	Clergy
Monica, St.	4th	Africa	Laity, Married
Oscar Romero, Bishop	20th	N. America	Clergy
Padre Pio, Bl.	20th	Europe	Clergy
Patrick, St.	5th	Europe	Clergy
Paul, St.	1st	Asia	Clergy
Philip Neri, St.	16th	Europe	Clergy
Pierre Toussaint, Ven.	19th	N. America	Laity, Married
Raymond of Capua, Bl.	14th	Europe	Clergy
Robert Bellarmine, St.	17th	Europe	Clergy
Rose Philippine Duchesne, St.	19th	Europe, N. America	Laity, Religious
Seraphina Sforza, Bl.	15th	Europe	Laity, Married, Religious
Stanislaus Kostka, St.	16th	Europe	Clergy
Teresa of Calcutta, Mother	20th	Asia	Laity, Religious
Thérèse de Soubiran, Bl.	19th	Europe	Laity, Religious
Thérèse of Lisieux, St.	19th	Europe	Laity, Religious
Thomas Aquinas, St.	13th	Europe	Clergy
Thomas Becket, St.	12th	Europe	Clergy
Thomas More, St.	16th	Europe	Clergy
Vincent de Paul, St.	17th	Europe	Clergy

Bibliography

Ahern, Patrick. *Maurice and Thérèse. The Story of a Love*. New York: Doubleday and Co., Inc., 1998.

Alacoque, Margaret Mary. *The Autobiography of Saint Margaret Mary*. Tr. by Vincent Kerns. Westminster, Md.: The Newman Press, 1961.

Augustine of Hippo. *The Confessions of St. Augustine*. Tr. by John K. Ryan. New York: Image Books, 1960.

Bacci. *The Life of Saint Philip Neri: Apostle of Rome, and Founder of the Congregation of the Oratory*. Ed. and rev. by Frederick Ignatius Antrobus. St. Louis: B. Herder, 1903. Two volumes.

Baldwin, Lou. *A Call to Sanctity: The Formation and Life of Mother Katherine Drexel*. Philadelphia: The Catholic Standard and Times, 1987.

Ball, Ann. *Modern Saints: Their Lives and Faces*. Rockford, Ill.: Tan Books and Publishers, Inc., 1983.

Battersby, William John. "La Salle, John Baptist De, St." *New Catholic Encyclopedia*. Vol. 8, pp. 390-392.

Baunard, Msgr. *Ozanam in His Correspondence*. Tr. by a member of the council of Ireland of the Society of St. Vincent de Paul. Dublin: Catholic Truth Society of Ireland, 1925.

Bazin, René. *Charles de Foucauld: Hermit and Explorer*. Tr. by Peter Keelan. New York: Benziger Bros., 1923.

A Benedictine monk of Stanbrook Abbey, ed. *Letters from the Saints*. New York: Hawthorne Books, Inc., 1964.

The Benedictine monks of Ramsgate Abbey, eds. *The Book of Saints*. Wilton, Conn.: Morehouse Publishing, 1989.

Bernardin, Joseph. *The Gift of Peace: Personal Reflections*. Chicago: Loyola Press, 1997.

Biblioteca Sanctorum. Rome: Instituto Giovanni XXIII Della Pontificia Universita Lateranense, 1961.

Blain, John Baptist. *The Life of John Baptist de la Salle: Founder of the Brothers of the Christian Schools*. Tr. by Richard Arnandez. Rouen, France: John Baptist Machuel, 1733.

Boniface, Archbishop of Mainz. *The English Correspondence of Saint Boniface: Being for the Most Part Letters Exchanged Between the Apostle of the Germans and His English Friends*. Tr. and ed. by Edward Kylie. New York: Cooper Square Publishers, Inc., 1966.

Boresky, Theodosia. *Life of St. Josaphat: Martyr of the Union*. New York: Comet Press Books, 1955.

Borgia, Franciscus. *Sanctus Franciscus Borgia, Quartus Gandiae Dux Et Societatis Jesu*. Vol. II (1530-1550). Matriti, Typis Augustini Avrial, 1903.

Bourke, Mary Carmel. *A Woman Sings of Mercy: Reflections on the Life and Spirit of Mother Catherine McAuley, Foundress of the Sisters of Mercy*. Sydney, Australia: E. J. Dwyer, 1987.

Bourke, Vernon J. *Aquinas' Search for Wisdom*. Milwaukee: The Bruce Publishing Co., 1965.

Broughton, Rosemary. *Praying with Teresa of Ávila. Companions for the Journey* series. Winona, Minn.: St. Mary's Press, 1990.

Burbach, Mauer Ralph. "Vianney, Jean Baptiste Marie, St." *New Catholic Encyclopedia*. Vol. 14, p. 637.

Burns, Helen Marie and Sheila Carney. *Praying with Catherine McAuley. Companions for the Journey* series. Winona, Minn.: St. Mary's Press, 1996.

Butler's Lives of the Saints. Ed. by Herbert Thurston and Donald Attwater. Four volumes. Westminster, Md.: Christian Classics, 1990.

Cabrini, Frances Xavier. *Letters of Saint Frances Xavier Cabrini*. Tr. by Sr. Ursula Infante. Private publication, 1970.

Cabrini, Frances Xavier. *The Awakening*. New York: Missionary Sisters of the Sacred Heart, 1996.

Callan, Louise. "Duchesne, Rose Philippine, Bl." *New Catholic Encyclopedia.* Vol. 4, pp. 1088-1089.

Callan, Louise. *Philippine Duchesne: Frontier Missionary of the Sacred Heart.* Abridged Edition. Westminster, Md.: The Newman Press, 1965.

Camm, Bede, ed. *Lives of the English Martyrs Declared Blessed by Pope Leo XIII in 1886 and 1895.* Vol. 1. *Martyrs Under Henry VIII.* London: Burnes and Oates Limited, 1904.

Carrouges, Michel. *Soldier of the Spirit: The Life of Charles de Foucauld.* Tr. by Marie-Christine Hellin. New York: G. P. Putnam's Sons, 1956.

Carson, R. E. "Damien, Father (Joseph De Veuster)." *New Catholic Encyclopedia.* Vol. 4, pp. 626-627.

Carty, Charles Mortimer. *Who Is Padre Pio?* Tr. by Laura Chanler White. Rockford, Ill.: Tan Books and Publishers, Inc., 1974.

Catechism of the Catholic Church. Liguori, Mo.: Liguori Publications (copyright 1994 by United States Catholic Conference and Libreria Editrice Vaticana).

Catherine of Genoa. *Life and Doctrine of Saint Catherine of Genoa.* Ed. and tr. by Isaac Thomas Hecker. New York: Catholic Publication Society, 1874.

Catherine of Genoa. *The Spiritual Dialogue.* Tr. by Serge Hughes. *Classics of Western Spirituality.* New York: Paulist Press, 1979.

Catherine of Siena. *Saint Catherine of Siena, As Seen in Her Letters.* Tr. by Vida D. Scudder. New York: E. P. Dutton and Co., 1911.

Champlin, Joseph M. *Together for Life.* Notre Dame, Ind.: Ave Maria Press, 1994.

Chervin, Ronda de Sola. *The Kiss from the Cross.* Ann Arbor, Mich.: Servant Publications, 1994.

Clare of Assisi. *Clare of Assisi: Early Documents.* Tr. and ed. by Regis J. Armstrong. New York: Paulist Press, 1988.

Claret, Anthony Mary. *The Autobiography of St. Anthony Mary Claret.* Tr. by Louis Joseph Moore. Compton, Calif.: Claretian Major Seminary, 1945.

Code, Joseph Bernard. "Seton, Elizabeth Ann, St." *New Catholic Encyclopedia.* Vol. 13, p. 136.

Colledge, Edmund. *Saint Thomas Aquinas, Commemorative Studies: The Legend of Saint Thomas Aquinas.* Toronto: Pontifical Institute of Mediaeval Studies, 1974.

Couve de Murville, M.N.L. *Slave from Haiti: A Saint for New York? The Life of Pierre Toussaint.* London: Incorporated Catholic Truth Society, 1995.

Cumming, John, ed. *Letters from Saints to Sinners.* New York: The Crossroad Publishing Co., 1996.

Current Biography. Ed. by Charles Mortiz and others. New York: The H. W. Wilson Co., 1982.

Cyprian of Carthage. *St. Cyprian: The Lapsed, and the Unity of the Catholic Church.* Tr. by Maurice Bevenot. Vol. 25 of *Ancient Christian Writers* series. Westminster, Md.: The Newman Press, 1957.

Daws, Gavan. *Holy Man. Father Damien of Molokai.* New York: Harper and Row, Publishers, 1973.

Dawson, Christopher. *The Making of Europe.* Cleveland: Meridian Books, 1968.

Day, Dorothy. *The Eleventh Virgin.* New York: Albert And Charles Boni, 1923.

De Castro, Francis. *The Life of St. John of God.* Tr. by Benignus Callan. Published privately by the Irish Province of the Hospitaler Order of St. John of God, 1983.

De la Salle, John Baptist. *The Letters of John Baptist de la Salle.* Tr. by Colman Molloy. Ed. by Augustine Loes. Romeoville, Ill.: Lasallian Publications, 1988.

De la Salle, John Baptist. *De la Salle: Letters and Documents.* Ed. by William John Battersby. London: Longmans, Green and Co., 1952.

De Lellis, Camillus. *The Writings of St. Camillus: 1584-1614.* Tr. by C. Dyer from the Italian version of Germana Sommaruga. Manila: St. Camillus College Seminary, 1992.

De Marillac, Louise. *Spiritual Writings of Saint Louise de Marillac.* Tr. by Louise Sullivan. Albany, N.Y.: De Paul Provincial House, 1984.

Dempsey, Martin. *John Baptist de la Salle: His Life and His Institute.* Milwaukee: The Bruce Publishing Co., 1940.

De Paul, Vincent. *Correspondence, Conferences, Documents.* Vol. 1. *Correspondence I (1607-1639).* Tr. by Helen Marie Law and others. Ed. by Jacqueline Kilar. Brooklyn: New City Press, 1985.

De Robeck, Nesta. *Saint Elizabeth of Hungary. A Story of Twenty-four Years.* Milwaukee: The Bruce Publishing Co., 1954.

De Sales, Francis and Jane de Chantal. *Letters of Spiritual Direction.* Tr. by Peronne Marie Thibert. Ed. by Wendy M. Wright and Joseph F. Power. *The Classics of Western Spirituality.* New York: Paulist Press, 1988.

Devos, Paul. "Cyril (Constantine) and Methodius, SS." *New Catholic Encyclopedia.* Vol. 4, pp. 579-581.

Dictionary of Quotations. Ed. by Bergen Evans. New York: Delacorte Press, 1968.

Dirvin, Joseph I. *Louise de Marillac: Of the Ladies and Daughters of Charity.* New York: Farrar, Straus and Giroux, 1970.

Dirvin, Joseph I. *Mrs. Seton, Foundress of the American Sisters of Charity.* New York: Farrar, Straus and Cudahy, 1962.

Dirvin, Joseph I. *Saint Catherine Labouré of the Miraculous Medal.* New York: Farrar, Straus and Cudahy, 1958.

The Documents of Vatican II. General ed.: Walter M. Abbott. Translation ed.: Joseph Gallagher. New York: Guild Press, 1966.

Doherty, Catherine de Hueck. *Fragments of My Life.* Combermere, Ontario: Madonna House Publications, 1996.

Donne, John. *John Donne: Selections From Divine Poems, Sermons, Devotions, and Prayers.* Ed. by John Booty. *The Classics of Western Spirituality.* New York: Paulist Press, 1990.

Dorcy, Mary Jean. "Joan of France (Valois), St." *New Catholic Encyclopedia.* Vol. 7, p. 993.

Downey, Michael, ed. *The New Dictionary of Catholic Spirituality.* Collegeville, Minn.: The Liturgical Press, 1993.

Duffy, Sister Consuela Marie, SBS. *Katharine Drexel: A Biography.* Bensalem, Pa.: Mother Katherine Drexel Guild, 1987.

Duquin, Lorene Hanley. *They Called Her the Baroness: The Life of Catherine de Hueck Doherty.* Staten Island, N.Y.: Alba House, 1995.

Durka, Gloria. *Praying with Julian of Norwich. Companions for the Journey* series. Winona, Minn.: St. Mary's Press, 1989.

Durka, Gloria. *Praying with Hildegard of Bingen. Companions for the Journey* series. Winona, Minn.: St. Mary's Press, 1991.

Dvornik, Francis. *Byzantine Missions Among the Slavs. SS. Constantine-Cyril and Methodius.* New Brunswick, N.J.: Rutgers University Press, 1970.

Egan, Eileen. *Such a Vision of the Street: Mother Teresa — The Spirit and the Work.* Garden City, N.Y.: Doubleday and Co., Inc., 1985.

Elliott, Lawrence. *I Will Be Called John: A Biography of Pope John XXIII.* New York: E. P. Dutton and Co., Inc., 1973.

Erdozain, Placido. *Archbishop Romero: Martyr of Salvador.* Tr. by John McFadden and Ruth Warner. Maryknoll, N.Y.: Orbis Books, 1981.

Eusebius. "The Life of Constantine." Tr. and rev. by Ernest Cushing Richardson. *A Select Library of Nicene and Post-Nicene Fathers of the Christian Church.* Tr. and ed. by Philip Schaff and Henry Wace, and others. Vol. 1, pp. 405-465. Grand Rapids, Mich.: Wm. B. Eerdmans Publishing Co., 1961.

Fitts, Mary Pauline. *Hands to the Needy. Blessed Marguerite d'Youville: Apostle to the Poor.* Garden City, N.Y.: Doubleday and Co., Inc., 1971.

Flores, Miguel Perez and Antonio Orcajo. *The Way of St. Vincent Is Our Way.* Tr. and ed. by Charles T. Plock. Cape Girardeau, Mo.: Concord Publishing House, Inc., 1995.

Foley, Leonard. *Saint of the Day. A Life and Lesson for Each of the 173 Saints of the New Missal.* Two volumes. Cincinnati: St. Anthony Messenger Press, 1974.

Foster, Kenelm Francis. "Catherine of Siena, St." *New Catholic Encyclopedia.* Vol. 3, pp. 258-260.

Francis of Assisi. *St. Francis of Assisi: Writings and Early Biographies; English Omnibus of the Sources for the Life of St. Francis*. Tr. by Raphael Brown and others. Ed. by Marion A. Habig. Third Revised Edition. Chicago: Franciscan Herald Press, 1973.

Fremantle, Anne. *Desert Calling*. New York: Henry Holt and Co., 1949.

Friske, Joseph. "Bellarmine, Robert, St." *New Catholic Encyclopedia*. Vol. 2, pp. 250-252.

Gaffney, John Patrick. "Grignion de Montfort, Louis Marie, St." *New Catholic Encyclopedia*. Vol. 6, p. 805.

Genevieve of the Holy Face, Sister. *The Father of the Little Flower (Saint Thérèse of the Child Jesus)*. Tr. by Michael Collins. Dublin: M. H. Gill and Son Ltd., 1959.

Gettemeier, Loretto. "Louise: A Life in Her Own Words." *Vincentian Heritage*. Cape Girardeau, Mo.: Concord Publishing House, Inc. Vol. 12, no. 2, pp. 105-113.

Gibson, Audrey and Kieran Kneaves. *Praying with Louise de Marillac. Companions for the Journey* series. Winona, Minn.: St. Mary's Press, 1995.

Giles, J. A. *The Life and Letters of Thomas à Becket*. London: Whittaker and Co., 1846.

Goodier, Alban. *Saints for Sinners*. San Francisco: Ignatius Press, 1993.

Gregory the Great, Pope. *Life and Miracles of St. Benedict*. Tr. by Odo J. Zimmermann and Benedict R. Avery. Westport, Conn.: Greenwood Press, Publishers, 1980.

Gregory Nazianzen. "Four Funeral Orations." Tr. by Leo P. McCauley. *Funeral Orations by Saint Gregory Nazianzen and Saint Ambrose*. Tr. by Leo P. McCauley and others. Vol. 22. The Fathers of the Church. New York: Fathers of the Church, Inc., 1953.

Grignion de Montfort, Louis Marie. *The Collected Writings of St. Louis Marie de Montfort: God Alone*. Bayshore, N.Y.: Montfort Publications, 1988.

Guerri, Severino Giner. *Saint Joseph Calasanz*. Tr. by S. Cudinach. Second Edition. Kochi, India: Argentinian Piarist Fathers, 1993.

Habig, Marion A. *Secular Franciscan Companion*. Chicago: Franciscan Herald Press, 1961.

Habig, Marion A. and Francis Borgia Steck. *Man of Greatness: Father Junípero Serra*. Chicago: Franciscan Herald Press, 1963.

Harkins, Paul William. "John Chrysostom, St." *New Catholic Encyclopedia*. Vol. 7, pp. 1041-1044.

Harkins, Paul William. "Oak, Synod of the." *New Catholic Encyclopedia*. Vol. 10, p. 589.

Hebblethwaite, Peter. *Pope John XXIII: Shepherd of the Modern World*. Garden City, N.Y.: Doubleday and Co., Inc., 1985.

Hildegard of Bingen. *Hildegard of Bingen: Scivias*. Tr. by Mother Columba Hart and Jane Bishop. *The Classics of Western Spirituality*. New York: Paulist Press, 1990.

Hildegard of Bingen. *Hildegard of Bingen's Book of Divine Works with Letters and Songs*. Ed. by Matthew Fox. Santa Fe, N.M.: Bear and Co., 1987.

Hinchliff, Peter. *Cyprian of Carthage and the Unity of the Christian Church*. London: Geoffrey Chapman Publishers, 1974.

Honore, Jean. *The Spiritual Journey of Newman*. Tr. by Mary Christopher Ludden. Staten Island, N.Y.: Alba House, 1992.

Hug, Pacific Lawrence. "Catherine of Genoa, St." *New Catholic Encyclopedia*. Vol. 3, pp. 254-256.

Ignatius of Loyola. *A Pilgrim's Journey: The Autobiography of Ignatius of Loyola*. Tr. by Joseph N. Tylenda. A Michael Glazier Book. Collegeville, Minn.: The Liturgical Press, 1985.

Iranyi, Ladislaus Anthony. "Joseph Calasanctius, St." *New Catholic Encyclopedia*. Vol. 7, pp. 1115-1116.

Jerome. *The Principal Works of St. Jerome*. Tr. by W. H. Fremantle, G. Lewis, and W. G. Martley. Vol. VI in the series of *Nicene and Post-Nicene Fathers of the Christian Church*. Grand Rapids, Mich.: Wm. B. Eerdmans Publishing Co., 1961.

John Chrysostom. "Correspondence of St. Chrysostom with the Bishop of Rome." Vol. IX, pp. 309-314. *A Select Library of the Nicene and Post-Nicene Fathers of the Christian Church*. Ed. by Philip Schaff. New York: The Christian Literature Co., 1889.

John of the Cross. *The Collected Works of St. John of the Cross*. Tr. by Kieran Kavanaugh and Otilio Rodriguez. Washington, D.C.: ICS Publications, Institute of Carmelite Studies, 1979.

Jourdain, Vital. *The Heart of Father Damien: 1840-89*. Tr. by Francis Larkin and Charles Davenport. Milwaukee: The Bruce Publishing Co., 1955.

Julian of Norwich. *Showings*. Tr. by Edmund Colledge and James Walsh. New York: Paulist Press, 1978.

Kearns, J. C. *The Life of Martin de Porres: Saintly American Negro and Patron of Social Justice*. New York: P. J. Kenedy and Sons, 1937.

Kelly, Ellin and Annabelle Melville, eds. *Elizabeth Seton: Selected Writings*. New York: Paulist Press, 1987.

Kelly, J.N.D. *The Oxford Dictionary of Popes*. New York: Oxford University Press, 1986.

Knowles, David. *Thomas Becket*. Stanford, Calif.: Stanford University Press, 1971.

Kreeft, Peter. *Making Sense Out of Suffering*. Ann Arbor, Mich.: Servant Books, 1986.

Lambrecht, Jan and Raymond F. Collins, eds. *God and Human Suffering*. Louvain Theological and Pastoral Monographs no. 3. Louvain: Eerdmans, Peeters Press, 1989.

Lappin, Peter. *Halfway to Heaven*. New Rochelle, N.Y.: Don Bosco Publications, 1981.

Laurentin, René. *Bernadette of Lourdes*. Tr. by John Drury. Minneapolis: Winston Press, 1979.

Leclerc, Eloi. *Exile and Tenderness*. Tr. by Germain Marc'hadour. Chicago: Franciscan Herald Press, 1965.

Lefevre, Marie Cecilia and Rose Alma Lemire. *A Journey of Love: The Life Story of Marguerite d'Youville*. Buffalo: D'Youville College, 1990.

Leo, Brother and Brothers Rufinus and Angelus. *We Were With St. Francis*. Tr. and ed. by Salvator Butler. Chicago: Franciscan Herald Press, 1976.

Leo the Great, Pope. *The Letters and Sermons of Leo the Great, Bishop of Rome*. Tr. by Charles Lett Feltoe. Vol. XII. *Nicene and Post-Nicene Fathers of the Christian Church*. Second Series. Ed. by Philip Schaff and Henry Wace, 1956. New York: The Christian Literature Co., 1889. Vol. XII.

The Liturgy of the Hours. 4 volumes. New York: Catholic Book Publishing Co., 1975.

Liturgy of the Hours: Proper of the Congregation of the Mission. New York: Catholic Book Publishing Co., 1978.

Lorit, Sergius C. *Charles de Foucauld: The Silent Witness*. Tr. by Ted Morrow. New York: New City Press, 1983.

Marie-Eugene of the Child Jesus, Rev. *Under the Torrent of His Love*. Tr. by Mary Thomas Noble. New York: Alba House, 1995.

MacDougall, Angus J., ed. *Martyrs of New France*. Midland, Ontario: Martyrs' Shrine Publication, 1972.

Madigan, Shawn. "Saints, Communion of Saints." *The New Dictionary of Catholic Spirituality*. Ed. by Michael Downey. Collegeville, Minn.: The Liturgical Press.

Mallet, Françoise. "Benedict, St." *New Catholic Encyclopedia*. Vol. 2, pp. 271-273.

Martin, Céline; a.k.a. Sister Genevieve of the Holy Face and of St. Teresa. *The Father of the Little Flower*. Tr. by Michael Collins. Dublin: M. H. Gill and Son Ltd., 1959.

Martindale, Cyril Charlie. *Life of Saint Camillus*. New York: Sheed and Ward, 1946.

Maynard, Abbé. *Virtues and Spiritual Doctrine of Saint Vincent de Paul*. Rev. by Carlton A. Prindeville. St. Louis: Vincentian Foreign Mission Press, 1961.

McCarty, Shaun. "Frederick Ozanam: Lay Evangelizer." *Vincentian Heritage*. Cape Girardeau, Mo.: Concord Publishing House, Inc. Vol. 17, no. 1, pp. 5-34.

McKenna, Thomas. *Praying with Vincent de Paul*. Winona, Minn.: St. Mary's Press, 1994.

McNeill, Betty Anne. "Last Will and Testament of St. Louise de Marillac." *Vincentian Heritage*. Cape Girardeau, Mo.: Concord Publishing House, Inc. Vol. 15, no. 2, pp. 97-112.

Miller, William D. *Dorothy Day: A Biography*. San Francisco: Harper and Row Publishers, 1982.

Mitchell, Estelle. *Marguerite d'Youville. Foundress of the Grey Nuns*. Tr. by Helena Nantais. Montreal: Palm Publishers, 1965.

Murphy, Francis Xavier. "Ignatius of Antioch, St." *New Catholic Encyclopedia*. Vol. 7, pp. 353-354.

Neumann, John. *The Autobiography of St. John Neumann*. Tr. by Alfred C. Rush. Boston: Daughters of St. Paul, 1977.

Newman, John Henry. *John Henry Newman: Autobiographical Writings*. Ed. by Henry Tristram. New York: Sheed and Ward, 1957.

Newman, John Henry. *Parochial and Plain Sermons*. San Francisco: Ignatius Press, 1987.

Nuth, Joan M. *Wisdom's Daughter: The Theology of Julian of Norwich*. New York: The Crossroad Publishing Co., 1991.

O'Malley, Vincent J. *Saintly Companions*. New York: Alba House, 1995.

Ong, Walter Jackson. "Humanism." *New Catholic Encyclopedia*. Vol. 7, pp. 215-224.

Orsenigo, Cesare. *Life of St. Charles Borromeo*. Tr. by Rudolph Kraus. St. Louis: B. Herder Book Co., 1943.

Papasogli, Benedetta. *Wisdom of the Heart: The Story of Marie Louise Trichet*. Bayshore, N.Y.: Montfort Publications, 1993.

Patrick of Ireland. *The Works of St. Patrick: St. Secundinus Hymn on St. Patrick*. Tr. by Ludwig Bieler. No. 17 of *Ancient Christian Writers* series. Ed. by Joannes Quasten and Joseph C. Plumpe. Westminster, Md.: The Newman Press, 1953.

Petitot, L. H. *The Life and Spirit of Thomas Aquinas*. Chicago: The Priory Press, 1966.

Piat, Stephane-Joseph. *The Story of a Family. The Home of the Little Flower*. Tr. by a Benedictine of Stanbrook Abbey. New York: P. J. Kenedy and Sons, 1948.

Pole, Reginald. *Pole's Defense of the Unity of the Church*. Tr. by Joseph G. Dwyer. Westminster, Md.: The Newman Press, 1965.

Pontifex, Dunstan. "St. Dunstan in His First Biography," *Downside Review*. 1933. Vol. 51, pp. 20-40.

The Positio of the Historical Section of the Sacred Congregation of Rites on the Introduction of the Cause for Beatification and Canonization and on the Virtues of the Servant of God: Katharine Tekakwitha, The Lily of the Mohawks. New York: Fordham University Press, 1940.

Ravier, André. *Saint Jeanne de Chantal: Noble Lady, Holy Lady*. Tr. by Mary Emily Hamilton. San Francisco: Ignatius Press, 1983.

Raymond of Capua. *The Life of St. Catherine of Siena*. Tr. by George Lamb. New York: P. J. Kenedy and Sons, 1960.

Rey-Mermet, Theodule. *St. Alphonsus Liguori: Tireless Worker for the Most Abandoned*. Tr. by Jeanne-Marie Marchesi. Brooklyn: New City Press, 1989.

Rigault, George. *Saint Louis-Marie Grignion de Montfort: His Life and Work*. Tr. by D.M.D.B. Port Jefferson, N.Y.: The Montfort Fathers, 1947.

Roman Missal. New York: Catholic Book Publishing Co., 1985.

Royle, Roger and Gary Woods. *Mother Teresa: A Life in Pictures*. San Francisco: Harper San Francisco, 1992.

Scarre, Chris. *The Penguin Historical Atlas of Ancient Rome*. London: Penguin Books, 1995.

Short, William J. "Stigmata." *The New Dictionary of Catholic Spirituality*. Ed. by Michael Downey. Collegeville, Minn.: The Liturgical Press, 1993.

Schug, John A. *Padre Pio: He Bore the Stigmata*. Huntington, Ind.: Our Sunday Visitor, Inc., 1975.

Smith, John Holland. *Constantine the Great*. New York: Charles Scribner's Sons, 1971.

Sparks, Richard. "Suffering." *The New Dictionary of Catholic Spirituality*. Ed. by Michael Downey. Collegeville, Minn.: The Liturgical Press, 1993.

Stein, Edith. *Life in a Jewish Family, 1891-1916. Her Unfinished Autobiographical Account*. Vol. I. *The Collected Works of Edith Stein*. Ed. by L. Gelber and Romaeus Leuven. Tr. by Josephine Koeppel. Washington, D.C.: ICS Publications, 1986.

Stein, Edith. *Self-Portrait in Letters: 1916-1942*. Vol. V. *The Collected Works of Edith Stein*. Ed. by L. Gelber and Romaeus Leuven. Tr. by Josephine Koeppel. Washington, D.C.: ICS Publications, 1993.

Stella, Pietro. *Don Bosco: Life and Work*. Tr. by John Drury. New Rochelle, N.Y.: Don Bosco Publications, 1985.

Sticco, Maria. *The Peace of St. Francis*. Tr. by Salvator Attanasio. New York: Hawthorn Books, Inc., 1961.

Stubbs, William. *Memorials of Saint Dunstan, Archbishop of Canterbury*. Munich, Germany: Kraus Reprint Ltd., 1965. In the series *Chronicles and Memorials of Great Britain and Ireland During the Middle Ages*.

Stuhlmueller, Carroll. "The Gospel According to Luke." *The Jerome Biblical Commentary*, pp. 115-164.

Sullivan, Mary Louise. *Mother Cabrini: "Italian Immigrant of the Century."* New York: Center for Migration Studies, 1992.

Sylvestre, André. *John Gabriel Perboyre, C.M.: China's First Saint*. Tr. by John E. Rybolt, C.M. Strasbourg, France: Editions du Signe, 1996.

The Tablet. News Briefs: "Pope Approves Heroic Virtues of Pierre Toussaint." December 28, 1996. Vol. 89, no. 40, p. 2.

Teresa of Ávila. *The Complete Works of Saint Teresa of Jesus*. Tr. and ed. by E. Allison Peers. Three volumes. New York: Sheed and Ward, 1957.

Thérèse of Lisieux. *The Autobiography of St. Thérèse of Lisieux: The Story of a Soul*. Tr. by John Beevers. Garden City, N.Y.: Image Books, 1957.

Thérèse of Lisieux. *Her Last Conversations*. Tr. by John Clarke. Washington, D.C.: Institute of Carmelite Studies, 1977.

Thomas of Celano. *St. Francis of Assisi: First and Second Life of St. Francis, with Selections from Treatise on the Miracles of Blessed Francis*. Tr. by Placid Hermann. Chicago: Franciscan Herald Press, 1962.

Thompson, Edward Healey. *The Life of St. Stanislaus Kostka, Of the Society of Jesus*. New York: P. J. Kenedy and Sons, n.d.

Treece, Patricia. *A Man for Others: Maximilian Kolbe, Saint of Auschwitz, In the Words of Those Who Knew Him*. San Francisco: Harper and Row Publishers, 1982.

Trexler, Richard C. *Naked Before the Father: The Renunciation of Francis of Assisi*. Vol. 9. *Humana Civilitas*. Under the auspices of the Center for Medieval and Renaissance Studies, at the University of California, Los Angeles. New York: Peter Lang, 1989.

Tripp, Rhoda Thomas. *The International Thesaurus of Quotations*. New York: Thomas Y. Crowell Co., 1970.

Trochu, Francis. *The Curé D'Ars. St. Jean Marie Baptiste (1786-1859) According to the Acts of the Process of Canonization and Numerous Hitherto Unpublished Documents*. Tr. by Ernest Graf. London: Burns, Oates and Washbourne, Ltd., 1927.

Trombley, Fay. "Toward Eternity: Elizabeth's Experience of Suffering and Hope." *Vincentian Heritage*. Cape Girardeau, Mo.: Concord Publishing House, Inc. Vol. 14, no. 2, pp. 349-362.

Tuchman, Barbara. *A Distant Mirror: The Calamitous 14th Century*. New York: Alfred A. Knopf, 1978.

Turks, Paul. *Philip Neri: The Fire of Joy*. Tr. by Daniel Utrecht. New York: Alba House, 1995.

Vanti, Mario. *St. Camillus de Lellis and His Ministers of the Sick*. Tr. by Charles Dyer. Manila: St. Camillus College Seminary, n.d.

Von Stamwitz, Alicia. *Women of Valor: The Trials and Triumphs of Seven Saints*. Liguori, Mo.: Liguori Publications, 1986.

Von Stamwitz, Alicia. *The Liguorian*, May 1986; p. 2.

Wallace, Susan Helen. *Matt Talbot: His Struggle and His Victory Over Alcoholism*. Boston: St. Paul Books and Media, 1992.

Wallace, William A. and J. A. Weisheipl. "Thomas Aquinas, St." *New Catholic Encyclopedia*. Vol. 14, pp. 102-115.

Webster's New World Dictionary of the American Language. College Edition. Cleveland: The World Publishing Co., 1962.

Wintz, Jack. "Dorothy Day: Father Kieser's New Film," *St. Anthony Messenger*, January 1996; pp. 28-32.

Wise, Winifred E. *Fray Junípero Serra and the California Conquest*. New York: Charles Scribner's Sons, 1967.

Wouters, Anthony Joseph. "Foucauld, Charles Eugene De." *New Catholic Encyclopedia*. Vol. 5, p. 1040.

Wysochansky, Demetrius E. *Josaphat Kuntsevych: Apostle of Church Unity*. Detroit: Basilian Fathers Publications, 1987.

Yeo, Margaret. *The Greatest of the Borgias*. London: Sheed and Ward, 1936.

Index of Proper Names

Note: This specialized index consists of names of the subjects of this work, with their names appearing as first and last names (e.g., Thomas Aquinas) instead of the conventional last names first (e.g., Aquinas, Thomas), although many of them are cross-referenced (e.g., Aquinas — *see* Thomas Aquinas). For the main entries (the subjects of this work), the page references are all-inclusive (i.e., they include the entire story in which each entry appears); however, references to the subjects in the endnotes are excluded.

About the Author

Rev. Vincent J. O'Malley, C.M., Senior Assistant to the President of Niagara University, is no stranger to the publishing world. He has several works under his belt, the latest being *Saintly Companions*, published by Alba House. He has also written for *The Priest*, one of many publications of Our Sunday Visitor.

Ordinary Suffering of Extraordinary Saints covers topics ranging from abortion to assassinations, from abandonment to addictions — in short, every type of human suffering imaginable.

Father O'Malley has succeeded in presenting "the humanness of the saints so that readers," as he puts it, "can more easily identify with and experience the saints' threefold role" of being "exemplary, intercessory, and inspirational."

The author has been a priest for more than twenty-five years and during that time has been involved in preaching, teaching, and giving retreats on the themes of saints and suffering.

Our Sunday Visitor. . .
Your Source for Discovering the Riches of the Catholic Faith

Our Sunday Visitor has an extensive line of materials for young children, teens, and adults. Our books, Bibles, booklets, CD-ROMs, audios, and videos are available in bookstores worldwide.

To receive a FREE full-line catalog or for more information, call **Our Sunday Visitor** at **1-800-348-2440**. Or write, **Our Sunday Visitor** / 200 Noll Plaza / Huntington, IN 46750.

- -

Please send me: ___A catalog
Please send me materials on:
___Apologetics and catechetics ___Reference works
___Prayer books   ___Heritage and the saints
___The family   ___The parish
Name_____
Address_____Apt._____
City_____State____Zip_____
Telephone (   ) _____

                                               A03BBABP

- -

Please send a friend: ___A catalog
Please send me materials on:
___Apologetics and catechetics ___Reference works
___Prayer books   ___Heritage and the saints
___The family   ___The parish
Name_____
Address_____Apt._____
City_____State____Zip_____
Telephone (   ) _____

                                               A03BBABP

- -

Our Sunday Visitor
200 Noll Plaza
Huntington, IN 46750
Toll free: 1-800-348-2440
E-mail: osvbooks@osv.com
Website: www.osv.com

Your Source for Discovering the Riches of the Catholic Faith